The Music Producer's Guide to Social Media Content

The Music Producer's Guide to Social Media Content offers essential insights into the role of audio in content creation for social media platforms. It provides advice on succeeding in the music industry through the successful adoption of social media practices, and on creating high-quality content as a vehicle of career growth.

Introducing both industry-standard tools, including DAWs, plug-ins and hardware, and an array of advanced techniques—such as consideration of immersive and spatial audio as well as live-streaming systems—the book equips readers to create audio for uploaded and streamed media. With a focus on maximizing quality, the book explores destinations and distribution with contemporary case studies, while focusing on principles that can be transferred to new technologies as they are released. Throughout, readers gain an understanding of the technology behind media creation, methods of using social media platforms to expand career opportunities, and the process of monetizing content.

This is an invaluable companion for both novice and experienced music producers who are seeking to promote their work on social media, as well as those looking to master the art of creating audio content for social media.

Sam McGuire is a long-time faculty member at the University of Colorado Denver. He specializes in audio production and social media, and has extensive experience in both academia and the industry. McGuire's contributions include numerous publications and innovative projects in the music industry.

SAM MCGUIRE

The Music Producer's Guide to Social Media Content

The Science, Business, and Art of Building a Musical Career

Routledge
Taylor & Francis Group

NEW YORK AND LONDON

Designed cover image: Sam McGuire

First published 2025
by Routledge
605 Third Avenue, New York, NY 10158

and by Routledge
4 Park Square, Milton Park, Abingdon, Oxon, OX14 4RN

Routledge is an imprint of the Taylor & Francis Group, an informa business

Library of Congress Cataloging-in-Publication Data
Names: McGuire, Sam, author.
Title: The music producer's guide to social media content : the science, business, and art of building a musical career / Sam McGuire.
Description: New York : Routledge, 2025. | Includes bibliographical references and index.
Identifiers: LCCN 2024043872 (print) | LCCN 2024043873 (ebook) |
ISBN 9781032542911 (hardback) | ISBN 9781032542874 (paperback) |
ISBN 9781003416180 (ebook)
Subjects: LCSH: Music trade--Vocational guidance. |
Social media--Vocational guidance. | Sound recordings--Production and direction. |
Music--Production and direction.
Classification: LCC ML3795. M355 2025 (print) | LCC ML3795 (ebook) |
DDC 780.23--dc23/eng/20240918
LC record available at https://lccn.loc.gov/2024043872
LC ebook record available at https://lccn.loc.gov/2024043873

ISBN: 978-1-032-54291-1 (hbk)
ISBN: 978-1-032-54287-4 (pbk)
ISBN: 978-1-003-41618-0 (ebk)

DOI: 10.4324/9781003416180

Typeset in Joanna
by SPi Technologies India Pvt Ltd (Straive)

Access the Support Material: https://www.youtube.com/playlist?list=
PLIezNGtdLioi9MKcvPwqZyOk9WKsDMIK7

To my partner and children, for their patience while I hide and write. I could write 19 more ...

Thanks to the College of Arts & Media at CU Denver for their support in writing this book through a development grant.

Contents

One

The art of music production is simultaneously reliant on traditional music skills and the ever-changing technical landscape. In order to enhance the chances of your own version of success in the music industry, you may find it helpful to learn, adopt, and refine a set of vibrant social media skills along the way. In this chapter we start with the fundamental concepts of the platforms which have helped define the social media experience for musicians.

A BRIEF HISTORY OF YOUTUBE

YouTube (see Figure 1.1) wasn't the first platform to play a critical role in the toolkit of music industry professionals, but it certainly has grown into the most important one.

Figure 1.1 YouTube.com

DOI: 10.4324/9781003416180-1

The Evolution of Audio/Video Specs and Quality

Let's dive into the fascinating world of YouTube's audio and video specifications and quality, tracing how these technical advancements have not only revolutionized the user experience but also shaped modern content creation and consumption. From its humble beginnings with basic video uploads to today's high-resolution streams and cutting-edge audio technologies, YouTube's evolution reflects broader trends in digital media and has had a surprising impact on global culture.

Timeline of Audio/Video Specifications and Quality on YouTube

2005: Launch of YouTube with basic 320×240 pixel video support.

2006: Introduction of 480×360 pixels, enhancing visual clarity for a growing audience.

2008: YouTube supports 720p HD video, making high-definition content accessible.

2009: The 1080p HD setting is rolled out, offering viewers significantly improved video quality.

2010: YouTube begins supporting 4K video, staying ahead in the digital media race.

2011: Launch of YouTube Live, integrating live-streaming with up to 720p video quality.

2012: 1080p live-streaming becomes available, catering to professional broadcasters and gamers.

2014: YouTube announces support for 60 frames per second, enhancing video smoothness.

2015: Introduction of 8K video support, although content availability remains low.

2016: HDR video support is added, improving color accuracy and contrast.

2018: YouTube adds support for immersive 360-degree videos and VR content.

2019: Introduction of AV1 codec for better compression without compromising quality.

2020: Enhanced live-streaming capabilities introduced due to increased demand during the COVID-19 pandemic.

2021: Launch of experimental features in YouTube Labs, including better integration of spatial audio.

2022: Implementation of machine learning algorithms to optimize video delivery based on user bandwidth.

Here's a Detailed Explanation for Each of the 14 Key Developments in YouTube's Audio and Video Specifications and Quality:

1) Initial Video Upload Limit

Initially, YouTube set a 10-minute limit for video uploads to manage storage and because of bandwidth considerations. This restriction influenced the early content, encouraging creators to focus on short-form videos. As infrastructure improved, YouTube expanded this limit, enabling longer-form content, which attracted a broader range of creators and audiences. The change significantly impacted how narratives and information were structured and presented.

2) HD-Ready 720p Launch

When YouTube introduced 720p HD video in 2008, it marked a significant upgrade from the previously implemented standard definition. This enhancement allowed creators to upload higher-quality videos, appealing to a more discerning audience and elevating the viewer's experience. It also set a new standard for online video content, pushing competitors to also adopt higher resolutions. This shift was critical in transforming YouTube into a serious platform for film and video enthusiasts.

3) 1080p Full HD

The rollout of 1080p HD in 2009 provided an even sharper video quality that was particularly appealing for professional content creators and media companies. This resolution became the new standard for quality in online video, enabling YouTube to host content that could rival traditional television and cinema in terms of clarity. The introduction of 1080p helped to solidify YouTube's position as a key player in digital entertainment. Additionally, it improved the attractiveness of the platform for advertising, boosting its economic viability.

4) 4K Ultra HD

Introducing 4K video in 2010, YouTube stayed ahead of the curve, offering resolution four times that of 1080p. This capability not only catered to professional videographers and photographers but also set a high standard that pushed the boundaries of internet video streaming. The adoption of 4K also prepared the platform for future technologies and trends, such as ultra-high-definition television broadcasts. This move reinforced YouTube's commitment to leading innovation in digital video.

5) High Frame Rate (HFR)

YouTube's support for videos at 60 frames per second, introduced in 2014, significantly improved the smoothness of video playback, which was especially beneficial for content involving high-speed actions like sports and video gaming. Higher frame rates reduce motion blur and provide a more fluid viewing experience, which is critical for maintaining viewer engagement in fast-paced content. This development was crucial for YouTube's gaming community and sports broadcasters. It also demonstrated YouTube's adaptability to the needs of different content genres.

6) High Dynamic Range (HDR)

By adding HDR video support in 2016, YouTube enabled a wider color and contrast spectrum, bringing a more vivid and immersive visual experience to viewers. HDR enhances the realism of videos, making bright areas brighter and dark areas darker, which is especially noticeable in scenes with complex lighting. HDR has become an important feature for filmmakers and viewers who value cinematic quality in video content.

7) 360-Degree Video Capability

Launched in 2015, 360-degree video support opened up new possibilities for content creators, allowing them to offer viewers an interactive experience where the viewer controls the camera angle. This feature has been particularly influential in fields like tourism, education, and real estate, in which immersive experiences add substantial value. It has also paved the way for more experimental and engaging storytelling techniques. The introduction of 360-degree videos (see Figure 1.2) significantly broadened the creative possibilities available to YouTube creators.

8) Virtual Reality (VR)

Integrating VR technology, YouTube provided a platform for sharing and viewing VR content, further extending its capabilities in providing immersive experiences. This move not only catered to tech enthusiasts but also encouraged creators to explore new forms of content that could be more engaging and interactive. VR on YouTube

Figure 1.2 What a 360° Frame Looks Like

has allowed viewers to experience events and places in a completely novel way, from concerts to remote travel destinations. The platform's support for VR reflects its ongoing commitment to embracing cutting-edge technologies.

9) Live-Streaming Technology

The introduction of YouTube Live in 2011 democratized live broadcasting, making it accessible to a wide array of creators, from individuals to large media organizations. This feature enabled real-time interaction with audiences, which is crucial for community building and engagement. Live-streaming has become a staple for events, tutorials, gaming, and more, creating new opportunities for monetization and viewer participation. YouTube's continual improvements in live-streaming technology have helped it maintain its competitive edge in the increasingly popular live content domain.

10) Adaptive Bit-Rate Streaming

Adaptive bit-rate streaming, implemented by YouTube, adjusts video quality in real time based on a user's internet speed, ensuring the best possible viewing experience under varying network conditions. This technology minimizes buffering and enhances user satisfaction, which is critical for maintaining the platform's vast and globally diverse user base. It has significantly reduced viewer frustration during periods of low bandwidth, making video content more accessible and enjoyable for all. This adaptability is essential for retaining viewers in regions with varying internet infrastructure.

11) AV1 Codec

The adoption of the AV1 codec in 2019 was a clever move by YouTube to reduce data usage without compromising video quality. The AV1 codec offers better compression efficiency than other options, which is vital to reducing bandwidth costs and improving streaming performance, especially in regions with limited connectivity. This advancement supports YouTube's goal of making high-quality video more accessible worldwide.

12) Spatial Audio

Spatial audio on YouTube, introduced with immersive 360-degree video, creates a sound experience that mimics real life, where the audio comes from all directions. This technology enhances the realism of videos, particularly in immersive and VR content, making the audio experience equally as dynamic as the visual. Spatial audio allows creators to produce more engaging and enveloping content, offering viewers a more compelling reason to use headphones and immerse themselves fully. It represents a significant step towards more sensory-rich online experiences.

13) Enhanced Accessibility Features

Over the years, YouTube has significantly improved its accessibility features, including more sophisticated subtitles and closed captions. These enhancements have made content more accessible to a wider audience, including those who are deaf or hard of hearing. By supporting multiple languages and refining the accuracy of automatic captions, YouTube has expanded its global reach and inclusivity. These improvements align with broader trends towards digital inclusivity and ensure that content is accessible to all users.

14) Content ID System

The Content ID system is a pivotal development in how YouTube manages copyright issues, allowing for automatic detection and handling of copyrighted content. This system helps protect the rights of content owners while ensuring that creators can share compliant videos more freely. It has been crucial for maintaining the quality and legality of the platform, safeguarding both creators and copyright holders. The Content ID system also supports YouTube's monetization model by ensuring that revenue is appropriately distributed among creators and rights owners.

The Growth and Evolution of the YouTube Platform

This next section explores the remarkable growth and evolution of YouTube as a platform, charting its journey from a simple video-sharing website to a global media powerhouse. We will examine how strategic decisions, technological advancements, and community engagement have played pivotal roles in shaping YouTube's trajectory. The platform has not only revolutionized how videos are consumed and shared but has also emerged as a crucial space for cultural expression, educational content, and social interaction, influencing everything from pop culture to politics.

Timeline of the Growth and Evolution of YouTube

2005: YouTube is founded, offering a new platform for user-generated video content.

2006: Google acquires YouTube for $1.65 billion, integrating it with its vast technology and advertising networks.

2007: Introduction of the Partner Program, allowing creators to earn revenue from their videos.

2008: YouTube global expansion begins, launching local versions in nine countries.

2010: YouTube reaches 2 billion views a day, highlighting its rapid growth in popularity.

2011: Launch of YouTube Live, which adds streaming capabilities to the platform.

2012: YouTube reaches 4 billion video views per day and introduces skippable ads.

2013: YouTube announces channels with paid subscriptions, diversifying revenue options for creators.

2014: YouTube acquires Maker Studios, a major multichannel network, for $500 million.

2015: Introduction of YouTube Kids, a dedicated platform for children's content.

2016: Launch of YouTube Red (later YouTube Premium), offering ad-free viewing and exclusive content.

2017: YouTube TV is launched, offering live television streaming as a new service.

2018: YouTube Music and YouTube Premium are rebranded and expanded globally.

2019: YouTube reaches 2 billion logged-in monthly users, underscoring its vast global reach.

2020: Amid the COVID-19 pandemic, YouTube becomes a vital platform for remote learning and entertainment.

Key Developments in the Growth and Evolution of YouTube

YouTube was created as a simple platform for users to upload and share videos, quickly gaining attention for its accessibility and user-friendly interface. The idea was born out of the founders' personal desire to share videos easily online, which resonated with millions globally, filling a significant gap in the market.

- Google's acquisition of YouTube just a year after its launch was a key turning point, providing YouTube with the necessary resources and infrastructure to scale rapidly. This acquisition integrated YouTube into Google's extensive advertising network, significantly boosting its revenue potential and global presence.
- The YouTube Partner Program was revolutionary as it allowed content creators to earn money from their videos through ad revenue sharing. This initiative not only attracted more creators to the platform but also incentivized them to produce higher-quality and more engaging content.
- In 2008, YouTube began its global expansion by launching local versions in countries around the world. This localization strategy was crucial to increasing its global user base and making content more accessible and relevant to international audiences.
- YouTube reached 2 billion views a day in 2010, demonstrating its rapid growth and its increasing importance as a media consumption platform. This milestone highlighted the platform's capacity to engage vast audiences worldwide daily.
- The addition of live-streaming capabilities with YouTube Live allowed the platform to tap into the growing demand for real-time content and interaction. This feature significantly enhanced community engagement and has been instrumental in covering live events, adding a new dimension to content on YouTube.

- The achievement of 4 billion video views per day and the introduction of skippable ads in 2012 were key developments. Skippable ads improved the user experience by providing viewers with control over advertising, which in turn helped sustain viewer engagement and satisfaction.
- The move to allow channels to offer paid subscriptions in 2013 provided content creators with an additional revenue stream, further professionalizing and monetizing the platform. This feature diversified the ways in which creators could earn from their content, beyond traditional advertising.
- By acquiring Maker Studios, a leading multichannel network, YouTube strengthened its relationships with high-profile content creators and improved its content offerings across various genres. This acquisition also enhanced YouTube's ability to manage and support its content creators.
- The launch of YouTube Kids in 2015 targeted young viewers with content curated specifically for children, addressing parents' concerns about the suitability of content on the main platform. This move helped secure a new generation of viewers, providing a safe and educational space for children to explore videos.
- The introduction of YouTube Red, rebranded later as YouTube Premium, marked an important step towards offering a more diverse viewing experience. It not only provided ad-free viewing and access to exclusive content but also included a music-streaming service, further enhancing its value proposition.
- YouTube TV expanded the platform's offerings into live television streaming, including sports, news, and entertainment channels. This service provided an alternative to traditional cable TV, aligning with the broader trend towards cord-cutting and streaming.
- By rebranding and expanding YouTube Music and Premium in 2018, YouTube aimed to enhance the user experience and compete more directly with other music-streaming services. This rebranding was critical in consolidating YouTube's services under a more unified and recognizable brand.
- YouTube reached 2 billion logged-in monthly users in 2019, demonstrating its enormous scale and influence as a global platform. This milestone underscored its role as a central hub for digital content, attracting a vast and diverse audience.

- During the global crisis of COVID-19, YouTube's role expanded significantly as it became a go-to resource for educational content, entertainment, and information dissemination. Its capacity to connect people and provide continuous content despite physical distancing measures highlighted its critical role in the digital age.

Each of these developments highlights how YouTube has adapted and evolved to meet the changing needs of viewers and creators, maintaining its position as a leader in the digital media landscape.

The Implementation of Ad Revenue

This section delves into the critical role of advertising in YouTube's business model, tracing the evolution of ad revenue mechanisms and their impact on content creators and the platform as a whole. Since introducing monetization features, YouTube has continually adapted its advertising strategies to balance the needs of advertisers, viewers, and creators. These developments have not only fueled YouTube's growth but have also been instrumental in shaping the digital marketing landscape (see Figure 1.3).

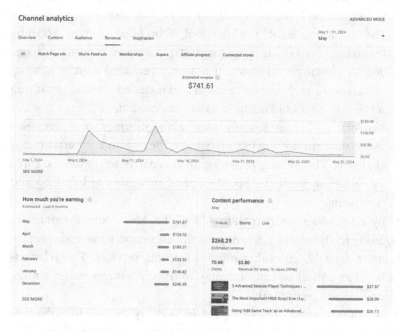

Figure 1.3 AdSense control panel

Timeline of Ad Revenue Implementation on YouTube

2006: Introduction of the first basic ads on YouTube.

2007: Launch of the Partner Program, allowing content creators to earn ad revenue.

2008: Overlay ads introduced, offering non-intrusive advertising options.

2010: TrueView ads launched; viewers can skip ads after 5 seconds, enhancing user experience.

2012: Introduction of skippable ads for all creators, expanding monetization opportunities.

2014: Google introduces Google Preferred, designed to compete with traditional broadcast advertising by giving recognized brands easier access to the most popular content on YouTube.

2016: YouTube starts offering unskippable 6-second bumper ads.

2018: Adaptation of machine learning to better target ads and optimize ad performance.

2020: Expansion of ad formats to include more interactive and integrated options.

Key Developments in Ad Revenue Implementation

First basic ads and Partner Program: YouTube's introduction of basic ads in 2006, followed by the Partner Program in 2007, marked the beginning of monetization on the platform. The Partner Program was particularly revolutionary as it allowed content creators to receive a share of the ad revenue generated from their videos. This not only incentivized content creation at a larger scale but also established YouTube as a viable career path for many.

- In 2008, YouTube introduced overlay ads, which are transparent advertisement banners that appear on the lower portion of the video. These ads were less intrusive than traditional commercials and allowed viewers to engage with content without significant disruption. This format was a nod towards balancing advertiser interests with user experience.
- Launched in 2010, TrueView ads were a significant innovation, as they allowed viewers to skip ads after 5 seconds. This model empowered viewers to choose whether or not to watch ads, which

improved their viewing experience and engagement. For advertisers, TrueView was beneficial as they only paid for ads that were watched for at least 30 seconds or to completion.

- Extending skippable ads to all creators in 2012 democratized revenue opportunities across the platform. This change enabled more creators to monetize their content effectively, fostering a more vibrant and diverse content ecosystem. It also helped YouTube scale its advertising model by increasing the volume of monetizable views.

- Google Preferred, introduced in 2014, and the 6-second unskippable bumper ads introduced in 2016, were both aimed at increasing the value proposition for advertisers seeking more engagement and impact. Google Preferred allowed brands to target ads on the most popular and engaging content, while bumper ads provided a short format that was ideal for mobile viewing, offering a guaranteed audience reach without the option to skip.

- The adoption of machine learning technologies in 2018 to optimize ad targeting and performance represented a significant advancement in YouTube's advertising capabilities. This technology allowed for more precise targeting based on viewer preferences and behavior, increasing the relevance of ads and thereby enhancing their effectiveness.

- In 2020, YouTube expanded its ad formats to include more interactive and integrated options, such as display and shopping ads that appear directly in the video interface. These developments provided advertisers with new ways to engage viewers and integrated seamlessly with the viewing experience, further blurring the lines between content and commerce.

These key developments illustrate how YouTube has continually evolved its ad revenue strategies to support its growth and meet the needs of its diverse stakeholders, significantly influencing the way digital content is monetized.

Addition of Spatial Audio and Immersive Video

This section explores YouTube's foray into spatial audio and immersive video technologies, enhancing how content is experienced on the platform. These innovations have significantly transformed the

Figure 1.4 Examples of a 360° Camera

viewer's experience by providing more depth, realism, and engagement through audiovisual enhancements. The implementation of these technologies marks a pivotal evolution in content consumption, catering to a growing demand for more immersive and interactive media (see Figure 1.4).

Timeline of Spatial Audio and Immersive Video Implementation on YouTube

2015: YouTube introduces support for 360-degree videos, laying the groundwork for more immersive experiences.
2016: Launch of spatial audio for on-demand YouTube videos, enhancing 360-degree video playback.
2017: Introduction of VR180 format, simplifying VR content creation while maintaining immersion.
2018: YouTube rolls out live-streaming in 360-degree video, enabling real-time immersive experiences.
2019: Expansion of VR180 capabilities and improvement in spatial audio algorithms for better sound localization.

360-degree video support: Introduced in 2015, 360-degree video support on YouTube was a significant milestone in creating more engaging and interactive content. This feature allows viewers to control their perspective within the video, offering a panoramic view of the scene. It opened new creative possibilities for content creators in various sectors, including tourism, events, and education, by allowing them to craft experiences that engage viewers on a more interactive level.

- Spatial audio, launched in 2016 for on-demand videos, complements 360-degree video by adding a three-dimensional sound field. This means that viewers can experience audio that corresponds with the direction they are looking within a video, mimicking real-life auditory experiences. Spatial audio significantly enhances the realism of immersive videos, making them more compelling and engaging, especially when used in conjunction with VR headsets.
- In 2017, YouTube introduced the VR180 format, designed to make VR content creation more accessible while still offering an immersive experience. This format focuses on a 180-degree view rather than a full 360-degree view, making it easier for creators to produce high-quality VR content without the need for specialized equipment. VR180 also supports stereoscopic 3D video, adding depth to the viewing experience, which is particularly effective in personal or close-up content scenarios.
- The ability to live-stream in 360-degree video, rolled out in 2018, marked another advancement in YouTube's immersive content offerings. This technology allows creators to broadcast events in real time with a panoramic view, giving viewers the ability to choose their viewing angle and more actively participate in the experience. It has been especially popular for live events, such as concerts and sports events, where being able to look around adds a new layer of immersion.
- In 2019, YouTube continued to refine its immersive video technologies by enhancing its VR180 capabilities and improving the algorithms it used for spatial audio. These improvements focused

on better sound localization, which is crucial for maintaining the illusion of depth and space in virtual environments. The ongoing development in spatial audio technology aims to create even more lifelike audio experiences, further bridging the gap between virtual and physical realities.

Through these initiatives, YouTube has significantly pushed the boundaries of how content can be consumed, making it a pioneer in the adoption of immersive technologies. These advancements not only enhance user engagement but also set new standards for media consumption in the digital age.

A BRIEF HISTORY OF FACEBOOK

Facebook (see Figure 1.5) is a common platform for growing musical communities, although in my limited experience student-aged musicians are using this less than the other available platforms. It is still worth exploring the history and current offerings since it has an extensive worldwide reach.

The Evolution of Audio/Video Specs and Quality

This section examines the evolution of audio and video specifications and quality on Facebook, highlighting the platform's journey from its origins as a site hosting simple text-based posts to its current status as a multimedia powerhouse. As Facebook has expanded its features to include videos, live-streaming, and interactive media, the

Figure 1.5 Facebook Landing Page

improvements in audio and video quality have significantly shaped how people connect and share experiences. This evolution has not only enhanced user engagement but also opened new avenues for advertisers and content creators.

Timeline of Audio/Video Specifications and Quality on Facebook

2007: Facebook introduces video uploading, allowing users to share personal video content.

2010: Introduction of HD video support, enhancing visual quality for uploaded videos.

2011: Rollout of Facebook Live, offering live video streaming to public figures and brands.

2013: Implementation of autoplay for videos in the News Feed, increasing video views and engagement.

2014: Upgrade to include 1080p HD videos, improving clarity and detail in video content.

2015: Support for 360-degree videos, enabling immersive viewing experiences.

2016: Introduction of Facebook Live to all users, democratizing live-streaming on the platform.

2017: Deployment of 4K support for uploaded videos and live broadcasts.

2018: Facebook launches Watch, a dedicated platform for video content.

2019: Introduction of HEVC (high-efficiency video coding) to improve video compression and quality.

2020: Enhanced audio quality for Facebook Live, ensuring clearer and more reliable sound.

2021: Rollout of Live Audio Rooms, catering to the growing popularity of audio content.

2022: Introduction of spatial audio features for more immersive video experiences.

2023: Support for 8K video uploads, pushing the boundaries of video quality on social media.

2024: Development of advanced AI-driven filters and effects for real-time video enhancements.

Key Developments in Audio/Video Specs and Quality

Video uploading feature: Introduced in 2007, this feature marked Facebook's first foray into multimedia, transforming the platform's function from text and image sharing to a more dynamic form of personal expression through video. Further developments in this area have included the following:

- Starting in 2010, HD video support allowed users to upload and view content in higher definition, significantly enhancing visual quality and viewer engagement, aligning Facebook with emerging standards in digital video.
- At its launch in 2011, Facebook Live was initially only available to celebrities and brands, offering them a new way to engage with audiences in real time, which significantly increased user interaction and content reach.
- The introduction of autoplay in 2013 for videos in the News Feed boosted video views and engagement by reducing the barrier to content consumption, although it also sparked discussions about user control and data usage.
- By 2014, Facebook Live upgraded to 1080p HD video support, which allowed for clearer and more detailed video content, catering to professional content creators and enhancing the user experience on the platform.
- Support for 360-degree video in 2015 marked a significant step towards more immersive content, allowing users to view and interact with video content from all angles.
- Expanded to all users in 2016, Facebook Live democratized livestreaming, making it a standard feature for personal and professional use across the platform.
- The introduction of 4K video support in 2017 for both uploaded videos and live broadcasts catered to professional filmmakers and video marketers, significantly improving visual fidelity (see Figure 1.6).
- In 2018, Facebook created a dedicated video platform, through which it aimed to centralize and monetize video content, competing with other video streaming services and creating a new venue for professional content creators.

Figure 1.6 Quality Comparison

- Adopting HEVC in 2019 improved video compression techniques, allowing for better video quality at lower data rates, which is crucial for mobile viewing and bandwidth conservation.
- In 2020, the audio quality for Facebook Live was upgraded, addressing the needs of creators for clearer sound during live broadcasts and enhancing both music performances and dialogue-driven content.
- Introduced in 2021, Live Audio Rooms tapped into the rising trend of audio content, such as podcasts and live discussions, offering users a new format through which to connect over shared interests without the need for video.
- Launched in 2022, spatial audio brought a more realistic and immersive audio experience to videos, enhancing the sense of presence and engagement for viewers, particularly in virtual-reality contexts.
- By supporting 8K video uploads in 2023, Facebook pushed the limits of video quality on social media, catering to future technologies and ultra-high-definition content.
- The development of advanced AI-driven filters and effects in 2024 revolutionized real-time video enhancements, allowing users to create high-quality, visually striking content directly within the Facebook platform.

These developments showcase Facebook's commitment to enhancing its multimedia capabilities, thus ensuring that it remains at the forefront of digital communication and media sharing.

The Growth and Evolution of the Facebook Platform

This section explores the growth and evolution of Facebook, from its inception as a college networking site to becoming one of the world's largest and most influential social media platforms. We will examine how strategic innovations, acquisitions, and policy changes have shaped its expansive user base, diversified its services, and continuously adapted to the changing landscape of digital communication and social networking.

Timeline of the Growth and Evolution of Facebook

2004: Launch of Facebook at Harvard University.

2006: Introduction of the News Feed, revolutionizing how content is shared and consumed.

2007: Launch of the Facebook Platform, allowing third-party apps and services.

2009: Implementation of the "Like" button, enhancing user interaction.

2010: Introduction of Facebook Pages, expanding tools for businesses and brands.

2012: Facebook goes public and acquires Instagram.

2013: Introduction of Graph Search, improving the search functionalities.

2014: Acquisition of WhatsApp and Oculus VR, diversifying its business.

2015: Launch of Instant Articles and video monetization options.

2016: Introduction of Facebook Live, bringing real-time video to millions.

2017: Overhaul of the News Feed algorithm to prioritize personal content.

2018: Major privacy and security updates following global scrutiny.

2019: Introduction of Facebook Dating and the redesign of the Facebook interface.

2020: Expansion into e-commerce with Facebook Shops.

2021: Rebranding of the parent company to Meta, focusing on building a metaverse.

Key Developments in the Growth and Evolution of Facebook

Launch at Harvard: Originally launched in 2004 for Harvard students, Facebook quickly expanded to other universities, laying the groundwork for its global network. This initial exclusivity created a buzz around the platform, contributing significantly to its early growth. In Figure 1.5 you can see a screenshot of my own initial account in 2005!

- In 2006, the introduction of the News Feed changed how content was distributed and consumed, allowing users to see updates from friends all in one place, dramatically increasing user engagement and time spent on the platform.
- The 2007 launch of the Facebook Platform enabled third-party developers to create applications that operated within Facebook, significantly enhancing the functionality and stickiness of the social network.
- Introduced in 2009, the "Like" button was a simple yet powerful tool for users to interact with content, becoming an iconic part of the Facebook experience and a new metric for engagement.
- In 2010, Facebook Pages gave businesses, celebrities, and brands a presence on the platform, facilitating a new level of interaction between companies and consumers and opening up new opportunities for targeted advertising.
- Going public in 2012 and acquiring Instagram marked a strategic expansion in Facebook's capabilities and audience, positioning it at the forefront of social media innovation and market dominance.
- Launched in 2013, Graph Search allowed users to search their connections for more specific information, enhancing the utility of the network and integrating social context into searches.
- In 2014, the acquisitions of WhatsApp and Oculus VR diversified Facebook's portfolio beyond traditional social media, as it ventured into messaging and virtual reality, respectively.
- These features, introduced in 2015, aimed to keep users and content creators within the platform, optimizing the user experience and content reach while boosting advertising revenue.
- Launched in 2016, Facebook Live introduced live-streaming capabilities to the masses, significantly enhancing user engagement and opening up new content-creation possibilities.

- In 2017, changes were made to feeds to ensure that they prioritized content from friends and family over brands and media; this was done with the aim of improving the user experience and address concerns about content saturation and quality.
- Following intense scrutiny over privacy practices, the 2018 updates aimed to regain user trust and comply with new regulations like GDPR, reflecting a shift towards greater user data protection.
- Launched in 2019, Facebook Dating ventured into the online dating market, while a significant redesign of the interface aimed to simplify navigation and improve usability.
- In 2020, the launch of Facebook Shops represented a significant move into e-commerce, allowing businesses to set up online stores within Facebook and Instagram.
- The 2021 rebranding to Meta highlighted a strategic pivot towards building immersive digital experiences in the Metaverse.

Addition of Spatial Audio and Immersive Video

This section examines Facebook's integration of spatial audio and immersive video technologies, key advancements that have significantly enriched the user experience by adding depth and realism to audiovisual content. These innovations reflect Facebook's commitment to enhancing multimedia interactions and fostering more engaging and interactive forms of communication on the platform.

Timeline of Spatial Audio and Immersive Video Implementation on Facebook

2016: Introduction of 360-degree videos with spatial audio on Facebook.

2017: Launch of Facebook Spaces, a VR app integrating spatial audio for a more immersive social experience.

2018: Rollout of 3D posts that allow interaction with 3D objects, including spatial audio components.

2021: Enhancement of audio capabilities in Facebook's virtual-reality environments to support more realistic spatial sound.

360-degree videos with spatial audio: Facebook first introduced 360-degree videos with spatial audio in 2016. This feature enabled viewers to experience sound from all directions, enhancing the realism of the 360-degree viewing experience. The spatial audio component meant that as users moved their viewing angle, the audio would adjust to match the direction of the video, mimicking real-world sound perception. Other developments in this area have included the following:

- Launched in 2017, Facebook Spaces was a virtual reality application designed to let users meet and interact in VR. The integration of spatial audio within this environment was crucial to creating a lifelike presence, allowing users to hear sounds from specific locations in the virtual space, which enhanced the feeling of being physically together with others in a shared virtual environment.
- In 2018, Facebook introduced the ability to interact with 3D objects in posts, which could be accompanied by spatial audio. This development meant that users could not only view but interact with 3D models by dragging to rotate or zoom, with audio cues changing accordingly based on the interaction—adding a layer of depth and engagement previously unachievable in standard posts.
- By 2021, Facebook had further enhanced the spatial audio capabilities within its virtual-reality platforms, aiming to support even more realistic audio experiences. These improvements were part of Facebook's broader strategy to create more immersive and interactive virtual environments, essential for the development of the metaverse, where spatial audio plays a critical role in delivering an authentic sensory experience.

These advancements demonstrate Facebook's ongoing efforts to push the boundaries of how social interactions and content consumption can be experienced, leveraging cutting-edge technology to create more immersive and engaging digital environments.

The Metaverse

This section explores the development and impact of Meta's Quest headset and its role in pioneering the metaverse, a digital universe offering immersive virtual experiences. The Quest headset, known for its standalone operation and advanced VR capabilities, has been instrumental in making virtual reality accessible and enjoyable for a broader audience. The evolution of this technology, coupled with an ambitious vision for the metaverse, underscores Meta's commitment to setting new standards in how we interact with digital environments.

Timeline of Quest Headset and the Metaverse

2019: Release of the Oculus Quest, Meta's first standalone VR headset.

2020: Launch of Quest 2, an improved version with higher resolution and better processing power.

2021: Announcement of the Meta rebranding, aligning the company's focus on the metaverse.

2022: Introduction of Horizon Worlds, a VR social experience platform within the metaverse.

2023: Rollout of advanced development tools for creating content in the metaverse.

Key Developments in Quest Headset and the Metaverse

Oculus Quest Launch: In 2019, Meta (then Facebook) launched the Oculus Quest, a standalone VR headset that did not require a PC or wires, significantly lowering the barrier to entry for high-quality VR. The Quest came equipped with Oculus Insight, using onboard cameras for tracking movements in real time, which was a major leap in VR technology. Further developments in this area have included the following:

- The Quest 2, introduced in 2020, marked an improvement over its predecessor, with a more powerful XR2 chipset, higher resolution display, and a lighter design, making it more comfortable for extended use. These enhancements helped solidify Quest's position in the market as one of the leading VR headsets, offering both affordability and high performance.

- In 2021, Facebook rebranded as Meta, signifying a strategic pivot towards building immersive digital experiences beyond traditional social media. This rebranding emphasized the company's commitment to developing the metaverse, a unified virtual environment for users to interact, work, and play in.

- Horizon Worlds was launched in 2022 as a platform within the metaverse where users can create, share, and explore virtual spaces in a community setting. This platform was designed to be a cornerstone of Meta's vision for the metaverse, showcasing the potential for new forms of social interaction and digital creativity.

- By 2023, Meta had introduced a suite of advanced development tools designed to empower creators to build more dynamic and interactive experiences in the metaverse. These tools were aimed at facilitating the creation of a diverse range of content, from games and educational tools to virtual meetings and social events, further expanding the ecosystem of the metaverse.

These developments highlight Meta's leadership in pushing the boundaries of virtual reality and its vision for the metaverse. By continually enhancing the capabilities of the Quest headset and developing a rich, interactive virtual world, Meta aims to redefine how people connect and experience digital content.

Oculus Before Meta

This section traces the origins and early history of Oculus, a pioneering company in the field of virtual reality. From its inception, Oculus was instrumental in revitalizing interest in VR technologies with innovative designs and accessible platforms. The company's journey from a groundbreaking Kickstarter campaign to becoming a leader in VR, leading up to its acquisition by Meta, showcases its significant impact on the industry and technology. See Figure 1.7 for an image of the original Oculus Quest headset next to the Meta Quest versions 2 and 3.

Figure 1.7 Quest Versions 1–3

Timeline of Oculus Before Acquisition by Meta

2012: Launch of Oculus's Kickstarter campaign for the Rift VR headset.

2013: Oculus Rift DK1 (Development Kit 1) ships to backers.

2014: Introduction of the Oculus Rift DK2 with improved tracking and resolution.

2014: Acquisition by Facebook (now Meta), marking a pivotal moment in Oculus's history.

Key Developments in Oculus's Early History

- In 2012, Oculus initiated a Kickstarter campaign to fund the development of its first VR headset, the Oculus Rift. The campaign was an immediate success, raising over $2.4 million and far exceeding the initial goal. This overwhelming support highlighted the public's interest and belief in the potential of VR, setting the stage for Oculus's rapid growth.
- The first version of the Oculus Rift, the Development Kit 1, was released to Kickstarter backers in 2013. This initial model provided developers and early adopters with a glimpse into Oculus's vision for VR, featuring head tracking and a stereoscopic 3D view. Despite its limitations, such as low resolution and a lack of positional tracking, it sparked widespread interest in VR development.
- With the release of the Oculus Rift Development Kit 2 in 2014, Oculus made significant improvements, including a higher resolution display, positional tracking, and a more comfortable design.

The DK2 incorporated an external camera for positional tracking, greatly enhancing user experience by allowing for more natural movements within a 3D space.

- In March 2014, Oculus was acquired by Facebook for approximately $2 billion. This acquisition not only provided Oculus with the resources and infrastructure to accelerate its product development but also signaled the importance of VR as an emerging technology in the broader tech landscape. The acquisition was a testament to Oculus's leading role in the VR industry and highlighted the potential for VR to extend beyond gaming into various other fields.

These developments showcase Oculus's role as a trailblazer in the VR industry, driven by innovation and a clear vision for the future of immersive technology. Its early products and subsequent acquisition by Meta paved the way for VR to become a mainstream technology with applications across entertainment, education, and beyond.

A BRIEF HISTORY OF INSTAGRAM

Starting as a photo-sharing platform, Instagram has come a long way as a popular tool for musicians and producers.

The Evolution of Audio/Video Specs and Quality

This section explores the evolution of audio and video specifications and quality on Instagram, illustrating how the platform has significantly enhanced its multimedia capabilities since its inception. From merely supporting photo sharing to embracing a wide array of video features, Instagram's developments in audio and video have been central to its transformation into a dynamic social media powerhouse. These improvements have reshaped user interactions, enabling more engaging and creative content sharing.

Timeline of Audio/Video Specifications and Quality on Instagram

2010: Launch of Instagram with photo sharing.
2013: Introduction of video posting capabilities.
2016: Debut of Instagram Stories.
2017: Launch of live video streaming.
2018: Release of IGTV for longer videos.

2020: Expansion of live features with Live Rooms.
2021: Rollout of Instagram Reels for short, edited video content.
2023: Enhancement of video and audio editing tools.

Key Developments in Audio/Video Specs and Quality on Instagram

- In 2013, Instagram introduced the option to post 15-second videos. This feature marked the platform's first major step beyond static images, meeting the growing user demand for more dynamic content. The move was pivotal in transforming Instagram into a multimedia platform, significantly expanding its user engagement.
- In 2016, Instagram Stories was launched, allowing users to post photos and videos that disappear after 24 hours. This feature rapidly became popular, increasing daily user engagement and providing a new way for users to share more spontaneous and less curated content. Stories enhanced the interactive nature of the app, encouraging frequent visits and prolonged usage.
- Introduced in 2017, live video streaming on Instagram allowed users to broadcast videos in real time. This addition helped Instagram keep pace with competing platforms like Snapchat and Facebook, which already offered similar features. Live-streaming on Instagram fostered real-time interaction between broadcasters and viewers, deepening community ties and engagement.
- In 2018, Instagram launched IGTV, a feature designed for longer videos up to an hour in length, aimed at creators who wanted to publish more extensive content. IGTV represented Instagram's move into the digital video space dominated by YouTube, offering a new avenue for influencers and content creators to engage with their audience. This feature supported vertical videos, which are optimized for mobile viewing, aligning with user behavior on mobile devices.
- Expanding its live-video capabilities, Instagram introduced Live Rooms in 2020, allowing up to four users to broadcast live together. This feature was designed to foster greater interaction and collaboration between users, multiplying the ways in which content could be co-created and shared. Live Rooms also expanded audience reach, as followers of each participant could join the live session, significantly increasing engagement.

- In 2021, Instagram rolled out Reels, a new video format that allows users to create and edit 15–30-second multi-clip videos with audio, effects, and new creative tools. Reels was a direct response to the rising popularity of TikTok and aimed to capture the trend of short, entertaining video content. This feature added a significant layer of versatility to Instagram's video offerings, enhancing user engagement with fresh, creative possibilities.
- In 2023, Instagram significantly enhanced its video and audio editing tools, improving the quality of production accessible directly from the app. These enhancements included better filters, cutting-edge effects, and superior audio editing capabilities that catered to professional content creators and casual users alike. By offering advanced editing tools, Instagram has continued to encourage content creation within the app, ensuring that users have a seamless and integrated experience.
- Instagram progressively increased the resolution of videos that could be uploaded and viewed on the platform. Initially supporting only standard definition, Instagram now supports high-definition video uploads, providing a clearer, more detailed viewing experience, which is crucial for creators who prioritize video quality.
- Instagram has improved its analytics for video content, giving creators detailed insights into viewer engagement, watch times, and interaction rates. This data is invaluable for content creators and marketers, who rely on performance metrics to tailor their content strategies and maximize engagement.
- As part of its effort to support creators, Instagram introduced monetization features for video content, including ads in IGTV videos. This allowed creators to earn revenue directly from the platform, incentivizing them to produce more high-quality, engaging content.
- Instagram implemented video autoplay in the Explore tab, which helped to increase video views and user engagement. This feature allows users to discover new content seamlessly as they scroll, enhancing content visibility and engagement without requiring active searches by the user.
- Instagram incorporated the ability to add soundtracks to videos from a vast library of licensed music. This feature not only enriched the quality of video content but also simplified the process of creating more engaging and professional-looking videos.

- Leveraging Facebook's technology, Instagram integrated augmented reality (AR) filters into video recording and posting features. These AR capabilities allow users to create more fun and interactive videos, boosting creativity and sharing rates.
- Instagram has continually expanded the types of video formats supported on the platform, including slow-motion, time-lapse, and cinemographs. These formats offer users more creative freedom and diversify the types of content that can be produced and shared.
- Instagram introduced features that allow multiple users to collaborate on video posts and Stories. This functionality enhances community interaction and content richness, providing a platform for collective creativity and shared experiences.

These key developments in Instagram's audio and video capabilities demonstrate its ongoing commitment to enhancing user experience and maintaining its status as a leading platform in the social media landscape.

The Growth and Evolution of the Instagram Platform

This section explores the remarkable growth and evolution of Instagram (see Figure 1.8) from a simple photo-sharing app to a complex, multifaceted social media platform. We examine how strategic innovations, acquisitions, and updates have shaped its expansive user base, diversified its services, and continuously adapted to the changing landscape of digital communication and social interaction.

Timeline of the Growth and Evolution of Instagram

2010: Instagram is launched, focusing solely on photo sharing.
2012: Acquisition by Facebook.
2013: Introduction of video-sharing capabilities.
2016: Launch of Instagram Stories.
2018: Introduction of IGTV for longer-form video content.
2019: Launch of Instagram Checkout feature for direct purchases.
2020: Implementation of Reels to compete with TikTok.
2021: Enhancement of shopping features and expansion of monetization options for creators.

Figure 1.8 My Own Instagram Account

Key Developments in the Growth and Evolution of Instagram

- Instagram was launched in October 2010 and quickly gained popularity due to its user-friendly interface and unique focus on photo sharing. Its simplicity and the ability to instantly apply filters made it a favorite among smartphone users, significantly impacting how people interacted with digital photography.
- In April 2012, Instagram was acquired by Facebook for approximately $1 billion. This acquisition provided Instagram with the resources to scale its operations and expand its features rapidly. Facebook's extensive user base also helped accelerate Instagram's growth and integration with social networking features.
- In June 2013, Instagram added video-sharing capabilities, allowing users to post 15-second videos. This move was significant, as it

broadened the scope of content creation beyond static images and helped Instagram stay competitive with platforms like Vine and Snapchat.

- Launched in August 2016, Instagram Stories introduced ephemeral video and photo sequences that disappear after 24 hours. Inspired by Snapchat, this feature significantly increased daily user engagement and opened new avenues for creative storytelling and advertising.
- In June 2018, Instagram launched IGTV, a standalone app integrated within Instagram, allowing for the uploading of videos up to one hour long. IGTV aimed to attract content creators used to platforms like YouTube, offering them a new audience on Instagram.
- Introduced in March 2019, Instagram Checkout allowed users to complete purchases directly within the app. This feature marked a major step towards turning Instagram into a significant e-commerce platform, integrating shopping with a social media experience.
- In August 2020, Instagram launched Reels, its answer to the growing popularity of TikTok. Reels allows users to create and discover short, entertaining videos, further diversifying Instagram's video content offerings.
- Throughout 2021, Instagram continued to enhance its shopping capabilities, integrating more e-commerce features directly into the platform. This included expanded shopping options in Reels, Stories, and IGTV, making it easier for brands to connect with consumers.
- Also in 2021, Instagram expanded monetization options for creators through features like badges in Live videos and IGTV ads. These initiatives provided new revenue streams for creators, fostering a more sustainable ecosystem for content production.
- In 2016, Instagram transitioned from a chronological feed to an algorithmic feed, prioritizing content based on user engagement. This change was designed to show users more content they were likely to be interested in, increasing engagement and time spent on the app. However, it was also controversial, as many users felt it could diminish the visibility of posts from friends and family in favor of promotional content.
- Instagram has introduced features aimed at improving mental health and well-being, such as warnings on potentially upsetting

content and the ability to hide public like counts to reduce social pressure. These initiatives reflect a growing recognition of the platform's impact on mental health, and aim to create a safer and more supportive online environment.

- Utilizing Facebook's technology, Instagram integrated augmented reality (AR) filters into Stories and posts. These filters allow users to add interactive, dynamic visual effects to their content, enhancing creativity and user engagement. The popularity of AR filters has also opened new avenues for advertisers and brands to create novel marketing experiences that are highly engaging and shareable.

- In response to concerns over online safety, Instagram has implemented features to combat bullying, such as comment filtering, the ability to disable comments, and tools that let users restrict another user's interactions. These measures are part of Instagram's broader efforts to foster a more inclusive and respectful community.

- Instagram has continued to expand globally, localizing the app into dozens of languages and adjusting its features to meet regional preferences and cultural norms. This global strategy has not only helped Instagram increase its user base but has also made the platform more accessible and relevant to a diverse audience worldwide.

- Instagram has heavily invested in AI and machine learning to enhance content discovery, streamline ad targeting, and automate moderation tasks. These technologies help improve the user experience by personalizing content feeds, detecting and removing inappropriate content, and optimizing advertising to be more relevant to users. AI and machine learning are central to Instagram's strategy of maintaining its position as a leading social media platform.

These key developments highlight Instagram's ongoing evolution as it adapts to user needs, market trends, and technological advancements, continuously shaping its growth strategy to enhance user engagement and expand its global reach.

Future Growth of Audio/Video Offerings

This section discusses potential future developments in audio and video offerings on Instagram, based on extrapolation from current trends and emerging technologies. As Instagram continues to adapt and innovate within the dynamic digital media landscape, these speculative enhancements could significantly improve user engagement, enrich content quality, and open new avenues for creators and businesses.

Speculative Key Developments in Audio/Video on Instagram

Advanced AI-Driven Editing Tools

Instagram may introduce more sophisticated AI-driven editing tools that enable users to produce professional-quality videos directly within the app. These tools could automatically enhance video elements such as lighting, stabilize shaky footage, and optimize audio quality based on the video environment and content type.

VR Integration in Stories

Considering the rising interest in virtual reality, Instagram might integrate VR features into Stories, allowing users to create and share experiences in a fully immersive environment. This integration could revolutionize storytelling on the platform, making it more engaging and interactive.

AR Concerts and Live Events

Augmented-reality concerts and live events could become a part of Instagram, allowing users to attend performances virtually through the app. This would leverage AR to create interactive and immersive event experiences, expanding the boundaries of how live content is consumed and enjoyed.

Interactive 3D Content

Instagram could implement interactive 3D content for posts and advertisements, enabling users to engage with content in novel ways, such as by exploring products from all angles within a post, enhancing both user experience and commercial opportunities.

AI-Curated Personalized Video Feeds

Instagram might develop AI-curated personalized video feeds that use machine learning algorithms to tailor content to individual preferences and behaviors, ensuring that users are more likely to engage with content that aligns with their interests.

Enhanced Spatial Audio Capabilities

To complement advances in video quality, Instagram could enhance its spatial audio capabilities to provide a more immersive audio experience; this is especially critical for VR and AR content where audio plays a crucial role in creating believable and immersive environments.

360-Degree Video Support

As 360-degree video technology becomes more accessible, Instagram might support this format, allowing creators to produce and share fully immersive visual content that users can interact with by panning their device or through VR headsets.

Expansion of Video Formats

Instagram could continue to expand the variety of video formats it supports, including slow-motion, hyperlapse, and super-resolution videos, catering to professional filmmakers and hobbyists alike.

Real-Time Translation Features

With global interaction on Instagram, real-time translation for live and prerecorded videos could be introduced, breaking language barriers and enhancing the reach and engagement of content creators worldwide.

Deepfake Detection and Regulation

As deepfake technology advances, Instagram might implement more robust detection and regulation mechanisms to ensure the authenticity of content and protect user privacy and security.

Interactive Video Ads

To boost advertising effectiveness, Instagram could introduce more interactive video ad formats, such as embedded mini-games or interactive polls, offering advertisers creative ways to engage viewers and gather feedback.

Video Analytics Enhancements

Enhanced video analytics features could provide creators and advertisers with deeper insights into viewer behaviors, including heat maps of attention in videos and advanced performance metrics.

Holographic Video Features

Looking further into the future, Instagram could explore the integration of holographic video features, providing a three-dimensional viewing experience that could be projected into physical spaces.

Adaptive Streaming Technologies

Adaptive streaming technologies could be refined to deliver the best video quality based on the viewer's bandwidth, ensuring a smooth viewing experience regardless of internet speed.

Content Co-Creation Tools

Instagram might develop more advanced tools that facilitate content co-creation and collaboration remotely, allowing multiple users to edit and produce video content together in real time.

These speculative developments are based on potential technological advancements and market trends that could shape the future of Instagram as a leading platform in social media innovation.

A BRIEF HISTORY OF TIKTOK

This section explores the rapid growth and evolution of TikTok, a platform that has quickly risen to global prominence by revolutionizing short-form video content. We will examine how strategic innovations, global market penetrations, and continual updates have shaped its expansive user base and transformed it into a powerhouse of trend-setting and viral content creation.

The Growth and Evolution of the TikTok Platform

TikTok is the newest of these platforms, but as of this writing it is among the most influential.

Timeline of the Growth and Evolution of TikTok

2016: Launch of TikTok by ByteDance in China under the name Douyin.

2017: TikTok is launched internationally.

2018: Merger with the social media app Musical.ly, which significantly expands its global user base.

2019: TikTok becomes the most downloaded app on the Apple App Store.

2020: Introduction of TikTok For Business, which enhances its advertising capabilities.

2021: Launch of TikTok Shop in several markets, integrating e-commerce features.

2022: Rollout of longer video formats, allowing videos up to 10 minutes.

2023: Expansion into educational content with the introduction of Learning on TikTok.

Key Developments in the Growth and Evolution of TikTok

- Originally launched in 2016 under the name Douyin for the Chinese market, TikTok was introduced internationally by ByteDance in 2017 as a separate entity. This strategic move allowed TikTok to cater to international tastes while leveraging the robust technology and user interface of Douyin.
- In 2018, TikTok merged with Musical.ly, another popular short-form video app, primarily used in America. This merger was critical, as it combined TikTok's advanced technology with Musical.ly's large U.S. user base, fueling rapid growth and global expansion.
- By 2019, TikTok had become the most downloaded app on the Apple App Store, surpassing giants like Instagram and Snapchat. This milestone highlighted its increasing popularity and acceptance among a global youth demographic.
- In 2020, TikTok launched TikTok For Business, offering brands and advertisers a suite of tools and solutions to capitalize on the app's viral potential. This included branded effects, in-feed videos, and hashtag challenges, allowing businesses to engage with audiences in innovative ways.
- Expanding into e-commerce, TikTok launched TikTok Shop in 2021 in select markets. This feature allows users to buy products directly through the app, turning TikTok into a shopping destination and opening new revenue streams for creators and brands.
- Responding to user demand and competitive pressures, TikTok extended the maximum video length to 10 minutes in 2022, giving

creators more flexibility to produce diverse content types, from quick viral clips to more detailed and narrative-driven videos.

- In 2023, TikTok expanded its content categories by introducing Learning on TikTok, a dedicated platform for educational videos. This initiative aims to leverage TikTok's engaging format to make learning more accessible and entertaining, covering topics from science to cooking.

- Continual improvements to TikTok's content recommendation algorithm have been pivotal in maintaining user engagement. The algorithm's ability to quickly adapt to user preferences helps ensure that the most relevant and engaging content is prominently displayed.

- TikTok has localized its platform in over 150 markets and in 75 languages, tailoring content and user experience to regional cultures and trends. This localization strategy has been crucial in capturing a diverse global audience.

- As TikTok's popularity soared, so did scrutiny over user safety. In response, TikTok enhanced its safety features, including more robust content moderation, age restrictions, and privacy settings to protect its predominantly young user base.

- To support and retain top content creators, TikTok established a Creator Fund in 2020, which provides financial incentives based on engagement and viewership. This fund helps ensure that talented creators can earn revenue, encouraging them to continue producing high-quality content.

- TikTok has heavily invested in AR capabilities, allowing users to include interactive and immersive effects in their videos. This technology enhances the creative possibilities available to creators, further distinguishing TikTok from other social media platforms.

- TikTok has expanded its features to include live-streaming, enabling real-time interaction between creators and their audiences. This move into live content adds a new dimension to the platform, allowing for instantaneous community engagement and monetization through gifts and tips.

- Recognizing its platform's influence, TikTok has launched various environmental and social initiatives. These campaigns aim to raise awareness and drive action on global issues among its vast user base, reflecting a commitment to social responsibility.

- To help creators better understand their audience and performance, TikTok has developed advanced analytics tools. These tools provide detailed insights into viewership trends, engagement rates, and demographic data, helping creators optimize their content strategies.

These developments illustrate TikTok's dynamic evolution as it continues to innovate and adapt to changing market trends and user preferences, solidifying its position as a leader in the global social media landscape.

The Continued Evolution of Short-Format Content

This section delves into the continued evolution of short-format content on TikTok, exploring how the platform has not only embraced but also significantly influenced the rapid consumption trends of today's digital era. TikTok has been instrumental in defining the characteristics of successful short-format videos and has continually adapted and innovated to keep users engaged and creative within the constraints of brief video clips.

Key Developments in the Evolution of Short-Format Content on TikTok

Viral Dance Challenges
TikTok popularized the concept of viral dance challenges, where users recreate and adapt choreography to trending songs. This has become a hallmark of TikTok's content, driving massive engagement both on and off the platform.

Duet Feature
The Duet feature allows users to create content alongside another user's video, either adding to or responding to the original. This feature has fostered a collaborative environment and has been instrumental in amplifying the interactive nature of short-form content.

Hashtag Challenges
Hashtag challenges encourage users to create content around specific themes or prompts, which has proven highly effective for community building and engagement. Brands often sponsor these challenges, creating a lucrative marketing opportunity.

TikTok For Good

Through its "TikTok For Good" initiative, TikTok leverages short-form content for social advocacy, encouraging users to engage in content that promotes social causes and community welfare. This aligns the entertainment aspect with broader positive impacts.

Integration of AR Filters and Effects

TikTok has heavily invested in augmented reality (AR) filters and effects, allowing users to create more engaging and visually appealing videos. These tools have become essential in the creation of dynamic short-form content that stands out.

Sound Snippets

TikTok's extensive library of sound snippets, from popular songs to viral soundbites, allows users to create content that is culturally relevant and resonant. This audio integration is a core part of TikTok's identity and appeal.

Algorithm-Driven Personalization

The sophisticated algorithm of TikTok personalizes user feeds, ensuring that short-format content remains highly relevant and engaging to each user. This personalization drives longer viewing sessions despite the brevity of individual videos.

Creator Marketplace

TikTok's Creator Marketplace connects brands with TikTok creators for sponsored content creation, facilitating the monetization of short-form video content and enabling creators to sustainably leverage the platform's capabilities.

Mobile-First Editing Tools

TikTok provides advanced, mobile-first video-editing tools that allow users to create high-quality content directly from their phones. These tools are intuitive and accessible, reducing barriers to content creation.

Interactive Live-Streaming

TikTok has expanded into live-streaming, allowing creators to engage with audiences in real time. This feature enhances the dynamism of short-format content by adding the unpredictability and immediacy of live interactions.

E-Commerce Integration
The platform's integration with e-commerce capabilities, like direct product links and in-app purchases, turns short videos into a powerful sales tool, opening up additional revenue streams for creators and businesses.

Educational Content Initiatives
Initiatives like #LearnOnTikTok highlight educational content, proving that short-format videos can be both informative and entertaining. This broadens the scope of content beyond entertainment into practical, value-added uses.

Global Content Trends
TikTok influences global content trends by promoting diverse cultural content from around the world, thereby broadening the exposure and appeal of international content styles and themes within short-format videos.

Safety and Moderation Enhancements
As the platform grows, TikTok continues to enhance its safety and moderation policies to protect its community, especially its younger audience, making the platform safer for creating and sharing content.

Expansion of Video Length Options
Although primarily known for short videos, TikTok has experimented with allowing creators to produce longer videos, up to three minutes, giving them more flexibility to tell stories and convey messages without compromising the quick, engaging nature of traditional TikTok clips.

These developments reflect TikTok's ongoing innovation within the realm of short-format content, demonstrating its commitment to maintaining a dynamic and engaging platform that shapes how digital content is created and consumed globally.

Similarities to Other Platforms
This section examines the similarities between TikTok and other social media platforms, analyzing how TikTok has incorporated

and adapted features that are popular on platforms like Instagram, Snapchat, and YouTube. Understanding these similarities helps shed light on TikTok's strategy in positioning itself within the competitive landscape of social media, enhancing user engagement through familiar yet innovative functionalities.

Key Similarities to Other Platforms

Stories Format (Similar to Instagram and Snapchat)

Like Instagram Stories and Snapchat's original format, TikTok has integrated a stories feature that allows users to post content that disappears after 24 hours. This format is popular for its ephemeral nature, which encourages spontaneous and less polished content sharing.

Video Filters and Effects (Similar to Snapchat)

TikTok offers a wide range of AR filters and effects, reminiscent of Snapchat's pioneering use of AR technology. These features enhance user engagement and creativity, allowing TikTok users to create visually captivating content with ease.

Algorithmic Content Discovery (Similar to YouTube)

TikTok's "For You" page operates similarly to YouTube's recommendation algorithm, which suggests videos based on user preferences and engagement history. This feature keeps users engaged by continuously presenting highly tailored content.

Short-Form Video (Similar to Vine)

TikTok's core functionality of short-form video content bears a resemblance to Vine, which popularized the format of 6-second videos. TikTok has expanded on this concept by allowing videos of up to 60 seconds, and more recently up to three minutes, offering a new take on quick, loop-able content that is easy to consume.

Live-Streaming (Similar to Facebook and Instagram)

TikTok includes a live-streaming feature, which is similar to options available on Facebook and Instagram. This allows creators to engage with their audience in real-time, fostering a deeper connection and community feel.

Duet and Reaction Videos (Similar to YouTube's Response Videos)
TikTok's Duet and Reaction features allow users to interact with existing videos, either by adding their own video to appear in split screen alongside the original video or by recording their reactions separately. This interactive feature is akin to YouTube's video responses, and encourages a dynamic form of content collaboration.

Creator Monetization (Similar to YouTube and Twitch)
Like YouTube's Partner Program and Twitch's monetization options, TikTok has introduced several monetization strategies, including the Creator Fund and live gifting during streams, providing financial incentives for creators to produce engaging content.

Hashtag Challenges (Similar to Twitter)
TikTok utilizes hashtag challenges to promote trends and encourage user participation, similar to Twitter's use of hashtags to aggregate posts and foster community discussions around specific topics.

User Profiles and Follow System (Similar to All Major Platforms)
TikTok users have personal profiles where they can showcase their content, and a follow system that is similar to those of most social networks, allowing users to maintain a feed of content from creators they enjoy.

Content Moderation Policies (Similar to All Major Platforms)
Like other major platforms, TikTok has developed content moderation policies to ensure community safety and compliance with global standards, adapting these policies as the platform evolves and as needed based on the regulatory environment.

Advertising Platform (Similar to Facebook and Instagram)
TikTok has built a robust advertising platform that allows brands to place ads that appear in users' feeds, stories, and in-video formats, mimicking the advertising models of Facebook and Instagram with targeted ad capabilities.

E-commerce Integration (Similar to Instagram and Pinterest)
Taking cues from Instagram Shopping and Pinterest's Buyable Pins, TikTok is increasingly integrating e-commerce features, allowing users to shop directly from the app, and so linking content creation directly with sales opportunities.

Analytics Tools (Similar to Instagram and Twitter)
TikTok provides creators and businesses with analytics tools to track engagement and performance metrics, helping them optimize their content strategies based on data-driven insights, a feature that has been crucial for content creators on platforms like Instagram and Twitter.

Community Guidelines and Reporting Features (Similar to All Major Platforms)
TikTok enforces community guidelines and offers reporting features similar to those on other social media platforms, ensuring that users have a way to report inappropriate content and thus helping maintain a safe online environment.

Educational Content Initiatives (Similar to YouTube)
TikTok has been expanding its content categories to include educational and informational videos through initiatives like #LearnOnTikTok, similar to YouTube's educational channels, diversifying beyond entertainment to include value-added content.

These similarities highlight how TikTok has effectively incorporated and adapted successful features from other platforms, positioning itself strategically within the competitive social media landscape while maintaining a unique identity that appeals to a diverse, global audience.

Overview of Typical Musical Influencers

This section provides an overview of typical musical influencers on TikTok, exploring how these creators use the platform's features to innovate in the music industry and build substantial followings. TikTok has emerged as a powerful tool for musical artists, significantly impacting music discovery and promotion. This exploration will highlight the strategies employed by these influencers to engage audiences and create viral music content.

Key Characteristics of Musical Influencers on TikTok

- Musical influencers often gain popularity by creating short, catchy clips of their music that are easy to replicate or use in user-generated content. This strategy helps their music reach a broad audience quickly, as clips can go viral and be used in millions of videos across the platform.
- Many musical influencers collaborate with other TikTok users, including Duets or using features like "Stitch" to add their music to other users' content. This not only extends their reach but also embeds their music deeply into the TikTok community, fostering a sense of collaboration and community.
- Musical influencers frequently engage with current trends and challenges on TikTok to stay relevant and maintain visibility. They might create songs that fit with popular video themes or choreograph dances to their music, encouraging fans to create their own versions.
- Sharing behind-the-scenes content, such as songwriting sessions, music production processes, or personal stories about their music helps musical influencers on TikTok build a personal connection with their audience. This transparency fosters loyalty and a deeper interest in their music and personal brand.
- Influencers often strategically place their songs in TikTok's vast sound library, making them accessible for other creators to use in their content. This exposure can lead to organic growth in streams and popularity, as tracks become embedded in numerous videos across the platform.
- Musical influencers use TikTok's live-streaming feature to perform live, host Q&A sessions, and interact directly with fans. These live sessions can also include performances of new music or deep dives into the creation process, further engaging their audience.
- While they may start on TikTok, successful musical influencers typically maintain a presence on multiple social media platforms. They

use TikTok to funnel followers to platforms like Spotify, YouTube, and Instagram, where they can engage with fans more deeply and monetize their content in diverse ways.

- As their popularity grows, musical influencers often engage in sponsored content and brand partnerships. These deals can include creating music for commercials, promoting products in their videos, or participating in marketing campaigns that align with their image and audience.
- Many musical influencers on TikTok leverage the platform's global reach to share music that may represent their culture or unique style, attracting international audiences. This global exposure is pivotal for artists looking to break into new markets.
- Influencers on TikTok often experiment with merging different music styles or creating niche musical content that stands out. This innovation can lead to new trends and influence the music industry more broadly.
- Effective musical influencers actively engage with their followers through comments, challenges, and personalized content. This active engagement helps maintain a vibrant community that is invested in the influencer's success.
- To keep up with TikTok's fast-paced environment, musical influencers often post frequently and adapt their content strategies based on what is most effective at engaging their audience. This dynamic approach keeps their content fresh and engaging.
- Successful musical influencers on TikTok often maintain a consistent visual and aesthetic style that makes their content instantly recognizable. This branding consistency helps solidify their image and makes their content more attractive and shareable.
- Creating or participating in music challenges is a common tactic among musical influencers. These challenges, often involving specific songs or dances, can quickly become viral movements, significantly boosting the music's popularity.
- Savvy musical influencers utilize TikTok's analytics tools to understand audience preferences and optimize their content strategies. This strategic use of data allows them to maximize their impact and effectively grow their presence on the platform.

These characteristics and strategies highlight how musical influencers on TikTok have shaped the platform into a critical launchpad for music careers, influencing global music trends and creating new opportunities for artists around the world.

Summary of Other Related Social Media Platforms

This section offers a detailed examination of various other key social media platforms, each contributing uniquely to the digital ecosystem with distinctive features and targeted audience engagement. Exploring these platforms provides insight into the diversity of social media environments and their specific roles in shaping communication, culture, and business globally.

Detailed Overview of Other Related Social Media Platforms

Twitter

Microblogging: Specializes in short, concise posts called tweets.

Real-time updates: Ideal for breaking news and instant reactions.

Hashtags: Pioneered the use of hashtags for trending topics and discoverability.

Threads: Allows users to connect multiple tweets to create longer narratives.

Retweeting: Enables users to share others' content easily.

Public square: Known for public discourse and celebrity interactions.

Polls: Users can create polls directly in tweets.

Character limit: Encourages concise communication with a 280-character limit.

Verified accounts: Provides authenticity through verification badges.

Advertising: Offers targeted advertising and promotional opportunities.

Snapchat

Ephemeral content: Photos and messages disappear after being viewed.

Stories: Content that lasts 24 hours before disappearing.

Filters and Lenses: Wide range of dynamic visual effects.

Snap Map: Shows friends' locations and public stories geographically.

Discover: Platform for brands and media to share longer-form content.

Memories: Allows users to save snaps and stories.

Bitmoji: Integrated personal emoji creation.

Private and group chat: Supports multimedia messaging.
Screen minimization: Allows users to watch content hands-free.
Augmented reality: Continuously innovating with AR capabilities.

Pinterest

Visual discovery: Users can pin images and videos they find online.
Boards: Organize content into themed boards.
Shopping features: Direct links to purchase products.
Rich Pins: Provide more context than standard pins, such as recipe details.
Search by image: Users can search for similar items using images.
Personal recommendations: Suggests pins based on user activity.
Collaborative boards: Multiple users can contribute to boards.
Promoted Pins: Advertisements that look like regular pins.
Pinterest Trends: Provides insights into popular search terms.
Pinterest Lens: Uses the camera to find related objects and pins.

LinkedIn

Professional networking: Focuses on business connections and career development.
Resume profile: Users present their professional experience and skills.
Job listings: Comprehensive job search engine integrated into the platform.
Endorsements and recommendations: Peer validation of skills and qualifications.
LinkedIn Learning: Offers professional courses and skill development.
InMail: Allows users to send messages to others they aren't connected to.
Groups: Professional groups based on interests and industries.
Company pages: Businesses can create profiles to share updates and job openings.
Content publishing: Users can publish articles directly on the platform.
Networking events: Facilitates virtual and in-person professional events.

Reddit

Subreddits: User-created communities centered around specific topics.
Upvoting and downvoting: Community-driven content curation.

AMA (Ask Me Anything): Interactive Q&A sessions with experts and celebrities.

Threads: Detailed discussion threads that can grow extensively.

Anonymity: Users can participate without real-name identities.

Reddit Gold: Premium membership offering additional features.

Karma points: Earn points when your posts or comments are upvoted.

Customizable feeds: Tailor what content appears in your feed.

Moderation tools: Community moderators can manage subreddits.

Wide range of content: From light-hearted memes to deep technical advice.

These detailed points for each platform illustrate the varied ways social media can cater to different needs, from real-time updates and professional networking to ephemeral content and community discussions. Each platform's unique features contribute to its niche, allowing it to serve specific functions in the social media ecosystem.

The Impact of Release Timing on
Viewer Engagement on YouTube

Two

In the ever-evolving landscape of digital media, understanding the nuances of YouTube analytics has become essential for content creators aiming to maximize their reach and engagement. The following case study shows that the growth of YouTube channels is significantly enhanced when video releases are strategically coordinated with events in the music industry related to channel content. This chapter delves into the intricate relationship between video-release schedules and viewer engagement, highlighting how aligning content with relevant music industry events can lead to substantial increases in subscriber growth and overall channel performance. By leveraging data-driven insights, we aim to provide a comprehensive understanding for content creators to optimize their release strategies and harness the full potential of YouTube analytics.

1 BACKGROUND CONTEXT

The evolution of digital audio workstations (DAWs) has significantly impacted the music production landscape, offering musicians and producers unprecedented tools for creativity and efficiency. Among these DAWs, Logic Pro, currently developed by Apple Inc., stands out as a leading choice for professionals and enthusiasts alike. This case study explores the background of a YouTube channel dedicated to Logic Pro, examining its growth, its content strategy, and the impact of targeted video releases.

The YouTube channel in focus was launched and posted its first video on April 14, 2008. In its nascent stage, the channel experienced a modest trajectory, posting only 17 videos over the next eight years. Despite the relatively low output, the channel managed to amass 370 subscribers. This period of sporadic content creation highlighted the challenges

DOI: 10.4324/9781003416180-2

of maintaining viewer engagement and growing a subscriber base without a consistent publishing schedule or a strategic plan.

The videos posted during this initial phase varied in topic, covering fundamental tutorials, tips, and tricks for using Logic Pro. While the content was well received within its niche, the infrequency of uploads limited the channel's potential reach and growth. This stagnation prompted a reassessment and led to the formulation of a new content strategy aimed at leveraging the periodic updates of Logic Pro.

The revised approach centered around posting new content each time Logic Pro received a software update. This strategy aimed to capitalize on the heightened interest and search traffic surrounding each update, thereby increasing visibility and engagement. By aligning content releases with software updates, the channel sought to position itself as a timely and relevant resource for Logic Pro users eager to learn about the latest features and improvements.

This experimental shift not only aimed to boost subscriber growth and viewer retention but also sought to establish the channel as a credible and authoritative source within the Logic Pro community. The results of this experiment, including metrics such as subscriber growth, video views, and audience engagement, are explored in subsequent sections of this research.

2 RESEARCH QUESTIONS

1. How does aligning video content with Logic Pro updates influence viewer engagement and channel visibility?
2. Do these videos lead to increased individual video viewership and overall channel viewership over the short and longer term?
3. Does the concept of posting on the same schedule of updates translate to other related non-update topics?
4. How can scheduling video content and timing help musicians grow their own presence on YouTube?

This background section provides a foundation for understanding the context and rationale behind the strategic shift in content creation for the YouTube channel. The subsequent analysis delves deeper into the data and outcomes associated with this experiment, offering insights into effective content strategies for niche YouTube channels.

3 METHODOLOGY

The methodology employed in this research involved a comprehensive analysis of the YouTube channel's performance metrics following the implementation of a new content strategy aligned with Logic Pro updates. The analysis was conducted in several stages, incorporating both quantitative and qualitative approaches to gain a holistic understanding of the channel's growth and engagement.

3.1 Data Collection

1 Video Performance Tracking

Each video posted in conjunction with a Logic Pro update was meticulously tracked for key performance indicators (KPIs) such as views, watch time, and added subscribers. This data was collected from the YouTube analytics platform, ensuring accuracy and granularity.

2 Other Viewership Growth

Additional videos related to the music industry, following the same model of being posted on a timely schedule, were also posted, and tracked using the analytics platform.

3.2 Data Analysis

1 Logic Pro Update Correlation Analysis

A correlation analysis was performed to determine the relationship between video-release timing (aligned with Logic Pro updates) and various performance metrics. This helped to ascertain the effectiveness of the content strategy in driving engagement and growth.

2 Non-Update-Related Video Analysis

A correlation analysis was performed to determine the relationship between industry news (non-Logic Pro update) video-release timings and various performance metrics. This helped to ascertain the effectiveness of the content strategy in driving engagement and growth when not attached to the Logic Pro update schedule.

4 RESULTS INTERPRETATION

The results of the analysis were interpreted to draw meaningful conclusions about the effectiveness of the new content strategy. Key findings were summarized, highlighting the impact of video-release timing.

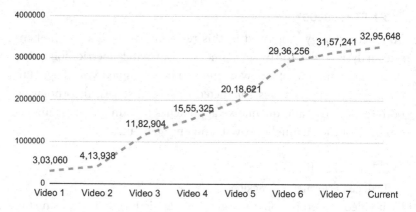

Figure 2.1 Video Views Aligned with 7 Key Video Posts

These findings provided actionable insights into optimizing content strategies for niche YouTube channels, particularly those focused on software updates.

The combination of quantitative and qualitative analysis methods ensured a robust and comprehensive evaluation of the YouTube channel's performance, offering valuable insights into the dynamics of content creation and audience engagement in the digital age. The overarching growth of the channel, as seen in Figure 2.1, demonstrates growth, but with various trajectories upward.

4.1 Results and Discussion

The analysis presented in this section revolves around the performance metrics of seven key video releases on various Logic Pro updates. These videos are pivotal to the project, representing significant milestones and driving substantial engagement on the channel. While these seven videos are crucial, it is essential to note that many other videos have been published on the channel. These additional videos have contributed to increasing traffic and engagement, complementing the impact of the main releases.

Research Question 1: How Does Aligning Video Content with Logic Pro Updates Influence Viewer Engagement and Channel Visibility?

The dataset comprises video views, immediate subscriber additions, channel views in the subsequent two weeks, and subscriber growth

Table 2.1 Detailed Breakdown of Video Releases

Video Topic / Date	Video Views	Subscribers Added	Channel Views— Next Two Weeks	Subscribers Added —Next Two Weeks
Logic Pro 10.31.18.17	3,114	1	8,716	163
Logic Pro 10.4 1.25.18	3,360	43	20,885	257
Logic Pro 10.5 5.12.20	16,322	150	90,790	1,411
Logic Pro 10.6 11.24.20	2,620	16	22,736	177
Logic Pro 10.7 10.18.21	2,912	23	45,930	408
Logic Pro 10.8 11.7.23	438	1	13,746	66
Logic Pro 11 5.7.24	43,355	309	135,036	1,005

over the same period. These metrics provide a comprehensive overview of each video's performance and the overall channel growth following the release of each update.

Among the seven videos analyzed as presented in Table 2.1, there are two notable outliers. The third video, covering Logic Pro 10.5, was released during the early stages of the COVID-19 pandemic, a period characterized by abnormally high YouTube viewership due to global lockdowns and increased online activity. This anomaly likely contributed to its elevated performance metrics. Conversely, the sixth video, detailing the Logic Pro 10.8 update, pertained to a relatively insignificant upgrade, which might explain its lower engagement figures.

The following analysis delves into these metrics, identifying patterns, trends, and key insights that inform future content strategies and highlight the factors driving successful engagement and growth on the channel.

Research Question 2: Do These Videos Lead to Increased Individual Video Viewership and Overall Channel Viewership Over the Short and Longer Term?

1 Initial Video Metrics vs. Two-Week Period Post-Release

The analysis of initial video metrics (immediate video views and subscriber additions) compared to the metrics observed in the two weeks following the release provides valuable insights into the dynamics of viewer engagement and channel growth.

2 Initial Video Metrics

The number of views a video accumulates shortly after its release serves as an immediate indicator of its popularity and relevance. Higher initial views suggest strong initial interest from the audience.

The number of subscribers added immediately following the release reflects the video's ability to convert viewers into long-term followers, indicating its effectiveness in engaging and retaining an audience.

3 Two-Week Period Post-Release

The increase in overall channel views in the two weeks following the video release demonstrates the video's broader impact on driving traffic to the channel. This metric highlights the sustained interest in the content and its ability to attract viewers to other videos on the channel.

The number of subscribers added during the two-week period provides insight into the video's longer-term impact on subscriber growth. It indicates the extent to which the video contributes to the channel's sustained growth beyond the initial surge.

4.2 Analysis

The comparison between initial video metrics and the two-week post-release period reveals several key trends:

1. Sustained Engagement: Videos that perform well initially tend to continue driving engagement, resulting in significant increases in both channel views and subscriber growth in the following weeks. This trend underscores the importance of capturing viewer interest immediately upon release.

2. Broader Impact: Successful videos not only attract views and sub-scribers immediately but also contribute to overall channel growth by encouraging viewers to explore additional content. This effect amplifies the video's impact beyond its initial release.

3. Effective Content Strategy: The data suggests that high-performing videos are often those that cover significant updates or feature content that resonates strongly with the audience. Focusing on such content can drive both immediate and sustained engagement.

4. Low-Performing Videos: Even the lowest-performing video still contributed to an increase in viewership over time.

By understanding these patterns, content creators can refine their strategies to maximize both initial impact and longer-term growth. The insights from this analysis highlight the importance of producing high-quality, relevant content that captures and retains viewer interest from the outset.

Research Question 3: Does the Concept of Posting on the Same Schedule of Updates Translate to Other Related Non-Update Topics?

In addition to posting videos in a coordinated fashion with the Logic Pro updates, other videos were also posted that lined up with various non-update industry occurrences to see how they affected subscriber counts, views/channel view counts, and the channel's performance in the two-week period after posting. Several other videos are also included that featured music videos not tied to any industry topics/timings.

The analysis of non-update video releases offers critical insights into the effectiveness of uploading content that is different than the videos focusing on the Logic Pro updates. The data, as summarized in Table 2.2, includes video views, subscriber growth, and overall channel performance in the two weeks following each video release.

4.3 Video Performance Analysis—Chronological Order

The "Friday Mix" video, posted on November 18, 2016, garnered a mere 56 views and did not add any subscribers initially. However, the sub-sequent two weeks saw an increase of 1,114 channel views and four new subscribers. This marginal increase indicates minimal engagement, likely due to the video's lack of specific industry relevance or appeal. This video is an original song with no specific mechanism to attract viewers.

Table 2.2 Detailed Breakdown of Non-Update Video Releases

Video Topic / Date	Video Views	Subscribers Added	Channel Views— Next Two Weeks	Subscribers Added— Next Two Weeks
Friday Mix 11.18.16	56	0	1,114	4
Billie Eilish Clone 4.23.19	23,599	214	9,909	86
Drummer Track 5.25.20	56,753	636	38,315	382
Get In Line Mix 3.5.21	1,053	2	22,574	124
CS12 3.6.24	6,809	50	18,420	94
Synthesizer V 3.18.24	31,824	167	19,949	142
Song Night Series 2.29.23 - 4.21.24 33 Videos	12,540 Mean: 380 per video	21	NA	NA

In contrast, the "Billie Eilish Clone" video, released on April 23, 2019, achieved significant success, with 23,599 views and 214 new subscribers. In the following two weeks, the channel experienced 9,909 views and an additional 86 subscribers. The considerable viewership and subscriber growth can be attributed to the video's association with Billie Eilish, a well-known figure, highlighting the effectiveness of leveraging popular names to boost engagement.

Furthermore, this period coincided with the aftermath of the release of her debut album, *When We All Fall Asleep, Where Do We Go?* on March 29, 2019. The album's success and the subsequent promotional activities, including tours and media appearances, kept Eilish in the spotlight. The combination of these high-profile engagements helped maintain her visibility and popularity, which in turn would have driven more traffic to related YouTube content, such as the "Billie Eilish Clone" video.

The "Drummer Track" video, posted on May 25, 2020, was the most successful among the non-update videos, attracting 56,753 views and

636 new subscribers. In the subsequent two weeks, it contributed to 38,315 channel views and 382 additional subscribers. This high engagement suggests that the technical content related to music production resonated strongly with the target audience, indicating the importance of topic relevance in driving viewer interest and channel growth.

The "Get In Line Mix" video, released on March 5, 2021, initially received 1,053 views and added only two subscribers. However, the following two weeks saw a substantial increase in channel activity, with 22,574 views and 124 new subscribers. This discrepancy suggests that viewers were coming to the channel to view other content independently of this specific video.

The "CS12" video, posted on March 6, 2024, had moderate success, with 6,809 views and 50 new subscribers. It led to 18,420 channel views and 94 additional subscribers in the following two weeks. The moderate performance indicates that while the video was engaging, its impact was not as pronounced as that of the top-performing videos.

The "Synthesizer V" video, released on March 18, 2024, attracted 31,824 views and 167 new subscribers. In the two weeks after its release, it contributed to 19,949 channel views and 142 additional subscribers. The substantial viewership and sustained interest underscore the appeal of specific technical topics, such as synthesizers, which draw a dedicated audience.

The "Song Night Series," spanning from February 29, 2023, to April 21, 2024, with a mean of 380 views per video, resulted in a total of 12,540 views and 21 new subscribers. Although the series did not generate viral individual videos, it maintained consistent viewer engagement over time, suggesting that series content can contribute to steady channel growth.

4.4 Key Observations

The analysis reveals that the most successful videos, such as "Drummer Track" and "Billie Eilish Clone," leveraged broad appeal or popular names to attract significant viewership and subscriber growth. These videos demonstrated sustained engagement in the weeks following their release, indicating that compelling content not only draws viewers but also retains their interest.

Videos like the "Get In Line Mix," despite low initial views, didn't prevent significant channel activity in the following weeks. The "Song Night Series" illustrates that while individual videos may not achieve high view counts, series content can foster consistent engagement and support overall channel growth.

The findings suggest that posting videos on topics related to industry trends or leveraging popular figures, even when not directly tied to Logic Pro updates, can enhance channel performance. Well-chosen non-update content can attract new subscribers and maintain viewer interest, thereby supporting the overall growth of the YouTube channel. This strategy emphasizes the importance of topic relevance and the potential for delayed engagement in driving long-term channel success.

Research Question 4: How Can Scheduling Video Content and Timing Help Musicians Grow Their Own Presence on YouTube?

To address how the findings from this research can assist musicians in growing their presence on YouTube, it is essential to distill the key insights and strategies derived from the data analysis. These strategies revolve around leveraging the principles of timely content release, relevance, and engagement, which have proven effective in the context of the studied YouTube channel.

Leveraging Timely Content Releases

The analysis clearly demonstrates that aligning video releases with significant updates or events in the music industry can substantially boost viewer engagement and subscriber growth. Musicians can apply this principle by timing their video releases to coincide with notable industry events, such as:

- Software and Gear Updates: For musicians who produce content related to music production, aligning videos with updates to popular software or new gear releases can attract a tech-savvy audience eager for the latest information.
- New Music Releases: Posting content around the release dates of new albums or singles, either their own or those of popular artists, can attract viewers searching for related content.

Creating Relevant and Engaging Content

The success of videos such as "Drummer Track" and "Billie Eilish Clone" highlights the importance of creating content that resonates with the target audience. Musicians should focus on:

- Educational and Informative Content: Tutorials, behind-the-scenes looks, and gear reviews can attract viewers interested in learning more about music production and performance.
- Leveraging Popular Names and Trends: Associating content with well-known figures or trending topics in the music industry can draw in a broader audience.

Consistent Content Creation

The data indicates that consistent content creation, even if individual videos do not go viral, can contribute to steady channel growth. Musicians should aim to:

- Ensure That All Videos Move in the Right Direction: The upload of videos focusing on Logic Pro updates came over 7 years and even the ones with smallest initial audience still added subscribers and contributed to the overall channel momentum.
- Maintain a Regular Posting Schedule: Consistency helps build a loyal audience base that knows when to expect new content. Each update video (excepting outliers) had a larger audience than its predecessor, and other videos that were focused on timely topics also helped follow the growth trajectory.
- Create Series or Themed Content: Series like the "Song Night Series" can foster ongoing engagement by providing viewers with a reason to return to the channel regularly. This also brought in a non-timely topic and took advantage of the other topics to build audience.

Engaging with the Audience

The study highlights the value of engagement metrics such as comments, likes, and shares in driving channel growth. Musicians can enhance their presence by:

- Responding to Comments: Engaging with viewers in the comment section helps build a community and encourages more interaction.
- Encouraging Viewer Participation: Inviting viewers to participate in challenges, ask questions, or share their own content can increase engagement and make the channel more interactive.

Utilizing Analytics

Finally, leveraging YouTube's analytics to track performance and adjust strategies is crucial.

Musicians should:

- Monitor Key Metrics: Keep an eye on views, and watch time, subscriber growth, and engagement rates to understand what types of content perform best.
- Experiment and Iterate: Use the data to experiment with different content formats and topics, iterating based on what resonates most with the audience.

By applying these strategies, musicians can optimize their YouTube content, enhance viewer engagement, and grow their subscriber base, ultimately building a more substantial and engaged online presence.

5 CONCLUSIONS, LIMITATIONS, AND RECOMMENDATIONS FOR FUTURE WORK

5.1 Conclusions

The analysis of the YouTube channel dedicated to Logic Pro content revealed several key insights:

- Strategic Content Release: Aligning video releases with significant Logic Pro updates significantly boosts viewer engagement and subscriber growth. This timing leverages the heightened interest and search traffic surrounding these updates, positioning the channel as a timely resource.
- Content Relevance: Videos covering major updates or featuring popular figures in the music industry attract substantial viewership and engagement. Educational and informative content, particularly tutorials and behind-the-scenes looks, resonates well with the audience.
- Consistency: Regular and consistent content creation fosters steady channel growth. Even videos that do not go viral contribute to overall viewer engagement and subscriber retention.
- Audience Engagement: Direct interaction with viewers through comments and participation in challenges enhances community building and increases engagement metrics, which are crucial for channel growth.

5.2 Limitations

- Data Scope: The analysis was limited to a specific YouTube channel focused on Logic Pro. Results may not be generalizable to channels with different content focuses or broader audiences.
- External Factors: External factors, such as global events like the COVID-19 pandemic, influenced the data. For example, increased online activity during the early part of the pandemic may have artificially inflated engagement metrics for certain videos.
- Content Variability: The nature and quality of content varied across videos, which could impact engagement metrics independently of the strategic timing. This variability was not fully accounted for in the analysis.
- Platform-Specific Insights: The findings are primarily applicable to YouTube and may not directly translate to other social media platforms with different algorithms and audience behaviors.

5.3 Recommendations for Future Work

- Broader Content Analysis: Future research should include a wider range of YouTube channels across different genres and topics to validate the findings and explore their applicability to other content types.
- Platform Comparison: Comparative studies across multiple social media platforms, such as Instagram, TikTok, and Facebook, would provide a more comprehensive understanding of effective content strategies and their impact on audience engagement.
- Longitudinal Studies: Conducting longitudinal studies to track long-term effects of content strategies on subscriber growth and engagement could offer deeper insights into sustained channel performance.
- Experimental Approaches: Implementing controlled experiments to isolate the impact of specific variables, such as content type, release timing, and audience interaction techniques, could help refine content strategies for optimal engagement.
- Advanced Analytics: Utilizing advanced analytics tools and machine learning algorithms to predict viewer behavior and optimize content recommendations could enhance the effectiveness of content strategies.

By addressing these limitations and pursuing the recommended future work, content creators and researchers can gain a more nuanced understanding of how to effectively leverage social media platforms to maximize audience engagement and channel growth.

Three

Chapter 3 unfolds as an essential starting guide for anyone venturing into the realm of long-format or short-format content creation, offering a treasure trove of insights and practical advice to enhance your storytelling process. It begins with the critical first step of capture, emphasizing not just the action but the deliberate choices behind selecting the right equipment, from cameras to indispensable accessories, that elevate your narrative. Aimed at filling the gaps in the skill sets of musicians and music producers, this chapter looks at the concepts and visual techniques that are commonly faced along the way.

LONG-FORMAT CONTENT

Whether you're a budding musician or seeking to enrich your content creation repertoire and an experienced producer/musician, the insights provided here are designed to help you navigate the complexities of producing compelling long-format content that resonates with audiences.

Capture

When embarking on the journey of long-format content creation, the very first step is capture—a process that sounds simpler than it actually is. It's not just about hitting the record button; it's about making deliberate choices on how and with what tools you capture your vision. Let's dive into the essential gear: cameras, audio tools, phone capture, screen capture, software content, and the not-to-be-forgotten accessories.

Cameras

In the realm of long-format content creation, selecting the right camera is akin to choosing a paintbrush for a canvas. It's not just about

DOI: 10.4324/9781003416180-3

what you capture, but how you capture it, which can elevate your storytelling.

Types: The choice of camera significantly affects the visual quality and feel of your content. Here's a closer look at the options:

DSLR Cameras: Digital Single-Lens Reflex (DSLR) cameras (see Figure 3.1) use a mirror mechanism to direct light from the lens to the viewfinder. They are renowned for their versatility, excellent image quality, and wide range of interchangeable lenses. Ideal for beginners and professionals alike, DSLRs like the line from Nikon offer robust manual controls, allowing for precise adjustments to exposure, focus, and more.

Mirrorless Cameras: These cameras do away with the bulky mirror system of DSLRs, making them lighter and more compact. They provide similar image quality and versatility, with interchangeable lenses, but with the advantage of a digital viewfinder. This feature allows for a real-time preview of your image with current exposure settings.

Action Cameras: Designed for adventurers, action cameras are compact, durable, and waterproof. They're perfect for capturing high-energy activities like sports, travel vlogs, and more. The GoPro series of cameras, for example, offers 5K+ video recording, hyper-smooth

Figure 3.1 My Nikon

Figure 3.2 DJI OSMO with Gimbal

stabilization, and the ability to capture breathtaking wide-angle shots. Other options such as the DJI OSMO series (see Figure 3.2) are excellent alternatives.

360-Degree Cameras: For creators aiming to produce immersive content, 360-degree cameras capture every angle of a scene simultaneously. This allows viewers to explore the video from different perspectives, making it a fantastic tool for virtual reality content. The Insta360 series of cameras (see Figure 3.3) is ever-expanding and is among the top products in this category, providing stunning 8K resolution, excellent stabilization, and user-friendly editing software.

Storage: The media you choose to store your footage on can impact your workflow and final product. Different cameras support various storage formats, and each has its pros and cons:

SD Cards: Secure Digital (SD) cards are widely used due to their affordability and compatibility with most cameras. They come in different speed classes, which is crucial for video capture. Higher class ratings (Class 10, UHS-I, and UHS-II) are recommended for

Figure 3.3 Insta360 X4 8K Camera

high-definition and 4K video recording to ensure smooth data writing without interruptions.

a. CFexpress Cards: CompactFlash Express cards are designed to support the high data rates of 4K and 8K video recording. They are ideal for professionals requiring fast read/write speeds for efficient editing workflows. Cameras like the Canon EOS-1D X Mark III use CFexpress cards to handle its high-resolution video capture capabilities.

b. SSDs: Solid State Drives (SSDs) offer the fastest data transfer rates and are used in external recorders or directly in cameras equipped with an SSD slot. They are particularly beneficial for extended recording sessions or when shooting in raw formats, where data files are significantly larger. The Blackmagic Pocket Cinema Camera 6K Pro, for instance, allows direct recording to an external SSD, enabling longer recording times and easier file management.

Brief Explanation of Settings

Mastery over your camera's settings can transform your videos from amateur to professional. Understanding the following key settings is essential.

- ISO: The ISO setting determines your camera's sensitivity to light. Lower values are used in bright conditions to prevent overexposure, while higher values allow for shooting in low light. However, increasing ISO can introduce noise or grain into your image, so finding a balance is key.
- Shutter Speed: Shutter speed controls how long your camera's sensor is exposed to light. In video, it's closely linked to the frame rate to achieve natural motion blur. A general rule is to set your shutter speed to double your frame rate; for instance, at 24 frames per second (fps), use a 1/48-second shutter speed.
- Aperture: Aperture affects the depth of field, which is the range of your scene in sharp focus. A lower f-number (e.g., f/2.8) creates a shallow depth of field, blurring the background and highlighting your subject. A higher f-number (e.g., f/16) keeps more of the scene in focus, useful for landscape shots.

By delving into these components, content creators can make informed decisions about their equipment and settings, setting a solid foundation for capturing high-quality long format content.

Audio Tools

In the cinematic world, audio is your narrative's heartbeat. It can convey emotion, set the scene, and engage your audience in ways visuals alone cannot. Understanding the types of audio tools at your disposal is pivotal in crafting a captivating auditory experience.

Microphones: Your microphone choice is contingent on your content's nature and the recording environment.

Lavalier Microphones: Often referred to as lapel mics, these are small, clip-on microphones that offer discrete audio capture. Ideal for interviews or situations where the speaker's voice needs to be clear and free from ambient noise. The RØDE GO lavalier (see Figure 3.4) is a popular choice for its crisp audio quality and compatibility with a wide range of devices.

Figure 3.4 RØDE GO Lavalier

Figure 3.5 Shotgun Microphone

Shotgun Microphones: Shotgun mics (see Figure 3.5) are highly directional and designed to capture sound from a specific area, minimizing side and rear noise. These are perfect for location shoots, where focusing on the subject's voice amidst background noise is crucial. The Sennheiser MKE 600 is known for its excellent directivity and clarity in outdoor environments.

Condenser Microphones: Favored in studio settings for their sensitivity and wide frequency response, condenser mics (see Figure 3.6) are superb for capturing vocal nuances and instruments. They require phantom power, usually supplied by audio interfaces or external recorders. The Audio-Technica AT2020 provides professional-quality

Figure 3.6 An Example of a Condenser Microphone

sound at an entry-level price, making it a favorite among podcasters and musicians.

Dynamic Microphones: Renowned for their durability and ability to handle high sound-pressure levels, dynamic mics (see Figure 3.7) are excellent for live performances and capturing loud sound sources. The Shure SM7B has gained legendary status for its warm, smooth sound profile and is a staple in radio stations and recording studios.

Recorders: For situations where in-camera audio isn't sufficient or when multitrack recording is needed, external audio recorders come into play.

• Handheld Recorders: Portable and versatile, handheld recorders like the Zoom H4n Pro can capture high-quality stereo or multi-track audio. They are ideal for on-the-go interviews, location sound effects, and as a backup audio source.

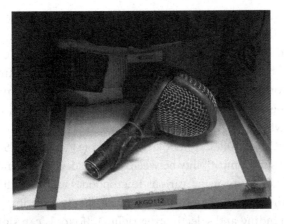

Figure 3.7 An Example of a Dynamic Microphone

Figure 3.8 Zoom LiveTrak L-8

- Multitrack Recorders: For complex productions requiring multiple audio sources to be recorded simultaneously, multitrack recorders are indispensable. Zoom has a line of portable, battery-powered mixer/recorders that are incredibly useful (see Figure 3.8.)

Cables: The unsung heroes that connect your audio universe. Quality cables ensure a clean signal path between your microphones, recorders, and cameras.

XLR Cables: The standard for professional audio, XLR cables are balanced, reducing noise and interference over long distances. They are essential for connecting professional microphones to recorders or audio interfaces.

TRS and TRRS Cables: TRS (Tip Ring Sleeve) cables are commonly used for stereo audio connections, while TRRS (Tip Ring Ring Sleeve) variants connect to smartphones and computers, accommodating microphones with built-in headphones. These are vital for simpler setups or when integrating audio into live streams.

Adapter Cables: Often overlooked, adapters (e.g., XLR to 3.5 mm, TRS to TRRS) ensure compatibility between different devices and inputs. They provide flexibility in using various microphones and recording equipment together, especially in makeshift or on-the-fly recording scenarios.

Understanding and selecting the right audio tools can significantly enhance the quality of your long-format content. Clear, crisp audio captures your audience's attention and holds it, making your message more impactful. Whether recording a documentary, interview, or narrative film, the right combination of microphones, recorders, and cables is key to achieving professional-level sound.

Phone Capture

In today's digital age, smartphones have evolved into powerful tools for video production, offering an array of features that rival traditional cameras. Understanding how to maximize these capabilities can transform your phone into a versatile filmmaking device.

Stabilization

The key to professional-looking footage is stability. Most modern smartphones are equipped with built-in stabilization technologies.

- Optical Image Stabilization (OIS): This hardware-based solution compensates for hand shake by physically moving the camera lens or sensor. It's especially effective for static shots or mild movements, ensuring your footage remains smooth and clear.
- Electronic Image Stabilization (EIS): Unlike OIS, EIS is a software-driven approach that stabilizes footage by cropping in and moving the video frame in opposition to any detected movements. It's useful for dynamic shots but can result in a slight decrease in video quality due to the cropping process.

- Gimbals: For even greater stability, smartphone gimbals are external devices that use motors to keep your phone steady. Products like the DJI Osmo Mobile series provide smooth, cinematic motion, making them indispensable for tracking shots, pans, and tilts.

Typical Phone Features
Modern smartphones come packed with features designed to enhance video production (see Figure 3.9).

- 4K Recording: Many smartphones now support 4K video recording, offering four times the resolution of 1080p HD video. This high resolution allows for clearer, more detailed footage, giving content creators the ability to crop or zoom into their footage without significant loss of quality.
- Slow Motion and Time-Lapse: These creative modes offer unique ways to capture motion and the passage of time. Slow motion is perfect for dramatizing action scenes, while time-lapse can beautifully compress hours into seconds, ideal for showcasing changes or movements too subtle for real-time video.
- Manual Controls: Several smartphone cameras offer manual settings, allowing users to adjust ISO, shutter speed, and focus, providing greater creative control over the look of their footage. Apps like Filmic Pro further extend these capabilities, turning your smartphone into a highly customizable video camera.

Figure 3.9 iPhone Video Interface

- App Workflow: The ecosystem of apps available for video editing and production on smartphones is vast and varied:
- Shooting Apps: Beyond the native camera app, third-party applications offer enhanced control and features. Filmic Pro, for example, provides users with a suite of professional-grade tools including logarithmic gamma curves, color grading, and focus peaking.
- Editing Apps: Editing on the go has never been easier thanks to mobile apps like Adobe Premiere Rush and LumaFusion. These apps offer powerful editing capabilities, from multitrack timelines to color correction, enabling creators to polish their footage directly on their phones.
- Collaborative and Cloud Apps: For projects involving multiple collaborators, cloud-based apps like Google Drive and Dropbox facilitate easy sharing and storage of video files. Additionally, collaboration platforms like Frame.io offer tools for real-time feedback and approval processes, streamlining post-production workflows.

By harnessing the power of smartphone technology, creators can produce stunning long-format content with a device that fits in their pocket. From capturing footage with advanced stabilization features to editing and collaborating through sophisticated apps, the possibilities for phone-based video production are virtually limitless.

Screen Capture

In the digital era, where online learning and video tutorials have become ubiquitous, mastering screen capture is indispensable for content creators. It's not just about recording what's on your screen; it's about crafting a narrative that guides your viewers through complex information with ease and clarity.

Basic Overview: Screen capture, or screencasting, (see Figure 3.10) involves recording the output of your computer screen, often accompanied by voice-over narration. This technique is widely used for creating tutorials, software demonstrations, and online courses. The simplicity of screen capture allows creators to efficiently share knowledge and instructions, making it a favorite among educators and tech reviewers.

Figure 3.10 ScreenFlow Capture Software

Software Options: Numerous tools are available for screen capture, and each has its set of features tailored to different needs. Free options like OBS Studio offer robust functionality, including high-definition recording and live-streaming capabilities. For those seeking more intuitive interfaces and enhanced editing features, paid software like Camtasia or ScreenFlow provide a comprehensive solution, from recording to final edits, including animations and quizzes.

Resolution and Frame Rate: When setting up for screen capture, selecting the right resolution and frame rate is crucial. Recording in 1080p is generally sufficient for clear, detailed visuals, while a frame rate of 30 fps ensures smooth playback. Adjusting these settings according to your content and delivery platform can optimize viewing experiences across devices.

Combining Screen, Camera, and Microphone Sources: To create more engaging and personal content, integrating multiple media sources is key. This approach not only conveys the information on the screen but also adds a layer of interaction through the creator's expressions and voice.

Picture-in-Picture (PiP): Many screen-capture tools allow for PiP, where a smaller frame (usually the webcam feed showing the creator) is superimposed over the main screen content (see Figure 3.11.) This feature is particularly effective in tutorials, where seeing the instructor adds a personal touch and aids in communication.

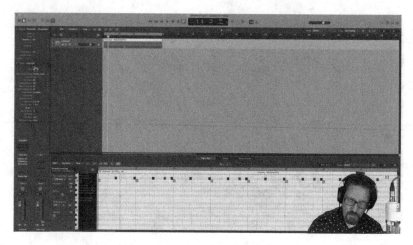

Figure 3.11 PiP Example

Audio Quality: Good audio quality is essential for keeping the audience engaged. Using a high-quality microphone and ensuring a quiet recording environment can dramatically improve the clarity of your voice-overs. External microphones, such as USB condenser mics, are preferred over built-in computer mics for their superior sound capture.

Synchronizing Sources: Ensuring that your video and audio sources are in sync is critical, especially when editing footage from different inputs. Most advanced screen-capture and editing software provide tools for aligning audio with video tracks, reducing echo, and synchronizing voice-overs with screen actions.

By understanding and applying these concepts, content creators can elevate their screen-capture projects beyond simple recordings, creating engaging, informative, and professional-quality videos. Whether for educational purposes, software tutorials, or online presentations, the ability to combine screen content with personal narration and video adds depth and personal connection to digital content, making it more relatable and easier to comprehend for the audience.

Software Content

In the vast ocean of content creation, software-based content stands out for its ability to convey complex ideas, narratives, and emotions through digital artistry. From the subtle nuance of animated characters to the sleek motion of graphics sweeping across the screen, this domain offers endless possibilities for creativity and expression.

- Animation: The art of bringing to life static images through movement, animation can range from simple 2D cartoons to intricate 3D models. It's a powerful tool for storytelling, capable of transporting viewers to new worlds filled with unique characters and vivid landscapes.
- 2D Animation: Utilizing software like Adobe Animate or Toon Boom Harmony, creators can design and animate characters, backgrounds, and objects in a two-dimensional space. This style is popular in cartoons, explainer videos, and educational content, offering a straightforward yet captivating way to engage audiences.
- 3D Animation: For content that requires a more realistic or complex visual approach, 3D animation software such as Blender or Autodesk Maya provides the tools to create lifelike scenes and characters. Though more time-consuming and resource-intensive, 3D animation opens up a universe of creative possibilities, from detailed character modeling to immersive environment design.
- Motion Graphics: Sitting at the crossroads of graphic design and video, motion graphics bring static designs to life through animation. This form is often used in advertising, title sequences, and information visualization, employing moving text, shapes, and imagery to convey messages in a dynamic and visually appealing manner.
- Tools and Techniques: Software like Adobe After Effects is synonymous with motion graphics, offering extensive features for compositing, animation, and effects. Learning keyframe animation, which allows for the precise control of movement and transformations over time, is fundamental. Additionally, understanding concepts like easing, which makes transitions more natural, can significantly enhance the fluidity and professionalism of your work.
- Whiteboarding: A favorite in educational and instructional content, whiteboard videos mimic the look of someone drawing on a whiteboard, progressively revealing information. This style is effective for breaking down complex concepts into digestible, engaging segments that retain the viewer's attention.
- Digital Creation: Whiteboard animation software, such as Videoscribe or Doodly, automates the drawing process, allowing

creators to focus on crafting their narrative. These tools offer a library of images and templates, as well as the ability to import custom artwork, making it easier to produce tailored content that resonates with your audience.

- Engagement Strategies: Incorporating storytelling elements, using relatable characters, and structuring information flow to build curiosity can turn educational content into a captivating experience. The key is to balance visual simplicity with narrative depth, guiding viewers through your content in an entertaining and informative way.

Embracing software content creation unlocks a realm of possibilities for video producers, allowing for the incorporation of elements that can enhance storytelling, explain complex subjects, and capture the audience's imagination. Whether through the whimsical charm of animation, the sleek sophistication of motion graphics, or the educational appeal of whiteboarding, software tools empower creators to push the boundaries of traditional video content, making it more engaging, informative, and visually compelling.

Accessories
In the world of content creation, the devil is in the details—and often, those details come down to the accessories you use. Whether you're filming a documentary, shooting a vlog, or creating an animated feature, the right accessories can transform your production from amateur to professional.

- Tripods: The cornerstone of stable, professional-looking video. A good tripod (see Figure 3.12) provides a steady base for your camera, eliminating unwanted shake and ensuring smooth panning and tilting movements.
- Types: From lightweight and portable to heavy-duty and feature-rich, tripods vary greatly to suit different needs. For fieldwork, a carbon fiber tripod offers the perfect balance of strength and lightness. In studio settings, heavier-duty tripods with fluid heads allow for precise, smooth movements, crucial for cinematic shots.
- Choosing the Right Tripod: Consider the weight of your camera setup, the environments you'll be shooting in, and the level of

Figure 3.12 Portable Tripod

movement you need. Features like quick-release plates, bubble levels, and adjustable legs can greatly enhance usability.

- Gimbals: For content creators on the move, a gimbal stabilizer (see Figure 3.13) is indispensable. Using motors and sensors, gimbals keep your camera level and stable, even when you're walking, running, or moving around unpredictably.
- Smartphone Gimbals: With the rising quality of smartphone cameras, smartphone gimbals have become increasingly popular. Lightweight and compact, they are perfect for vloggers and mobile filmmakers seeking cinematic smoothness in their handheld shots.
- Camera Gimbals: Larger than their smartphone counterparts, these are designed to handle the weight and balance of DSLRs or

Figure 3.13 iPhone Gimbal

mirrorless cameras. They are ideal for professional videographers looking to achieve steady footage without the confines of a tripod.

- Lights: Lighting can make or break your video. It's not just about making your scene visible; it's about shaping the mood, directing attention, and enhancing the overall aesthetic of your content.
  - Key Light, Fill Light, and Back Light: The three-point lighting setup is a fundamental technique, involving a key light to illuminate the subject, a fill light to soften shadows, and a back light to separate the subject from the background. This setup is versatile, working well for interviews, narrative filming, and product shots.
  - Ring Lights: Popular among vloggers and beauty content creators, ring lights (see Figure 3.14) provide even, flattering light directly around the camera. They're particularly effective for close-up shots, reducing shadows and highlighting details.
- Green Screens: By allowing you to change the background of your scene in post-production, green screens (see Figure 3.15) open up a world of creative possibilities. Whether you're adding an exotic location or creating a complex visual effect, what is important is a smooth, evenly lit green backdrop for easy keying.
- Setup Tips: Ensure your green screen is well lit and free from wrinkles or shadows. Lighting should be uniform, with no hot spots or dark areas, to facilitate clean keying in post-production.

Figure 3.14 Ring Light Example

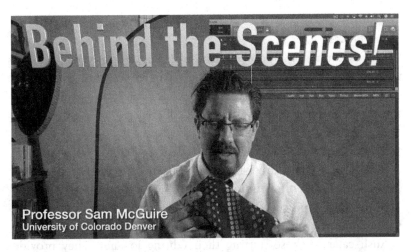

Figure 3.15 Green Screen in Action

- Dollies and Sliders: For dynamic shots that add drama and depth to your videos, dollies and sliders are the tools of choice. By smoothly moving the camera through space, they introduce motion that can enhance storytelling and visual interest.
- Use Cases: A slider can be used for smooth horizontal or vertical shots, adding a cinematic quality to interviews, establishing shots, or product showcases. A dolly setup, which requires more space and setup time, is ideal for longer tracking shots or scenes requiring complex movement.
- Miscellaneous: Don't overlook the small but mighty accessories that can save the day on set. Lens filters to control light and protect your lens, monitor screens for better visibility, and microphone windshields to improve audio quality are just a few examples of the unsung heroes in content creation.

Investing in and mastering the use of these accessories not only improves the technical quality of your videos but also expands your creative toolkit, allowing you to bring your artistic vision to life with greater precision and professionalism. Whether you're just starting or looking to upgrade your production value, the right accessories can make a significant difference in the impact and appeal of your long-format content.

Editing

The Process

Editing is not merely a post-production step but a creative process that weaves together visuals, sounds, and narrative to tell a compelling story. It's where the raw materials of your project are sculpted into something meaningful, engaging, and coherent.

- Software Editors: The digital toolset for any editor, software editors range from beginner-friendly applications to industry-standard platforms. Each offers unique features tailored to different aspects of the editing process.
- For Beginners and Enthusiasts: Tools like iMovie or Adobe Premiere Rush cater to those starting their editing journey. They provide intuitive interfaces and essential editing functionalities—cutting, transitions, simple color correction—that empower new creators to produce quality content with a shallow learning curve.
- Professional-Grade Software: Adobe Premiere Pro and Final Cut Pro (see Figure 3.16) represent the pinnacle of editing software, designed for those requiring advanced features and control. These platforms offer a depth of functionality including multi-cam editing, complex effect compositions, detailed audio editing, and extensive color-grading tools. Their powerful capabilities are best leveraged with a solid understanding of editing principles and techniques.

Figure 3.16 Final Cut Pro

- In-Camera Editing: While often overlooked, in-camera editing is a valuable technique for creators working with minimal resources or aiming for a raw, authentic aesthetic. It involves making deliberate choices about shots, sequences, and transitions during the filming process, reducing the need for extensive post-production. This approach requires a clear vision and precise execution but can significantly streamline the editing workload.
- Typical Editing Tools and Workflows: Mastery over your editing software's toolset is crucial for efficient and creative editing. Familiarity with the following tools and their applications can enhance your editing process:
- Cutting and Trimming: The backbone of editing, these tools allow you to select and refine the footage that makes it into your final product. Effective cutting and trimming remove unnecessary content, tighten the narrative, and ensure a smooth flow from one scene to the next.
- Transitions: Beyond the basic cut, transitions help to visually move from one scene to another. While cuts are most common, fades, wipes, and more creative transitions can be used sparingly to convey a specific mood or style.
- Color Correction and Grading: These tools adjust the footage's color balance and tone, ensuring consistency across shots and enhancing the visual appeal. Color correction standardizes colors and exposure, while color grading applies a stylistic look to your footage.
- Audio Mixing and Editing: Sound is half the experience in video content. Editing software (see Figure 3.17) provides tools to adjust levels, balance tracks, and clean up audio to ensure clarity and impact. Background music, sound effects, and voice-overs should be carefully balanced to complement the visual content without overwhelming it.
- Storytelling Through Editing: Ultimately, editing is about storytelling. It's about choosing which shots to use and how to arrange them to build tension, convey emotion, and guide the viewer through the narrative. Understanding the rhythm and pacing of scenes, how to use visual and audio cues to advance the story, and when to employ different editing techniques is what transforms raw footage into a compelling story.

The editing process is both technical and creative, requiring a blend of software skills, aesthetic judgment, and narrative intuition. By

Figure 3.17 Audio Editing in Final Cut Pro

mastering the tools and techniques of editing, you can unlock the full potential of your content, engaging your audience with stories that resonate and inspire.

Storytelling

At the heart of every memorable piece of content lies a compelling story. The editing process plays a pivotal role in storytelling, allowing creators to refine their narrative, emphasize key moments, and guide the audience through the emotional journey of the content.

- Storyboarding: Before diving into the editing process, storyboarding serves as a critical planning tool. It involves sketching out the sequence of scenes or key visuals on paper or digitally, providing a visual reference for the narrative flow. This preliminary step helps editors identify the core elements of the story, envision transitions, and organize content in a coherent manner.
- Importance: Storyboarding facilitates clear communication among all team members involved in the content creation process, ensuring everyone shares a unified vision of the final product. It also allows creators to experiment with different narrative structures and visual compositions before committing to edits, saving time and resources in the long run.
- Acts and Structure: Traditional storytelling often follows a three-act structure: the setup, the confrontation, and the resolution. This model can be adapted to fit the context of long-format content, helping to organize the narrative into a clear beginning, middle, and end.
- Application: In editing, this structure guides the arrangement of scenes, ensuring a smooth progression of the narrative. The first act introduces the characters, setting, and initial conflict. The second act escalates the conflict, presenting challenges and developments that drive the story forward. The final act resolves the conflict, offering closure and reflection on the journey.
- The Arc: The emotional or dramatic arc refers to the transformation or journey of the main subject(s) throughout the piece. Effective editing highlights this evolution, using pacing, music, and visual cues to reflect changes in tension, emotion, and stakes.
- Techniques: Key moments in the arc can be emphasized through close-ups, slow-motion, or music changes to heighten emotional

impact. Contrasting scenes or parallel editing can also illustrate the arc, juxtaposing the protagonist's lows with their eventual highs.

- Maintaining Mystery and Engagement: Keeping the audience engaged throughout the content is crucial, especially in long format where the risk of viewer drop-off is higher. Editors can employ various techniques to maintain interest and suspense.
- Pacing and Timing: Careful control of pacing, when to speed up action or slow down for reflection, can keep viewers on the edge of their seats. Strategic placement of revelations or twists ensures the audience stays curious and invested in the outcome.
- Visual and Audio Cues: Subtle visual or audio cues can foreshadow future events or reveal important information gradually, building anticipation and depth in the narrative. The use of motifs, recurring themes, or symbols enriches the storytelling, encouraging viewers to pay closer attention.

Storytelling through editing is a craft that combines technical skills with creative vision. By leveraging storyboarding, understanding narrative structure, and employing techniques to enhance the emotional arc and engagement, editors can transform raw footage into powerful stories that resonate with audiences. This intricate process not only brings the content to life but also showcases the editor's role as a storyteller, shaping the viewer's experience and emotional journey through deliberate, thoughtful choices in the editing room.

Advanced Topics

As you delve deeper into the editing process, mastering advanced techniques opens up new dimensions of storytelling and visual creativity. These skills allow for the crafting of content that not only tells a story but also captivates the audience with its polished aesthetics and compelling visuals.

- Effects: Effects in video editing are tools that can dramatically alter or enhance the appearance of footage. They range from simple color adjustments to complex composite images.
- Visual Effects (VFX): These are crucial in scenes that cannot be captured during filming, whether due to logistical challenges or the

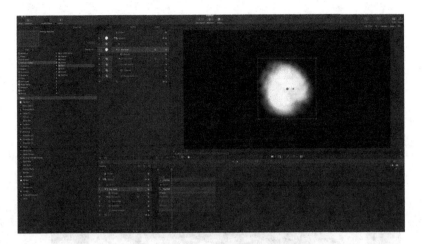

Figure 3.18 Apple Motion Creating an Explosion

fantastical nature of the content. Software like Apple Motion (see Figure 3.18) provides a plethora of options, from creating explosions to generating realistic weather conditions or crowd simulations.

- Transitional Effects: Beyond the conventional cut, transitions such as fades, wipes, and dissolves can be employed to signify changes in time, location, or mood. Used judiciously, these effects can add rhythm and fluidity to the narrative flow without distracting from the story.
- Masks and Keying: Masks and keying (see Figure 3.19) are powerful techniques for altering or selectively editing parts of a shot.
- Masks: By defining a specific area within a frame for adjustments or effects, masks enable editors to focus attention, blend shots seamlessly, or create intriguing visual compositions. Animating masks over time can also reveal or hide elements, adding a dynamic layer to the content.
- Chroma Key (Green Screen): Keying allows for the removal of a color (commonly green) to make it transparent, enabling the overlay of footage on different backgrounds. This technique is essential for placing characters in impossible locations, creating fantastical environments, or simulating depth and scale.
- Tracking and Motion Graphics: Integrating graphics that move with the elements of the footage can significantly enhance the narrative or provide supplementary information.

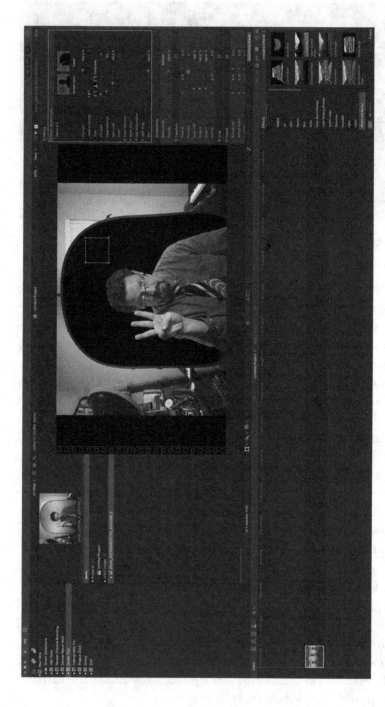

Figure 3.19 Keying a Green Screen in Final Cut Pro

- Motion Tracking: This allows for the attachment of graphical elements to moving objects within the video, ensuring that text, images, or effects follow the motion naturally. Whether it's highlighting a moving product or adding thought bubbles to a character, tracking maintains the coherence of motion between the graphic and the footage.
- Motion Graphics: These combine graphic design principles with video editing to create animated textual or graphical elements. From opening titles to informative graphics and dynamic lower thirds, motion graphics serve to engage viewers, convey information, and contribute to the visual identity of the content.
- Color Grading: The process of color grading involves adjusting the color palette of your footage to create a specific mood, style, or continuity across scenes.
- Tools and Techniques: Utilizing scopes and color wheels, editors can manipulate highlights, shadows, and midtones to warm up or cool down the image, enhance skin tones, or create a stylized look that supports the narrative theme or era.
- Look-Up Tables (LUTs): These are predefined color presets that can be applied to footage to achieve a particular look or to ensure consistency across various shots. LUTs are especially useful in projects with multiple shooting locations or lighting conditions, simplifying the color correction process.

Advanced editing techniques like these require time and practice to master, but they offer unparalleled control over the visual and narrative elements of your content. By skillfully applying effects, leveraging keying and masking, integrating motion graphics, and executing precise color grading, you can elevate your long-format content into a visually stunning and emotionally resonant masterpiece that captivates your audience from start to finish.

Exporting

The culmination of the editing process is the exporting stage, where your project transitions from a work in progress to a shareable video file. This step requires careful consideration of formats, quality settings, and platform requirements to ensure your content reaches your audience as intended, with the visual and auditory integrity intact.

- Formats: The digital container that holds your video, audio, and potentially subtitles and metadata. Choosing the right format affects compatibility, file size, and the quality of your content.
- Popular Formats:
  - MP4 (MPEG-4 Part 14): Universally compatible and efficient in terms of quality-to-file size ratio, MP4 is ideal for web distribution, including social media and video streaming platforms.
  - MOV (QuickTime File Format): Developed by Apple, MOV files offer high quality and are favored in professional settings, though they typically result in larger file sizes than MP4.
  - AVI (Audio Video Interleave) and WMV (Windows Media Video): Less commonly used for online content, these formats are better suited for specific uses, such as AVI for uncompressed video in post-production or WMV for Windows applications.
- Quality Expectations: Balancing file size and quality is crucial, especially for online distribution, as viewers may have varying internet speeds.
  - Resolution: Today's standard resolutions range from 1080p (Full HD) to 4K (Ultra HD), with 4K becoming increasingly common. Higher resolutions offer sharper detail but result in larger files. Consider your audience and the platforms you're targeting when deciding on resolution.
  - Bitrate: This determines the amount of data processed per unit of time in your video, affecting file size and quality. A higher bitrate means better quality but larger file sizes. Many platforms recommend specific bitrates for different resolutions to optimize for both quality and streaming performance.
  - Frame Rate: While 24fps (frames per second) is the cinematic standard, other common frame rates include 30fps for TV and web content and 60fps for high-definition slow-motion footage. Matching the frame rate to the content's intended use and aesthetic can enhance the viewer's experience.
- Export Settings for Different Platforms: Each social media platform and video hosting service has its own recommended settings for optimal video playback and quality.
  - YouTube: Recommends uploading content in high definition (1080p or 4K) with standard frame rates (24, 25, 30, 48, 50, 60) and using the MP4 format.

- Instagram: For Stories and Reels, vertical videos (9:16) with resolutions of at least 720p are preferred. IGTV allows for longer content, with similar quality recommendations.
- Vimeo: Prioritizes high-quality content, supporting up to 8K resolution uploads in various formats, but MP4 is recommended for its balance of quality and compatibility.

Understanding and implementing the appropriate export settings is a vital step in the post-production process, ensuring your content is delivered in the highest possible quality to your intended audience. By carefully selecting the right format, adjusting quality settings to suit your distribution channels, and adhering to platform-specific guidelines, you can maximize the reach and impact of your long format content, captivating your audience with both substance and style.

SHORTS/SHORT-FORMAT CONTENT

In the digital age, short-format content has surged to the forefront of social media consumption, driven by platforms like TikTok, Instagram Reels, and YouTube Shorts. These platforms have cultivated a new breed of content creators and audiences alike, who prize quick, impactful storytelling that fits into the palm of their hand. The following section moves into the art and science of producing short-format videos, highlighting the importance of mastering vertical video composition, understanding the unique interface of phone-based content creation, and utilizing editing tools that bring brevity and creativity together.

From conceptualizing ideas that fit within the tight confines of short videos to leveraging the advanced capabilities of smartphones, this section offers a roadmap for navigating the fast-paced world of short-format content. It underscores the creative and technical adjustments necessary to captivate an audience whose attention span is shorter than ever but which is eager for content that entertains, informs, and engages. Whether you're a novice looking to make your mark or an experienced creator aiming to refine your skills, understanding the dynamics of short-format videos is essential in the ever-evolving landscape of digital content.

Phone-Based Interface

Short-format videos have carved out a significant niche, driven by the rise of platforms like TikTok, Instagram Reels, and YouTube Shorts.

These platforms cater to audiences seeking quick, engaging content, and they have ushered in a new era of video production where creativity meets brevity.

The vertical video format (9:16 aspect ratio) is synonymous with short-format content on mobile platforms. This orientation (see Figure 3.20) aligns with the natural way users hold their smartphones, offering a full-screen viewing experience without the need to rotate the device.

Creating content in a vertical format necessitates a rethinking of traditional composition techniques. Subjects should be centered to capture viewer attention, and framing should be tight to utilize the limited space effectively. This format encourages a more intimate and direct connection with the audience, making it essential for content creators to adapt their visual storytelling strategies accordingly.

The vertical format opens up new creative possibilities for engaging the audience. Whether it's through direct address, leveraging the closer, more personal framing, or utilizing innovative transitions and effects that play with the vertical space, creators can experiment with various techniques to make their content stand out.

Modern smartphones are equipped with advanced cameras and editing software, making them powerful tools for content creation. High-resolution cameras, slow motion, time-lapse, and built-in stabilization are just a few features that can enhance short-format videos. Creators can experiment with these features to add variety and dynamism to their content.

Numerous mobile apps offer powerful editing capabilities, allowing creators to edit their videos directly on their smartphones. Apps like InShot, Adobe Premiere Rush, and Splice provide a range of tools, from basic trimming and cropping to advanced effects, transitions, and color grading. The integrated nature of smartphones with social media platforms facilitates seamless content sharing. Creators can shoot, edit, and upload their videos to their preferred platforms directly from their device, enabling rapid distribution and engagement with their audience.

Creating short-format content on a phone-based interface requires not only an understanding of the technical and compositional aspects of video production but also a creative mindset that embraces the unique constraints and possibilities of the vertical format. By leveraging the sophisticated features of smartphones and adapting

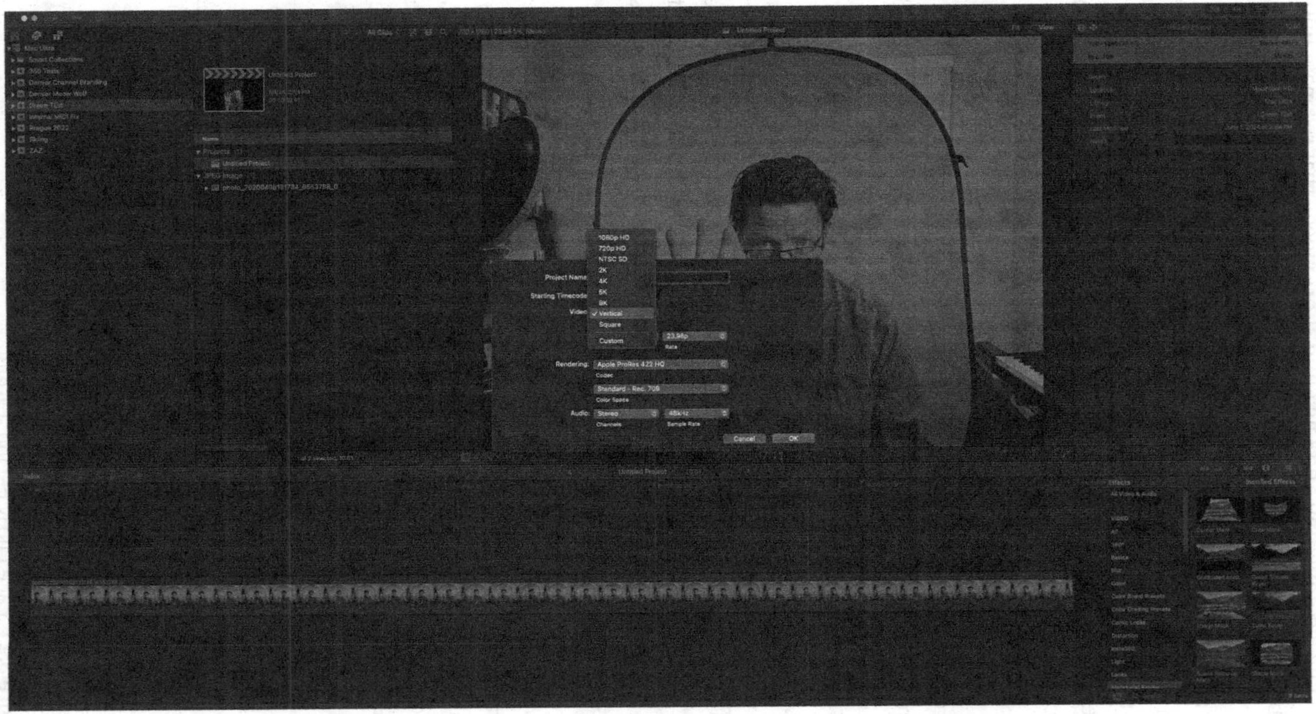

Figure 3.20 Vertical Video Example

storytelling techniques to this more personal, direct medium, creators can produce compelling and engaging short videos that resonate with a mobile-first audience.

Recording Procedures

Creating captivating short-format videos goes beyond having a good story to tell. The way you record your content, paying close attention to the interplay of light, sound, and environment, can significantly impact its appeal and effectiveness. Here, we explore key considerations and techniques for recording short-format videos that stand out.

Spatial Awareness for Sound and Light

The quality of your video is heavily influenced by your awareness and attention to the recording environment.

Sound

Good audio quality is paramount. Background noise can be distracting, if not outright detrimental to your video. When recording, choose a quiet location or use directional microphones to minimize ambient noise. Consider the acoustics of your environment; soft furnishings can help absorb echo, enhancing audio clarity.

Light

Natural light is a powerful ally in video production, offering a quality difficult to replicate with artificial sources. When recording indoors, position yourself near windows to make the most of natural light (see Figure 3.21), but be wary of direct sunlight, which can cause harsh

Figure 3.21 Face Lit By Facing a Window

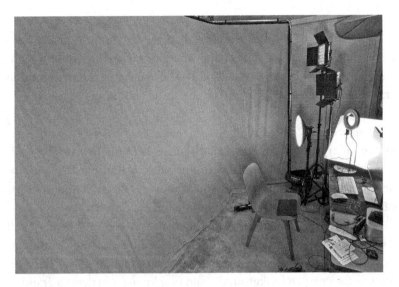

Figure 3.22 Well-Lit Green Screen

shadows. If shooting outdoors, overcast conditions offer diffuse, soft lighting, which can be flattering for subjects.

Green Screen

Incorporating a green screen (see Figure 3.22) can transport your audience to any location, real or imagined, without leaving your recording space. This technique, while advanced, opens up creative possibilities and adds a professional touch to your videos.

Setup Tips

Ensure the green screen is evenly lit and free from wrinkles or shadows, as these can complicate the keying process in editing. Your subject should be well lit and stand several feet in front of the green screen to avoid shadow casting and ensure a clean separation.

Creative Framing and Angles

The constraint of time in short-format content means every second—and every frame—counts. Experimenting with different camera angles and compositions can make your content more dynamic and visually interesting.

Experimentation

Don't be afraid to try unconventional angles or compositions. A low-angle shot can make a subject appear more powerful, while a high-angle shot might convey vulnerability. Close-ups can capture emotion and detail, whereas wide shots set the scene and provide context.

Equipment and Tools

While smartphone cameras can produce high-quality video, additional equipment like stabilizers or gimbals can improve the smoothness of your shots, especially if you're moving. External microphones can also significantly enhance audio quality.

Creating engaging short-format content is a blend of artistry and technique. By mastering the recording procedures, paying close attention to the nuances of sound and light, harnessing the power of green screens for creative backgrounds, and employing a variety of framing techniques, you can produce videos that are not only visually appealing but also resonate with your audience. The goal is to capture the viewer's attention quickly and keep them engaged through creative storytelling and technical prowess.

Editing Tools

In the realm of short-format content, where brevity meets creativity, the editing stage is where your footage is transformed into engaging narratives. This section outlines the essential tools and techniques for editing shorts, enabling creators to craft content that captivates and resonates with their audience.

Streamlined Editing Software

Given the fast-paced nature of short-format content creation, choosing editing software that is both powerful and intuitive is crucial. Mobile apps have risen to prominence, offering creators the flexibility to edit on the go without compromising on quality.

Popular Apps

Apps like Adobe Premiere Rush and InShot are favorites among short-content creators. They provide a suite of editing tools tailored for quick modifications, including trimming, splitting, and sequencing clips. These apps also offer a range of preset transitions, effects, and filters to enhance visual appeal.

Desktop Software

For creators looking for more advanced editing capabilities, desktop software like Adobe Premiere Pro and Final Cut Pro can be used to edit short-format videos as well. These programs offer a wider range of features for detailed editing, color grading, and audio mixing, suitable for projects that require a higher level of polish.

Music and Soundtrack

Audio plays a significant role in setting the tone and enhancing the emotional impact of your video.

Incorporating Music

A well-chosen soundtrack can elevate your content, adding rhythm and mood that complements the visual narrative. Many editing apps provide access to libraries of royalty-free music, allowing creators to integrate tracks without copyright concerns.

Sound Effects

Subtle sound effects can add realism or emphasis to specific moments in your video, making the experience more immersive for the viewer.

Speed Adjustments

Playing with the speed of your footage can create dynamic effects that draw the viewer's attention.

- Slow Motion: Slowing down footage can highlight a moment, adding drama or focusing on details that might otherwise go unnoticed.
- Time-Lapse: Conversely, speeding up footage can convey the passage of time, show a process from start to finish, or add energy to a transition.
- Concise Storytelling: The challenge of short-format content is to tell a compelling story within a limited time frame. Every second counts, and editing decisions should always serve the narrative.
- Trimming for Impact: Be ruthless in cutting anything that doesn't contribute directly to the story or message. The goal is to keep the pacing tight and maintain viewer engagement from start to finish.

- Visual Storytelling: Utilize visual cues and transitions to convey changes in time or setting, reducing the need for explanatory text or dialogue. This keeps the narrative moving and allows for a more visually driven storytelling approach.

Editing short-format content demands a balance between creativity and efficiency, leveraging the tools at your disposal to craft stories that engage and entertain within a concise format. By mastering streamlined editing software, integrating music thoughtfully, employing speed adjustments for effect, and focusing on concise storytelling, creators can produce standout shorts that captivate their audience and leave a lasting impression.

Creativity

In the competitive landscape of short-format videos, creativity isn't just an asset; it's a necessity. This final piece of the puzzle focuses on leveraging creative elements like titles, graphics, and visual effects to distinguish your content, making it not only memorable but also shareworthy.

- Titles: The first impression counts, and often, it's your title that captures initial viewer interest. In the fast-scrolling world of social media, a compelling title can be the difference between a view and a skip.
- Engaging and Informative: Titles should be concise yet descriptive, giving viewers a clear idea of what to expect while enticing them to watch. Use dynamic fonts or animations sparingly to catch the eye without overwhelming the content.
- Brand Consistency: If you're creating content as part of a series or under a brand, maintaining consistent title designs can help establish visual identity and viewer recognition over time.
- Graphics: Beyond mere embellishment, graphics can significantly contribute to storytelling, providing context, emphasizing key points, or evoking emotions.
- Motion Graphics: Incorporating motion graphics can bring static elements to life, adding depth to your narrative. Tools like Adobe After Effects or simpler app-based solutions allow creators to animate text, icons, and illustrations, enhancing viewer engagement.

- Overlay Graphics: Use graphics overlays such as pop-ups, annotations, or calls to action strategically to add information or encourage viewer interaction without detracting from the main content.
- Visual Effects (VFX): In short-format content, visual effects are not just about spectacle; they're tools for creative storytelling. They can transform the ordinary into the extraordinary, make the invisible visible, and convey complex ideas in visually engaging ways.
- Augmented Reality (AR): Many platforms now offer AR capabilities, allowing creators to incorporate interactive, immersive elements into their videos. Whether it's through filters, virtual backgrounds, or interactive animations, AR can create unique, engaging experiences for viewers.
- Transition Effects: Creative transitions can seamlessly link different parts of your video, maintaining momentum and keeping viewers hooked. From simple cuts to more elaborate effects that play with geometry or mimic social media interfaces, transitions are an opportunity to showcase creativity.
- Innovation and Experimentation: The essence of creativity in short-format content lies in experimentation. Don't be afraid to try new approaches, mix mediums, or break conventions. The most memorable content often comes from a willingness to explore and innovate.

Crafting creative short-format content is an iterative process that blends artistry with strategic thinking. By thoughtfully integrating titles, graphics, and visual effects, creators can produce videos that not only grab attention but also leave a lasting impact on their audience. This creative journey is about pushing boundaries, engaging viewers on multiple levels, and ultimately, telling stories that resonate in the fleeting moments of short-format media.

PLATFORM-SPECIFIC INFORMATION CHECKLISTS

Venturing into this next section, we shift our focus toward platform-specific considerations, beginning with the intricacies of creating content for YouTube. Much of this content is summarized from earlier in this chapter, but included as a quick reference checklist for easy reference. From selecting the appropriate video equipment, such as cameras and microphones, to understanding the importance of lighting and stabilization, this section delves into the technical prerequisites and creative strategies that elevate the quality and engagement of YouTube videos.

YouTube

Creating content for YouTube, a platform known for its diverse content and broad audience, requires a strategic approach to video production. From choosing the right equipment to understanding the nuances of creating videos that resonate with viewers, this section outlines key considerations for YouTube content creators.

1. Camera Choices: Your choice of camera significantly impacts the quality of your YouTube videos. While smartphones can produce suitable content for vlogs or casual videos, investing in a higher-quality camera can set your content apart.
   - DSLRs and Mirrorless Cameras: These are popular among YouTubers for their high image quality, versatility, and control over depth of field, allowing for more professional-looking results.
   - Webcams: For live-streaming or desktop-based content (e.g., gaming, tutorials), a high-quality webcam can provide clear video without the need for a complex setup. The Logitech Brio is known for its 4K resolution and excellent low-light performance.
2. Audio Equipment: Clear, crisp audio is crucial for keeping viewers engaged. Poor audio quality can detract from even the most visually stunning video.
   - Microphones: Depending on your recording environment and content type, options include shotgun mics for on-camera use, lapel mics for interviews, and condenser mics for voice-overs or podcasts. The RØDE VideoMic Pro, for example, offers great quality for on-camera use.
   - Audio Interfaces: For more advanced audio setups, especially involving multiple microphones or high-quality voice-overs, an audio interface can provide superior sound quality and flexibility.

3. Lighting: Proper lighting can dramatically improve the appearance of your videos, making them more appealing to viewers.
   - Softbox Lights: These diffuse light evenly, reducing harsh shadows, and are ideal for sit-down videos or interviews.
   - Ring Lights: Perfect for vloggers, ring lights offer even, flattering light directly in front of the subject, enhancing facial features and reducing blemishes.
4. Stabilization Tools: To ensure your footage is smooth and professional, stabilization tools can be invaluable, especially for dynamic shooting scenarios.
   - Tripods: A sturdy tripod is essential for static shots, ensuring your camera stays steady during filming.
   - Gimbals: For moving shots, a gimbal can stabilize your camera, eliminating shaky footage and allowing for smooth, cinematic movement.
5. Video Editing Software: Post-production is where your content comes to life. Choosing the right editing software is key to refining your footage and adding the final touches that enhance your narrative.
   - Adobe Premiere Pro: Offers comprehensive tools for editing, color correction, and effects. It's suitable for creators looking for extensive control and professional outcomes.
   - Final Cut Pro X: Known for its user-friendly interface and powerful editing capabilities, it's optimized for Mac users and offers efficient workflow options for rapid content creation.
6. Additional Accessories: Consider the role of accessories such as external monitors for better framing and focus, filters to enhance your footage aesthetically, and portable hard drives for ample storage of high-quality video files.

Creating content for YouTube involves a careful consideration of the technical aspects of video production. From selecting the right equipment to enhance the visual and auditory quality of your videos to understanding the post-production process that polishes your content, each decision plays a pivotal role in the success of your YouTube channel. By investing in the right tools and honing your technical skills, you can produce high-quality content that captivates and grows your audience.

Facebook

Facebook's platform offers a rich tapestry of content formats, from live videos and stories to standard video posts, each serving different audience engagement needs. Creators must navigate these formats effectively, leveraging Facebook's specific tools and algorithms to maximize content visibility and engagement.

1. Optimized Video Specifications: Facebook supports a wide range of video formats, but MP4 or MOV files are preferred for their compatibility. Videos should ideally be uploaded in high resolution (at least 1080p), and aspect ratios can vary from square (1:1) for feed posts to vertical (9:16) for stories and portrait-mode content. Keeping videos under 2 minutes can help maintain viewer engagement, as Facebook users often scroll through content quickly.

2. Engagement Strategies: Unlike YouTube, Facebook's algorithm heavily prioritizes user engagement and interaction, including reactions, comments, and shares. To enhance engagement:
   - Encourage Viewer Interaction: Ask direct questions in your video or caption, prompt viewers to share their thoughts, and actively engage with comments to foster a community around your content.
   - Utilize Captions and Thumbnails: Many Facebook users watch videos with the sound off, making captions essential for ensuring accessibility and engagement. Eye-catching thumbnails can also attract viewers' attention in a crowded newsfeed.
   - Facebook Live: This feature offers a powerful way to connect with your audience in real time, providing opportunities for Q & A sessions, behind-the-scenes looks, or live coverage of events. Live videos often receive higher engagement rates, as they trigger notifications to followers and encourage immediate interaction.

3. Content Strategy for Different Formats: Tailoring your content to fit Facebook's various formats can broaden your reach. For instance, shorter, more dynamic videos may perform better in the News Feed, while longer, more narrative-driven content can find a home on Facebook Watch, the platform's dedicated video space.

4. Video Series and Scheduling: Creating series or regularly scheduled content can help build anticipation and establish a routine with

your audience. Facebook's scheduling feature allows creators to plan their content release in advance, aiding in consistent engagement.

5. Analytics and Insights: Leveraging Facebook's built-in analytics tools can provide valuable feedback on your video's performance, including viewer demographics, engagement patterns, and reach. This data can inform future content creation, allowing you to tailor your videos to the preferences of your audience more effectively.

Creating engaging video content for Facebook involves a strategic blend of creativity, technical savvy, and social interaction. By optimizing video specifications, engaging with your audience, and making use of Facebook's diverse content formats, creators can enhance their visibility and foster a strong community around their content. As with any platform, understanding and adapting to the unique features and algorithms of Facebook is key to maximizing the impact of your video content.

Instagram

Instagram's appeal lies in its visual nature and the immediacy of its content, offering creators a canvas to express their creativity through photos, videos, and stories. As a platform that thrives on high-quality, visually appealing content, Instagram demands a particular focus on aesthetics, storytelling, and audience engagement.

1. Optimizing Video Content: Instagram supports several video formats, each serving different purposes. For standard posts, videos should be under 60 seconds, ideally in square (1:1) or vertical (4:5) formats to maximize screen real estate. Instagram Stories and Reels favor quick, engaging clips that capitalize on trends, music, and creative editing to catch the viewer's attention.

2. Visual Quality and Aesthetics: High-resolution, well-composed videos are essential on Instagram, where visual quality directly impacts engagement. Using a good camera, ensuring proper lighting, and applying thoughtful composition techniques can significantly enhance your content's appeal. Editing apps like Adobe Premiere Rush or InShot offer tools to refine your videos, adding filters, text, and effects that align with your brand or personal aesthetic.

3. Engagement Strategies: Instagram's algorithm favors content that generates high engagement, including likes, comments, shares, and views. To boost engagement:
   - Use engaging captions, ask questions, and include calls to action that prompt viewers to interact with your content. Utilizing Instagram's interactive features, like polls and questions in Stories, can also increase viewer participation.
   - Incorporate relevant hashtags to increase the discoverability of your content. Geotagging your location can also attract local viewers and contribute to broader exposure.
4. Leveraging Instagram's Features: Beyond standard posts, Instagram offers diverse content formats that can be utilized to keep your audience engaged:
   - Stories: Offer a behind-the-scenes look, quick updates, or interactive content. Stories are ephemeral, creating a sense of urgency and encouraging daily check-ins from your audience.
   - Reels: Instagram's answer to TikTok, Reels are short, entertaining videos set to music or audio clips. They're prominently featured on Instagram, offering significant visibility for trending or engaging content.
   - Consistency and Branding: Maintaining a consistent posting schedule and cohesive visual style helps in building a recognizable brand on Instagram. Your content should reflect a consistent theme or aesthetic that aligns with your brand identity or personal brand, aiding in audience retention and growth.

Crafting content for Instagram requires a keen eye for visual detail, a strategic approach to engagement, and a thorough understanding of the platform's various formats. By producing high-quality videos, leveraging Instagram's interactive features, and maintaining a consistent brand presence, creators can effectively captivate and grow their audience on one of the most popular social media platforms today.

TikTok

On TikTok, where creativity and quality collide to capture the audience's fleeting attention, the choice of equipment and editing tools plays a pivotal role in content creation. From selecting the appropriate filming gear to leveraging editing apps for that perfect TikTok video, here's what creators need to know:

1. Smartphone Camera: The cornerstone of TikTok content creation. Given the platform's mobile-first nature, a smartphone with a high-quality camera is essential. Newer models offering 4K video recording capabilities and advanced stabilization features can significantly enhance the visual quality of your videos without the need for bulky external equipment.

2. External Microphones: Audio clarity can elevate your TikTok content, making it more engaging and professional. Clip-on lapel mics or compact shotgun mics compatible with smartphones can drastically improve sound quality, especially in outdoor or noisy environments.

3. Ring Lights and Portable LED Lights: Lighting can make or break a video. A ring light or small LED panels can provide even, flattering lighting, crucial for capturing high-quality footage indoors or in low-light conditions. These lighting solutions are particularly beneficial for beauty, fashion, and talking-head videos where clarity and detail are key.

4. Gimbals and Stabilizers: For creators who love adding movement to their videos, a smartphone gimbal or handheld stabilizer can ensure smooth, cinematic shots. Whether you're walking, dancing, or moving around, these tools help prevent shaky footage, keeping the focus on your creative content.

5. Tripods with Smartphone Adapters: A versatile tripod can support a variety of shots, from static talking points to dynamic scenes. Look for tripods that come with smartphone adapters and offer flexibility in height and angle adjustments to accommodate different filming scenarios.

6. Creative Editing Apps: TikTok's built-in editing features are robust, but additional editing apps like InShot, Adobe Premiere Rush, or CapCut can offer greater control and creativity. These apps make possible advanced editing techniques, effects, and seamless transitions that can make your videos stand out.

7. Use of Effects and Filters: TikTok offers an array of built-in effects and filters that can enhance your content's appeal. Experiment with these to add flair to your videos, but use them judiciously to maintain authenticity and avoid overwhelming your audience.

Creating compelling TikTok content requires not just creative vision but also the right set of tools and equipment to bring that vision to life. High-quality visuals and clear audio are foundational to capturing and retaining viewer attention on a fast-paced platform like TikTok. By investing in and effectively utilizing these video production tools, creators can produce content that resonates with audiences, drives engagement, and harnesses the full potential of TikTok's dynamic platform.

Four

In the bustling world of social media, where musicians have unprecedented opportunities to share their art with a global audience, the importance of crystal-clear audio cannot be overstated. Understanding audio levels and the concept of gain staging is pivotal for artists aiming to produce content that stands out amidst the endless sea of digital noise. This guide, tailored specifically for social media musicians, demystifies these critical audio principles, ensuring your tracks not only capture attention but hold it, engaging listeners with professional-grade sound quality.

THE ESSENCE OF AUDIO LEVELS

At the core of every impactful social media post, live-stream, or video is the mastery of audio levels. Audio levels, simply put, are the measure of the strength of an audio signal. They dictate the clarity, volume, and overall presence of your sound. In the digital realm, understanding and manipulating these levels are crucial to preventing distortion (clipping) or an overly quiet mix (noise floor issues), as seen in Figure 4.1.

Navigating social media platforms means competing with a vast array of content. Your audio needs to be immediately engaging to ensure your music doesn't just play in the background but captivates the listener, encouraging them to interact, share, and follow. The right audio-level balance ensures your sound is consistent across various devices, from high-end sound systems to smartphone speakers, making your music accessible and enjoyable for everyone.

DOI: 10.4324/9781003416180-4

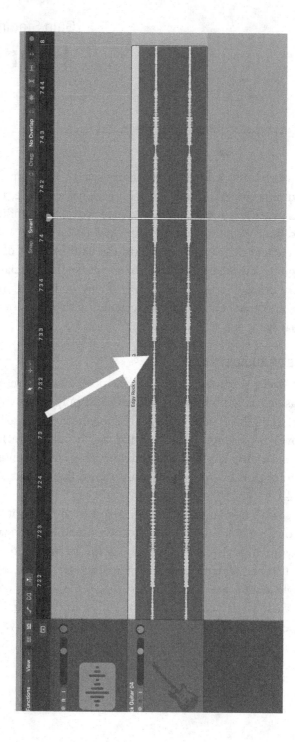

Figure 4.1 Noise Floor Example

The Journey of Gain Staging

Gain staging is the process of managing the volume levels of your audio signal throughout the recording, mixing, and mastering phases to ensure optimal sound quality. It's about control and precision, ensuring that each element of your track—from vocals to instruments—sits perfectly in the mix, clear, undistorted, and dynamically rich.

Recording

The first step in the gain staging process is capturing the sound. Whether you're miking an acoustic guitar or recording vocals (see Figure 4.2), setting the right input gain on your audio interface or recorder is paramount. The goal is to achieve a strong signal that's free from distortion, allowing enough headroom for dynamic performances without clipping. For social media musicians, this often means balancing the desire for a "loud" recording against the risk of digital distortion, which can be particularly jarring for listeners.

Mixing

Once you have your recordings, the mixing stage involves adjusting the levels of each track relative to one another. This is where

Figure 4.2 Recording a Guitar

Figure 4.3 A Control Surface Mixer

gain staging takes on a more nuanced role. It's not just about volume; it's about ensuring clarity and balance. Using trim plugins or input controls on each channel strip as seen in Figure 4.3 allows you to adjust the signal level feeding into your plugins and faders, maintaining a clean signal path. Proper gain staging during mixing ensures that your tracks breathe, each element clearly defined and contributing to the whole without muddiness or frequency overlap.

Mastering

The final polish of mastering involves adjusting the overall track's level to meet industry standards, optimizing it for playback across all media platforms. Here, gain staging is about ensuring your track's loudness matches that of other professional releases, particularly important in the realm of social media, where your music could be played back-to-back with top-charting tracks. Understanding the loudness normalization policies of platforms like YouTube, Spotify, and Instagram can help you set your master levels appropriately, preventing your music from being automatically turned down or compressed too much.

Gain Staging in the Digital Era

The digital era has transformed gain staging, making it both simpler and more complex. Digital audio workstations (DAWs) offer immense headroom, reducing the risk of analog-style distortion. However, the digital domain can be unforgiving; once a signal clips, it is distorted, often in a harsh, unpleasing way. This makes careful gain staging just as critical in digital recording and mixing.

Social media platforms apply their own processing to uploaded content, including compression and normalization, which can further alter the sound of your music. By adhering to good gain staging practices, you ensure that these platform-specific processes enhance rather than degrade the quality of your audio, allowing your music to sound its best, no matter where it's played.

Microphone Types and Output

In the journey of producing standout social media content, understanding how to masterfully set levels and stage gain for your microphones can significantly elevate the quality of your audio. This segment is designed for creators who have a fundamental grasp of different microphone types (see Chapter 3) and are ready to delve into the nuances of gain staging—a critical step to ensure your audio captures are pristine, balanced, and ready to engage your online audience.

Gain staging is the art and science of managing the volume levels of your audio signal from the microphone input through to the final mix, ensuring optimal quality and clarity. In the context of social media, where your content competes for attention against that of countless others, the clarity and quality of your audio can make your content stand out.

• Setting the Right Input Levels: The journey begins at the microphone, where setting the correct input gain is crucial. This stage involves adjusting the gain on your audio interface or mixer to ensure the microphone's signal is strong enough to be captured cleanly but not so strong that it clips and distorts. The goal is to find the sweet spot where the signal peaks at a healthy level on your meters. You should typically aim for peaks around -18 to -6 dBFS (decibels relative to full scale) in a digital system, allowing enough headroom for dynamic performances without risking clipping.

- Monitoring and Adjusting Levels: Constant monitoring is critical during recording. Many modern interfaces and digital audio workstations (DAWs) come equipped with visual metering tools that provide real-time feedback on signal levels. Use these tools to ensure that your levels remain consistent throughout the recording session, making adjustments as needed to accommodate variations in the performance intensity.
- Understanding the Role of Headroom: Headroom in audio production refers to the space left between the peak level of your audio signal and the maximum level that your equipment can handle before distorting. Proper gain staging ensures adequate headroom throughout the recording and mixing process, which is vital for maintaining audio quality, especially when processing or adding effects in post-production.

For social media musicians and creators, the practical application of gain staging extends beyond just capturing a clean signal; it's about crafting an audio experience that translates well across various playback systems, from high-quality top speakers to the limited poor-quality range of smartphone speakers.

- Adapting to the Environment: Social media content is consumed in diverse environments. Consider the acoustics of your recording space and how they interact with your microphone's pickup pattern. Adjust your gain staging to compensate for any environmental challenges, such as background noise or room reverberation, to ensure your primary sound source remains clear and prominent. Recording in a large cathedral has a large reverb tail (see Figure 4.4.)
- Leveraging Digital Tools: Leverage the capabilities of your DAW to fine-tune gain staging post-recording. Use clip gain or track automation to adjust levels of specific phrases or notes, maintaining a consistent volume throughout the track. This level of control is especially beneficial in creating content that needs to sound balanced and polished, regardless of where or how it's played back.

Figure 4.4 Recording in a Cathedral

- Preparing for Platform Processing: Social media platforms apply their own processing to uploaded content, including compression and normalization, which can affect the perceived loudness and dynamics of your audio. By mastering gain staging, you ensure your content maintains its intended quality and impact, even after platform-specific processing is applied.

Preamps

Preamps are essential tools in the audio recording chain, tasked with amplifying the relatively low-level signal from your microphone to a more robust line level that recording devices like better. This amplification stage is critical; it must be carefully managed to minimize noise and avoid horrible clipping, ensuring the cleanest possible signal is recorded.

- Understanding Preamp Gain: The gain on a preamp as seen in Figure 4.5, determines how much your microphone signal is amplified. Setting this gain correctly is a cornerstone of effective gain staging. Too low, and your recordings may be too quiet, getting lost amidst background noise. Too high, and you risk clipping, introducing distortion into your audio that can be challenging to ever fix.
- Finding the Sweet Spot: The "sweet spot" for preamp gain is where your signal is loud enough to be clear and above the noise floor but not so loud that it clips. For most social media content, aiming for peaks around -12 dBFS to -6 dBFS on your digital meters during the loudest parts of your recording is a good rule of thumb. This range provides a healthy balance between clarity and dynamic headroom.
- Utilizing Visual Metering: Many preamps, especially those integrated into audio interfaces, feature visual metering, as seen in Figure 4.6, to help you monitor your input levels in real time. Utilizing these meters allows you to adjust your gain staging on the fly, ensuring consistent levels that leverage the full dynamic range of your recordings.

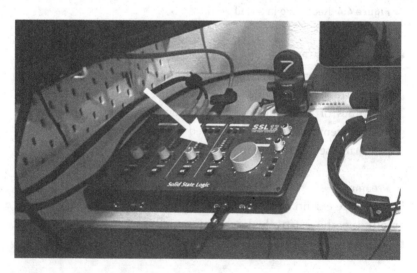

Figure 4.5 Preamp Knob

Figure 4.6 Meters on a RØDE GO Wireless Microphone

The unique demands of social media, where content is consumed on a vast array of devices, from high-end sound systems to smartphone speakers, require thoughtful consideration of how your audio is staged and processed.

a. Consistency Across Platforms: Social media platforms employ various compression and normalization algorithms that can affect your audio's perceived loudness and quality. By carefully gain staging with your preamp, you ensure that your recordings maintain their integrity, offering a consistent listening experience across all platforms.
b. Adapting to Content Needs: Different types of social media content may require different approaches to gain staging. For instance, a dynamic musical performance might benefit from slightly more conservative gain staging to preserve its dynamic range, while a spoken-word piece might afford to push closer to the -6 dBFS mark for clarity and presence.
c. Leveraging Preamp Characteristics: Some preamps impart a certain character or coloration to the signal they amplify, which can be creatively used to enhance your audio. The 4K knob on SSL preamp/ interfaces is a perfect example that adds very unique characteristics to the audio (see Figure 4.7). Understanding the tonal qualities of your preamp allows you not only to stage your gain effectively but also to add a layer of sonic personality to your recordings, making them stand out in the crowded social media space.

Figure 4.7 The SSL 12 Interface 4K Button

Line Level

Line level refers to the standard signal strength used to transmit audio between various devices in an audio recording chain, such as mixing consoles, effects processors, and audio interfaces. It is the level at which the signal is robust enough to be noise-resistant but not so strong that it risks distortion. Managing line level correctly ensures that the signal remains pristine and true to its source, a must for professional-grade social media content.

a. Balancing Signal and Noise: At the line level stage, the aim is to maintain a signal strength that balances between minimizing noise and avoiding distortion. This balance is crucial for social media, where audio might be played back on less-than-ideal speakers and headphones. A clear, clean signal ensures your content sounds great, regardless of how your audience tunes in.

b. Navigating Different Line Levels: There are two primary standards for line level: consumer (-10 dBV) and professional (+4 dBu). Understanding the equipment you're using and the standards it adheres to is crucial for effective gain staging. Misalignments in expected line level can lead to signals that are either too weak (resulting in noise) or too strong (causing distortion), diminishing the quality of your audio content.

c. Integrating Effects and Processors: In the realm of social media content creation, the use of effects and processors can add depth and character to your audio. Proper gain staging at the line level ensures that these enhancements contribute positively to your final sound, allowing for creative expression without compromising signal integrity.

Mastery of gain staging at the line level is a critical skill for any social media content creator aiming for professional-quality audio. This stage of the audio production process is where precision meets creativity, allowing you to prepare your audio for the final mix with clarity and definition. By carefully managing line level signals, you ensure that your audio not only captures the listener's attention but does so with the quality and professionalism that elevates your content above the rest.

THE PROCESS OF MASTERING

Mastering stands as the final, critical stage that bridges the gap between raw creativity and polished, shareable content. Focusing on the process of mastering delves into the nuanced art and science of refining your audio to meet professional standards and audience expectations alike. This segment explains the skills behind adjusting levels for consistency, implementing metering standards to ensure universal playback quality, optimizing the audio spectrum for clarity, and aligning the final product with your artistic vision and the sonic expectations of your listeners. Mastering, in the context of social media, transcends traditional audio engineering, adapting to the unique challenges and opportunities presented by digital platforms. It's about making strategic, informed decisions that enhance the listener's experience, ensuring your content not only captures but retains the audience's attention in a highly competitive space.

Adjusting Levels

The primary goal of adjusting levels during mastering is to ensure that your audio content maintains a consistent and engaging presence across all playback scenarios, from headphones to laptop speakers. For social media, this means crafting a mix that is immediately captivating, clear, and maintains the listener's interest from start to finish.

- Consistency Across Tracks: For creators releasing albums or EPs, consistency in loudness and tonal balance across all tracks is optimal. This consistency helps in delivering a professional and polished body of work that helps retains the listener's engagement throughout.

- Optimizing for Playback Devices: Given the diverse range of devices through which audiences consume social media content, adjusting levels to suit small speakers and headphones is crucial. This often involves ensuring that your mix translates well at lower volumes and across devices with limited frequency responses.
- Competing in the Loudness War: The "loudness war" refers to the trend of increasing audio levels to make music stand out. While social media platforms implement normalization to combat this, understanding how to make your track loud and clear without over-compression is key. This involves careful dynamic range management to preserve the emotional impact of your music.

Level adjustment, while seemingly straightforward, requires a nuanced approach to enhance the listener's experience on social media. Here are some strategies to consider:

- Use Reference Tracks: Comparing your mix to well-mastered tracks or similar posts on your platform can provide a benchmark for loudness and tonal balance. This comparison can guide your adjustments to ensure your content competes favorably in the crowded social media space.
- Dynamic Range Optimization: Rather than maximizing loudness, focus on optimizing the dynamic range. This ensures your audio has enough contrast between the soft and loud parts, enhancing emotional impact without causing listener fatigue.
- Monitor on Various Devices: Before finalizing your levels, listen to your mix on different devices, including smartphones, laptops, and earbuds. This will give you a better understanding of how your content will sound to your audience, allowing you to make necessary adjustments.
- Consider the Platform's Specifications: Each social media platform has its own audio specifications and normalization practices. Tailoring your level adjustments to these specifications can help your content maintain its intended quality and impact.

Mastering for social media requires a careful balance between technical precision and creative intuition. Adjusting levels is the cornerstone of this process, ensuring your audio content is primed for engagement and impact. By focusing on consistency, playback device optimization, and strategic loudness, you can create audio that both stands out on social media and provides a memorable and engaging experience for your audience. This approach not only elevates the quality of your content but also supports the establishment of your unique sonic brand in the digital realm.

Metering Standards

Metering (see Figure 4.8) goes beyond simple volume measurement; it provides a detailed analysis of how audio content will be perceived by listeners across various playback environments. For social media, where users may listen on anything from high-quality headphones to smartphone speakers, mastering with appropriate metering standards ensures your content delivers its intended impact regardless of the listening context.

- Loudness Normalization: Social media platforms like YouTube, Spotify, and Instagram implement loudness normalization to create a consistent listening experience. This process adjusts the playback

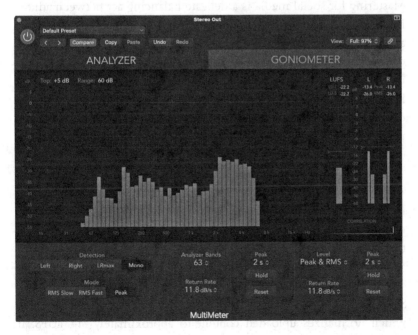

Figure 4.8 Multimeter Showing Audio

volume of all content to a target loudness level. By mastering your audio to these standards, you ensure that it neither sounds too quiet nor is unnecessarily attenuated by the platform's normalization process.

- LUFS—The Standard Measurement: LUFS (Loudness Units relative to Full Scale) has become the industry standard for measuring perceived loudness. This measurement considers the human ear's sensitivity to different frequencies, offering a more accurate representation of how loud audio content feels to the listener. Targeting the optimal LUFS level for your specific social media platform can help your content maintain its dynamics without falling victim to aggressive normalization.
- Peak and True Peak Metering: Understanding peak levels is crucial to avoid digital clipping, which can introduce distortion into your audio. True peak metering, an extension of standard peak metering, considers how digital-to-analog conversion might affect signal peaks, providing a safer margin to prevent clipping in the listener's playback device.

Mastering for social media is a delicate balancing act between adhering to technical standards and preserving the unique qualities of your audio content. By effectively employing metering standards, creators can ensure their content meets the expected auditory quality, stands up to platform normalization, and delivers a consistent and enjoyable listening experience across all devices. This mastery over metering not only elevates the professionalism of your content but also enhances its potential to engage and resonate with a global audience, turning casual listeners into dedicated followers.

Leveraging LUFS for Optimal Loudness

LUFS has emerged as a crucial standard for measuring perceived loudness in audio production, particularly for content destined for social media platforms.

Example

Suppose you're mastering a track intended for posting on YouTube, which normalizes uploaded content to approximately -14 LUFS. If your track is mastered to -8 LUFS, it will be perceived as significantly louder than most content on the platform. However, YouTube's normalization will automatically lower the volume of your track to match its target loudness level, potentially affecting the dynamic range and impact of your music. By mastering your track close to -14 LUFS, you ensure it retains its intended dynamic qualities and stands out for its clarity and balance, not just its loudness.

Understanding True Peak Metering
True Peak Metering measures the highest level that an audio signal reaches, accounting for how digital-to-analog conversion might introduce clipping in the analog domain.

Example
You are finalizing a podcast for Spotify, which has a loudness target of -14 LUFS with a -1 dBTP (True Peak) maximum. Using a true peak meter, you discover your podcast's loudest segment hits -0.8 dBTP, risking distortion upon playback through some streaming services. By applying limiting to ensure the true peak does not exceed -1 dBTP, you prevent potential clipping, ensuring your podcast sounds clean and professional across all devices.

Dynamic Range for Emotional Impact
Dynamic Range refers to the difference in loudness between the quietest and loudest parts of an audio track. Maintaining a healthy dynamic range is essential for preserving the emotional impact of your content.

Example
Imagine you are mastering an indie film trailer for Instagram, aiming for a dramatic, impactful sound. By carefully managing the dynamic range, ensuring it's neither too compressed (which would flatten the emotional peaks and valleys) nor too wide (which could result in lost details in quieter sections), you create a trailer that captures the audience's attention and conveys the intended emotional depth, fitting within Instagram's normalization standards without losing its dynamic impact.

Each social media platform has its own audio specifications, and tailoring your content to these can markedly improve its performance and listener experience.

Example for TikTok

Given TikTok's emphasis on short, engaging content, mastering your audio to suit mobile speakers and earphones becomes crucial. Suppose TikTok users typically engage with content that's around -15 LUFS, with a dynamic range that ensures clarity even on small smartphone speakers. By mastering your music or spoken-word content to align with these unofficial standards, you maximize its effectiveness on the platform, ensuring it's neither too quiet (and overlooked) nor too loud (and potentially distorted or normalized down), engaging viewers immediately and effectively.

Optimizing the Spectrum

In the realm of audio production for social media, optimizing the spectrum is a nuanced art that enhances the clarity, balance, and overall appeal of your content. This process involves careful adjustment of the frequency range to ensure that every element of your mix can be heard clearly, without any frequency overpowering another or muddying the mix. Given the diverse ways in which audiences consume media today, from high-end headphones to smartphone speakers, spectral optimization ensures your content translates well across all playback scenarios.

Understanding Spectral Optimization

Spectral optimization in mastering is about more than just balancing levels; it's about shaping the tonal characteristics of your audio to achieve a polished, cohesive sound. This involves a detailed analysis and adjustment of frequencies, as seen in Figure 4.9, to ensure that the bass is warm but not overwhelming, the mids are clear and present, and the highs are crisp without being piercing.

- Frequency Spectrum Analysis: The first step in spectral optimization is analyzing the frequency spectrum of your mix. This can

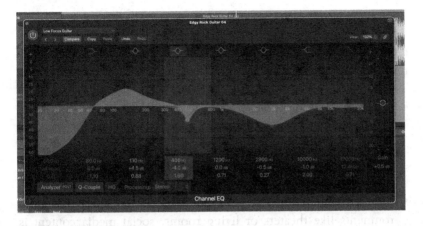

Figure 4.9 Equalization Example

reveal issues such as frequency masking, where one instrument's sound hides another's due to overlapping frequencies, or imbalances that could make the mix sound too bass-heavy or too bright on certain playback systems.

- Equalization (EQ): Equalization is the primary tool for spectral optimization. Strategic EQ adjustments can help carve out space for each element in the mix, ensuring clarity and preventing frequency masking. For social media content, where the final audio might be compressed by the platform, subtle boosts and cuts can help maintain intelligibility and impact.
- Harmonic Enhancement: Adding harmonic content to specific elements of your mix can make them sound better or blend better with the overall mix. This can be particularly effective for voice-over or music, ensuring they cut through the mix even on the smaller speakers commonly used for social media content consumption.
- De-essing and Taming Harsh Frequencies: Sibilance and harsh high frequencies can become exaggerated during compression, a common processing step for audio on social media platforms. De-essing and careful attenuation of these frequencies can prevent listener fatigue and ensure a more pleasant listening experience.

Strategies for Spectral Optimization in Social Media Content

Optimizing the audio spectrum for social media involves several strategic considerations, tailored to the unique challenges and opportunities these platforms present.

- Prioritize Midrange Clarity: Given the limited frequency response of many devices used to consume social media content, ensuring midrange clarity can significantly improve the overall perception of your audio. Voices, in particular, should be clear and present, as they often carry the core message of your content.
- Consider the End Listener's Environment: Unlike controlled environments like theaters or living rooms, social media content is often consumed in less-than-ideal acoustic conditions. Mixing with a slight emphasis on intelligibility and presence can help ensure your content communicates effectively, regardless of where it's played.
- Test on Multiple Playback Systems: Before finalizing your master, test the audio on various devices, including smartphones, tablets, laptops, and earbuds. This can provide valuable insights into how your adjustments translate across different playback systems, allowing you to make more informed decisions about spectral optimization.
- Use Reference Tracks: Comparing your content against professionally produced tracks that perform well on social media can offer benchmarks for spectral balance and dynamics. This comparative analysis can guide your EQ choices, helping you achieve a sound that stands up to the competition.

Spectral optimization is a critical component of mastering for social media, requiring a blend of technical skill, critical listening, and an understanding of the platforms' limitations and opportunities. By carefully adjusting the frequency spectrum of your audio, you can create content that not only sounds professional but also effectively engages and resonates with your audience, regardless of how or where they listen. This meticulous approach to mastering ensures that your social media content delivers the highest possible audio quality, enhancing your message and amplifying your reach in the digital arena. Through strategic use of EQ, harmonic enhancement, and mindful consideration of the listener's experience, creators can craft audio that stands out in the crowded social media landscape, capturing attention and leaving a lasting impression. Never assume your sound is good; take the time to critically listen and decide if it needs work.

Matching Expectations

Matching expectations in the mastering process is about aligning your audio content with the anticipated standards of your audience and the norms of the social media platforms where it will be shared. This crucial step ensures your content not only sounds professional but also resonates with listeners, fostering engagement and connection. For social media, where content consumption is vast and varied, understanding and meeting these expectations can significantly influence the success of your audio.

The Importance of Genre Conventions

Each musical genre carries its own set of sonic characteristics and listener expectations. For instance, a heavy metal track is expected to have a certain level of aggression and loudness, while a classical piece might prioritize dynamic range and clarity.

Example

A hip-hop track intended for SoundCloud promotion should possess a clear, punchy low end to emphasize the beat, crisp highs for the snares, and present vocals that stand out in the mix. Achieving this balance ensures the track meets the listeners' expectations for the genre, encouraging shares and saves.

Adapting to Platform Norms

Social media platforms have evolved into unique ecosystems with their own cultural and technical standards for audio. Tailoring your mastering approach to fit these norms can enhance the performance of your content.

Example

When preparing a track for TikTok, where content is often consumed on mobile devices without headphones, ensuring your mix is mono-compatible and retains its energy and presence in a smaller speaker environment is key. A track that sounds full and engaging, even on a smartphone speaker, is more likely to capture the listener's attention and go viral.

Understanding Audience Preferences

Audience preferences can vary widely across different social media platforms, influenced by factors like age demographics, listening environments, and cultural trends. Mastering your audio to cater to these preferences can greatly increase its appeal.

Example

YouTube viewers looking for relaxing background music will expect a different audio experience than Spotify listeners diving into an energetic workout playlist. For the former, mastering with a wider dynamic range and softer overall loudness might be more appropriate, providing a soothing background experience without overwhelming the listener.

Leveraging Technical Specifications

Each social media platform has specific audio specifications, including preferred file formats, bit rates, and loudness levels. Aligning your content with these specifications ensures optimal playback quality and user experience.

Example

Instagram stories are often consumed quickly, with users swiping through content at a fast pace. Mastering your audio to stand out in this environment, considering both loudness and the platform's compression algorithms, can make the difference between being skipped or noticed.

Matching expectations during the mastering process is a multifaceted endeavor that requires a deep understanding of genre conventions, platform norms, audience preferences, and technical specifications.

For creators and musicians looking to engage with their audience on social media, it's about striking the perfect balance between artistic integrity and the practical realities of digital consumption. By carefully considering these aspects, you can master audio that not only meets but exceeds expectations, driving engagement and fostering a deeper connection with your listeners. This attention to detail and audience insight is what transforms good content into great, memorable experiences that resonate across the digital landscape.

SOFTWARE MASTERING TOOLS

The tools at our disposal for mastering audio have evolved dramatically, offering unprecedented control and precision over the final sound. This section explores the realm of software mastering tools, shedding light on how these digital wonders can transform raw mixes into polished gems ready for social media. From dynamics processing that breathes life into flat recordings to spectral tools that ensure every frequency has its place and time-based effects that add depth and space to any track, the mastery of these tools is essential for any content creator looking to stand out in the crowded online space. This segment aims to equip you with the knowledge to navigate the vast array of software options, enabling you to make informed decisions that enhance your audio content, ensuring it captures and holds the listener's attention in the fast-paced world of social media.

Dynamics

Audio plays a pivotal role in capturing and maintaining the audience's attention. Unlike traditional music platforms where listeners may actively seek out and engage with content, social media platforms require content that immediately grabs attention. Dynamics processing, as shown in Figure 4.10, becomes a critical tool for content creators and audio engineers aiming to optimize their work for social media consumption.

The Challenge of Varied Playback Environments

One of the foremost challenges in mastering for social media is the wide range of playback environments. Content may be consumed

Figure 4.10 Typical Compressor

through high-quality headphones, budget earbuds, laptop speakers, or even the mono speaker of a smartphone. Each of these playback methods presents its own set of limitations and characteristics, particularly in terms of dynamic range and frequency response. Mastering audio for social media thus requires a careful balance, ensuring the content is impactful and clear across all devices.

Optimizing Dynamics for Engagement

Engagement on social media is often fleeting, making the first few seconds of any audio content crucial. Here, the manipulation of dynamics can play a significant role. For example, a sudden increase in volume or an unexpected dynamic shift can serve as an auditory hook, compelling the listener to stop scrolling and engage with the content. Similarly, the strategic use of compression can ensure that quieter details are still perceptible in noisier listening environments, such as a busy street or a crowded café.

Tools and Techniques for Social Media Mastering

Compression

Utilizing compression (Figure 4.11) to reduce the dynamic range of the audio can help ensure that all elements of the content are audible, regardless of the listening environment. However, over-compression must be avoided to prevent the audio from sounding flat and lifeless.

Limiting

A limiter (see Figure 4.12) can be employed to control the peaks of the audio, ensuring that the content meets the loudness standards of social media platforms without clipping or distortion.

Figure 4.11 Compression in Action

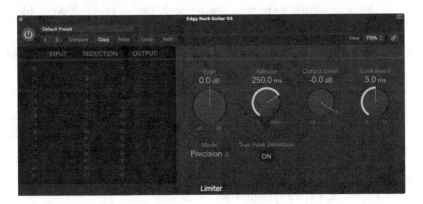

Figure 4.12 Limiting in Action

EQ and High-Pass Filtering

Applying EQ and high-pass filters can help clean up the lower frequencies—which are often less well reproduced by the smaller speakers common in mobile devices—thereby ensuring clarity and intelligibility of the audio content.

Detailed Case Study: Crafting a Viral Music Teaser for Instagram

Background

A music producer is set to release a new track that blends soulful melodies with energetic beats. The goal is to create a 15-second teaser for Instagram that encapsulates the essence of the track while ensuring it stands out amidst a sea of content. Given Instagram users' quick scrolling behavior, the teaser must instantly grab attention both visually and sonically.

The Role of Dynamics Processing

To achieve this, dynamic processing becomes a pivotal element of the audio mastering process. The focus here is on two main tools: parallel compression and limiting.

- Parallel Compression: Enhancing the Beat. The drums, being the backbone of the track's rhythm, need to be impactful without dominating the mix. To accomplish this, parallel compression is employed. This technique involves mixing a compressed version of the drum track with the uncompressed (or less compressed) original. The compressed version uses a high ratio and a moderate-to-fast attack time to reduce the dynamic range, making every hit consistently powerful. However, this often sacrifices the natural feel and subtleties of the drum performance. By blending this with the original, uncompressed signal, the result is drums that are both punchy and dynamic, retaining their natural character while ensuring they cut through the mix.

  This method is particularly effective for social media, where audio playback quality can vary significantly depending on the device. The enhanced presence of the drums ensures that even listeners on less capable speakers or headphones can feel the rhythm of the track, drawing them into the teaser.

- Limiting: Meeting Loudness Standards. The next step involves the strategic use of limiting to ensure the teaser's overall loudness is optimized for Instagram. Social media platforms have specific loudness standards to provide a consistent audio experience across all content. Exceeding these standards can result in automatic volume reduction, potentially diminishing the teaser's impact.

    A limiter with a fast attack time is applied to the master bus, carefully setting the threshold to catch only the loudest peaks without affecting the majority of the audio. This preserves the dynamic quality of the track while preventing distortion and ensuring compliance with Instagram's loudness norms. The key is to strike a balance where the audio is loud and engaging but not squashed or lifeless.

- Final Touches: EQ and Stereo Imaging. With dynamic processing in place, additional mastering steps are taken to tailor the teaser for social media. EQ adjustments are made to enhance clarity, particularly in the mid-to-high frequencies, ensuring the melody and vocals are intelligible on small speakers. Low-end frequencies are carefully managed to prevent muddiness, with a high-pass filter removing sub-bass elements that could be lost on phone speakers.

    Stereo imaging tools are used judiciously to widen the mix, creating an immersive listening experience for those using headphones. However, the mix is checked in mono to ensure that no phase cancellation occurs, preserving the integrity of the sound on mono playback devices.

- Conclusion: A Teaser Ready for Viral Success. The resulting teaser is a meticulously crafted piece of audio that immediately captures the listener's attention. The dynamic processing techniques ensure that the drums provide a solid rhythmic foundation that's both punchy and expressive. The careful balancing act performed with the limiter ensures the teaser is loud and proud, yet clear and distortion-free, adhering to the platform's standards.

    Upon release, the teaser successfully cuts through the noise of a crowded Instagram feed, compelling users to engage, share, and anticipate the full track release. This case study exemplifies the nuanced approach required to leverage dynamic processing in mastering audio specifically for social media, showcasing the importance of technical precision and creative strategy in achieving viral success.

Mastering audio for social media platforms requires a deep understanding of dynamics processing, not just as a technical necessity, but as a creative tool to engage and captivate an audience. By considering the unique challenges of social media, from varied playback environments to platform-specific loudness normalization, audio engineers can craft content that resonates with listeners, encourages engagement, and stands out in a crowded digital landscape. Whether for a viral TikTok video, a compelling Instagram story, or an informative YouTube tutorial, mastering the art of dynamics is essential for success in the ever-evolving world of social media.

Spectrum/Equalization

The spectrum refers to the distribution of frequencies within a sound or piece of music. From the deep bass (low frequencies) to the shimmering highs (high frequencies), achieving a balanced spectrum is crucial for creating an engaging and enjoyable listening experience. This balance ensures that all elements of a mix, from the kick drum to the lead vocals, are clearly audible and harmonically balanced.

The Challenge of Spectral Balance on Social Media

Social media platforms present unique challenges for spectral balance. The wide variety of playback devices, from high-end headphones to smartphone speakers, means that a mix must be carefully mastered to sound good on all potential listening devices. For example, small speakers on smartphones and laptops often cannot reproduce very low frequencies effectively, making it essential to ensure that the bass elements of a mix are still perceivable on these devices.

Techniques for Spectral Optimization

- EQ Adjustments: Equalization (see Figure 4.13) is the primary tool for sculpting the frequency content of a track. Strategic boosts and cuts can help ensure that every part of the audio spectrum is represented appropriately. For social media content, it might involve brightening the mid-to-high frequencies to ensure vocals and lead instruments cut through on small speakers.

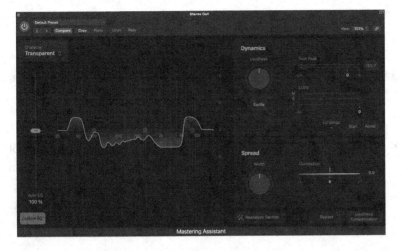

Figure 4.13 Equalizer

- Multi-band Compression: This allows for different parts of the frequency spectrum to be compressed independently, helping to balance the overall mix and ensure that no frequency range is too dominant or recessed. It's particularly useful for managing the low end in a mix, which can be challenging to translate well on smaller speakers (see Figure 4.14).

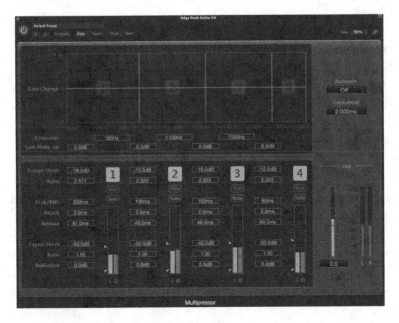

Figure 4.14 Multi-band Compression

Figure 4.15 Harmonic Exciter

- Harmonic Excitement: Adding harmonic content to certain parts of the frequency spectrum can help elements of a mix stand out on less capable playback systems. This is especially useful for enhancing the presence and intelligibility of vocals and key instruments within the higher frequency range (see Figure 4.15).

Practical Example: Mastering for Instagram Stories

When mastering audio for an Instagram story, one might focus on ensuring that the voice frequencies are prominent, considering that speech intelligibility is critical for engagement. This could involve using a combination of EQ to boost the clarity of the speech frequency range (around 2 kHz to 4 kHz) and multi-band compression to control the dynamics of the bass and midrange frequencies, ensuring a balanced mix that translates well across various playback devices.

Mastering the spectrum for social media involves a deep understanding of both the technical aspects of frequency management and the practical considerations of how content is consumed. By applying targeted EQ, multi-band compression and considering mono compatibility, audio content can be optimized for clarity, presence, and impact, ensuring it resonates with the diverse and dynamic audience on social media platforms.

Time/Space

Time/Space processing refers to the manipulation of audio signals (see Figure 4.16) in a way that affects their temporal and spatial characteristics. This can dramatically alter the listener's perceived space and time within a mix, creating environments ranging from intimate close-up settings to vast, expansive landscapes. In the context of social media, where the listener's attention must be captured quickly and

Figure 4.16 Reverb Example

maintained effectively, the creative use of Time/Space effects can significantly enhance the appeal of audio content.

Key Time/Space Processes

- Reverb: Adds a sense of space to a mix, simulating the natural acoustics of different environments. For social media content, where users often consume media via headphones or small speakers, a touch of reverb can add depth and life to a mix without making it sound washed out or distant.
- Delay: Echoes, which are the original audio repeated at various intervals, create a sense of movement and rhythm. In social media clips, delays can be used creatively to emphasize certain elements or create a signature sound that makes the content more memorable.
- Stereo Imaging: Adjusts the perceived width of the stereo field (see Figure 4.17), making a mix sound wider and more immersive. This is particularly effective for engaging headphone listeners, creating a sense of envelopment that can make audio content more captivating.

Challenges and Strategies for Social Media

- Ensuring Clarity: While time/space effects can enhance a mix, there's a fine line between adding depth and creating a cluttered or muddy sound. It's crucial to apply these effects judiciously, ensuring they complement rather than overwhelm the primary elements of the mix.

Figure 4.17 Stereo Imager

- Compatibility with Mono Playback: Many social media platforms and devices default to mono playback, which can collapse the stereo image and alter the impact of time/space effects. Mastering for social media thus requires careful consideration of how these effects translate in mono, ensuring the content remains engaging and balanced.
- Optimization for Short Formats: Social media content often comes in short, impactful formats. This limitation requires that time/space effects be used in a way that quickly establishes the desired atmosphere without detracting from the main message or hook of the content.

Practical Application: Enhancing a Promo Video for Social Media

Imagine a promotional video for a new music release, shared on a platform like TikTok. The goal is to immerse the viewer in the song's atmosphere within just a few seconds. A light, airy reverb might be added to the vocals, giving them a sense of space that draws the listener into the mix. Simultaneously, subtle stereo widening on key elements like synths or guitar lines can create an enveloping experience, especially for headphone users. However, ensuring that these effects don't compromise the mix's clarity or impact in mono playback is crucial, requiring careful tweaking and regular testing on various devices.

Crafting Immersive Audio for Social Media

The effective use of time/space effects in mastering for social media can transform a simple audio clip into an immersive experience, captivating the listener and enhancing the visual content. By carefully applying reverb, delay, and stereo imaging techniques, and considering the unique challenges of social media platforms, audio engineers can create content that not only sounds professional but also deeply engages the platform's diverse audience.

SUMMARY

The information included in this chapter is designed to be as general as possible, but what is clear in tech is that things will change in unexpected ways and that the change is constant. In order to provide you with the best book experience possible in these platform-specific areas, visit the accompanying YouTube playlist (see Figure 4.18) to discover updated related content.

Figure 4.18 Playlist QR Code

https://youtube.com/playlist?list=PLIezNGtdLioi9MKcvPwqZyOk9WKsDMIK7& si=VPC7sohBilr9S6Op

Five

While not solely focused on audio production techniques, this book tackles the topic in a way designed to help readers understand key principles as they apply to the larger topic of social media. Split into beginner, intermediate, and advanced topics, this chapter includes topics, skills, and equipment choices for every level of reader.

AUDIO PRODUCTION FOR BEGINNERS

The following ten workflow topics help illustrate key production techniques, with the aim of helping explain them to musicians and producers who are less initiated in the realm of technical audio.

1 Record Where It's Quiet

This principle is foundational for anyone stepping into the realm of audio production, whether for podcasts, music, or any form of digital media requiring clear, high-quality sound.

Imagine you're in your room, eager to start recording your first podcast episode or a cover of your favorite song. You have your script ready, and your energy is high. However, as you begin, you realize that the sound of cars passing by, the hum of your refrigerator, and even the distant chatter of people in your house are all creeping into your recording. This is where the principle of recording in a quiet space becomes crucial.

Recording in a quiet environment is the first step to achieving clean, professional-sounding audio. But why is this so important? At their core, sounds are vibrations traveling through the air that can be captured by microphones. In an ideal recording scenario, you want your microphone to pick up only the sound you intend to record, with minimal background noise. Noise can be distracting, reduce the clarity of your audio, and make it difficult for your listeners

DOI: 10.4324/9781003416180-5

Figure 5.1 Closet Filled with Clothes

to focus on your content. Later we'll also explore the reflections of sound and the critical role those reflections play in the capture of high quality audio.

How do you find a quiet place to record? Look for a room in your house that is far from noise sources like streets, common areas, or loud appliances. Sometimes, the quietest place might be a closet (see Figure 5.1), filled with clothes, which can naturally dampen sound. The goal is to find a space where the background noise is minimal, and the acoustics are favorable, meaning the sound does not echo too much.

Why bother with all this? Because the quality of your audio can make or break your project. In a world flooded with content, having crisp, clear sound can set your work apart from the rest. It's about giving your audience the best possible listening experience, showing them that you value their attention, and establishing your credibility as a skilled content creator.

This is more than just a tip; it's a foundational step in the journey of audio production. It underscores the importance of preparing your environment before hitting the record button, ensuring that your content starts off with the highest quality sound. Whether you're a college freshman venturing into audio production or a musician recording their songs at home, remembering to record in a quiet space is a simple yet effective way to enhance your work.

2 Use Furniture and Closets to Help Your Sound

This is another key piece of advice for beginners in audio production. This tip moves beyond just finding a quiet space; it's about optimizing that space with materials you already have to improve the sound quality of your recordings even further.

So, why focus on furniture and closets? These everyday items can be surprisingly effective in enhancing your audio quality by affecting the way sound behaves in a room. Sound waves can bounce off hard surfaces, leading to unwanted echoes and reverb that can muddle your recording. Furniture and closets, with varied surfaces and materials, can help absorb and scatter sound waves, reducing these unwanted audio artifacts.

Here's How to Use Furniture and Closets to Your Advantage

1. Closets as Recording Booths: Closets that are packed with clothes can act as a natural sound booth. Clothes absorb sound, preventing echoes. By recording in a closet, you create a makeshift recording studio that's isolated from external noise and less prone to reverb, resulting in clearer audio.

2. Furniture Arrangement: Arrange your furniture to create a space that's acoustically friendly. Sofas, cushions, bunk beds (see Figure 5.2), curtains, and bookshelves can absorb sound and reduce the reflection of sound waves. By strategically placing these items around your recording area, you can create a better sound environment. See the "Mirror Technique" side bar below for an explanation of an easy DIY method to help determine object placements.

3. DIY Sound Panels: If you're feeling a bit more ambitious, you can create your own sound-absorbing panels using materials like acoustic foam or even thick blankets. These can be hung on walls or

Figure 5.2 Bunk-Bed Option

placed around your recording space to further reduce echo. Trial and error may be required to accomplish a better sound.

4. Decoupling Devices: Sometimes, the problem isn't just about sound bouncing off walls but also vibrations traveling through furniture and stands. Using decoupling devices, such as isolation pads under speakers or microphones, can prevent these vibrations from affecting the recording.

Understanding and utilizing the acoustic properties of furniture and closets can significantly enhance the quality of your recordings. It's a testament to the idea that you don't always need expensive, professional equipment to start with audio production. Often, a little creativity and a keen ear for how your environment affects sound can lead you to create high-quality audio with minimal investment.

In essence, "Use furniture and closets to help your sound" is a principle that empowers beginners to take control of their recording environment. It's about making the best out of what you have, transforming everyday spaces into effective recording areas. Whether you're recording a podcast, a song, or any other audio project, understanding how to manipulate your environment for the best sound is a valuable skill in the journey of audio production.

Mirror Technique

Integrating a handheld mirror (see Figure 5.3) into the process of optimizing your recording space for sound quality is a creative and practical method to visually identify how sound waves might travel and reflect in your room. This technique is particularly useful for determining the best placements for absorptive and diffusive materials, such as furniture, curtains, bookshelves, and homemade sound panels, to minimize unwanted reflections and echoes.

Here's how it works:

1. Understanding Sound Reflection: Before diving into the use of a mirror, it's important to grasp the concept of sound reflection. When sound waves hit a flat, hard surface, they bounce back, much like a ball thrown against a wall. This can lead to echoes and reverb, which can muddy your recording. The goal is to interrupt these reflections using absorptive materials (which absorb sound) and diffusive materials (which scatter sound.)

2. The Mirror Test: Hold a handheld mirror against the walls of your recording space, starting at the height at which your microphone and speakers are positioned. Slowly move the mirror along the wall, while you sit or stand in your usual recording position.

3. Identifying Reflection Points: As you move the mirror, ask a friend to watch from your recording spot. Whenever they

Figure 5.3 Handheld Mirror in Action

can see the reflection of the microphone or speakers in the mirror, you've found a potential reflection point. These points are where sound waves from your speakers or your voice can directly bounce off the wall and travel back to the microphone, causing undesirable effects.

4. Placing Absorptive and Diffusive Materials: Once you've identified these reflection points, it's time to strategically place materials that will either absorb or scatter the sound. Absorptive materials, like acoustic foam, heavy curtains, or even a bookshelf filled with books, can be placed at these points to reduce reflections. Diffusive materials, such as uneven surfaces or objects that scatter sound in various directions, can also be used to break up sound waves and reduce the focus of reflections.

5. Optimizing Your Space: It's not just about the walls; ceiling and floor reflections can also affect your sound. Using the mirror technique on the ceiling (which might require a bit more effort and safety precautions) and considering rugs or carpets for the floor can further optimize your recording environment.

This mirror technique is a simple, yet effective, DIY approach to acoustically treating your recording space without needing specialized equipment to analyze the room's sound characteristics. By visually identifying where sound is likely to reflect, you can make informed decisions about where to place sound-absorbing and diffusing materials, ultimately improving the quality of your audio recordings. This approach is particularly beneficial for beginners in audio production who are looking to enhance their setup with a minimal budget, using everyday items creatively to achieve a more professional sound.

3 Add Some Affordable and Easy Audio Tools

This step is about enhancing the quality of your recordings with a few simple, budget-friendly tools that can make a significant difference in your audio production quality. As a beginner, diving into the world of audio equipment can be overwhelming, with an array of gadgets and software at various price points. However, focusing on a few essential tools can provide a solid foundation for your recordings without breaking the bank.

Figure 5.4 A Baffle

1. Baffles (Portable Isolation Booths): Baffles (see Figure 5.4) are portable screens placed around a microphone to isolate it from unwanted ambient noise and reflections. They work by absorbing sound before it can reflect off walls and other surfaces, preventing those reflections from entering the microphone. Baffles are particularly useful in untreated rooms where it's challenging to control the acoustics. They provide a semi-enclosed, quieter space for recording, making them ideal for vocals and acoustic instruments.

2. Microphone Isolation Shields: Similar to baffles, microphone isolation shields (see Figure 5.5) are designed to surround the back and sides of the microphone. These shields help to block and absorb

Figure 5.5 Microphone Shield

Figure 5.6 Microphone Stand

sound reaching the microphone from unwanted directions, focusing the pickup on the sound source directly in front of the mic. Isolation shields are a great way to improve recording quality in less-than-ideal environments, providing a cleaner, more focused sound capture.

3. Mic Stands: A reliable mic stand (Figure 5.6) is more than just a convenience; it's essential for proper microphone placement and stability during recording. Mic stands come in various designs, including straight stands, boom stands, and desktop stands, allowing for versatile setup options to match your recording environment and microphone type. A good stand will hold the microphone securely in the optimal position, helping to capture the best possible sound and reduce the risk of noise from movements or vibrations.

4. Shock Mounts: Shock mounts (see Figure 5.7) are crucial for isolating microphones from vibrations and handling noise. They hold the microphone in a suspended web of elastic bands, which absorb

Figure 5.7 Shock Mount

Figure 5.8 Pop Filter

vibrations before they reach the mic. This is particularly important for sensitive condenser microphones, which can pick up low-frequency rumble from footsteps, desk movements, or even the building's structural noise. Using a shock mount can significantly reduce these unwanted noises, ensuring a cleaner recording.

5. Pop Filters: These filters (Figure 5.8) are placed between the microphone and the sound source to diffuse air blasts from plosives, those hard "p" and "b" sounds, which can cause peaks in the audio recording. A pop filter is a simple yet effective way to smooth out your vocals for a professional sound quality.

6. Acoustic Treatment Panels and Foam: For a more comprehensive approach to controlling room acoustics, consider incorporating acoustic panels and foam (Figure 5.9). These materials can be used to treat walls, corners, and even ceilings to absorb excessive reverb and echoes. Proper placement of these panels can dramatically improve the sonic characteristics of your recording space, making it more conducive to capturing clean, dry audio that's ideal for professional projects.

7. Quality Headphones: A good pair of closed-back headphones (Figure 5.10) is invaluable for monitoring your recordings in real time. Closed-back headphones are recommended for recording because they prevent sound from leaking out and being picked up by the microphone. They also allow you to hear the details in your performance and the nuances of the audio, helping you make adjustments on the fly.

Figure 5.9 Acoustic Treatment

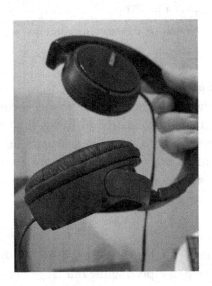

Figure 5.10 Quality Headphones

Audio Production Techniques

Incorporating these tools into your audio recording setup can lead to significant improvements in sound quality. By minimizing unwanted noise, echoes, and reflections, you create a more controlled environment that allows the true quality of your recordings to shine through. As with any equipment, it's essential to consider your specific needs and the acoustic challenges of your recording space when selecting the right tools for your setup.

4 Keep the Microphone Close

Diving deeper into the essentials of home audio production, the advice to "Keep the microphone close" is crucial for achieving the best sound quality in your recordings. This guideline isn't just about physical proximity; it's about understanding the relationship between the microphone, the sound source, and the recording environment. By keeping the microphone close to the sound source, you can enhance the clarity and quality of the audio captured, while also minimizing the pickup of unwanted ambient noise and room reflections.

Enhanced Sound Quality

The closer the microphone is to the sound source, the more direct sound it captures. This means a richer, clearer recording with more of the sound you want and less of the sound you don't. This is particularly important for vocals or acoustic instruments, where the nuances of the performance are key.

Reduced Background Noise

By positioning the microphone closer to the source, the relative level of the direct sound compared to background noise is higher. This helps in significantly reducing the pickup of unwanted ambient sounds, such as room reverberation (unless the sound of the room and reverb are desired), outside noise, or even the hum of computer fans and other electronic devices.

Controlled Dynamics

Close miking allows for better control over the dynamics of the recording. It can help in capturing the full range of the performance, from the softest whispers to the loudest crescendos, without losing detail or clarity.

Less Need for Gain

When a microphone is closer to the sound source, less gain is required from the preamp, which can reduce the noise floor of the recording. High gain settings can introduce noise, so minimizing this need helps in achieving a cleaner recording.

Tips for Effective Close Miking

1. Find the Sweet Spot: Experiment with the position of the microphone to find the best balance between clarity and naturalness of sound. Sometimes, moving the mic just a few inches can make a significant difference in sound quality.
2. Use the Right Microphone: Different types of microphones have different pickup patterns and characteristics. A cardioid pattern, for example, is good for isolating the sound source and minimizing room reflections.
3. Consider a Pop Filter: If you're recording vocals, using a pop filter can help in reducing plosives—those popping sounds from letters like "p" and "b"—without having to move the mic further away.
4. Be Mindful of Proximity Effect: For microphones with a directional pickup pattern (like cardioid), getting too close can boost low frequencies due to the proximity effect. While this is sometimes desirable, it can also muddy the sound if not controlled.

Practical Applications

Vocals

For vocal recordings, keeping the microphone about 6–12 inches away from the mouth, with a pop filter in between, is a good starting point. Adjust based on the desired sound and to control the proximity effect.

Acoustic Instruments

The ideal distance varies greatly depending on the instrument, but starting close and adjusting based on the sound and the room acoustics is a solid approach. For example, placing the microphone close to the 12th fret of a guitar can capture a balanced sound of the strings and the body of the instrument.

Podcasts and Voice-Overs

Clarity and intelligibility are key for spoken-word recordings. Keeping the microphone close, with careful attention to avoiding plosives and sibilance, ensures a professional-quality recording.

"Keep the microphone close" is a principle that underscores the importance of microphone technique in the quality of audio production. It's about more than just physical distance; it's about capturing the essence of the sound source with precision and clarity, making it a cornerstone of effective audio recording practices.

5 Learn to Listen

Developing a critical ear for audio quality is not just an advanced skill but a fundamental one that underpins every aspect of audio production. "Learn to listen" emphasizes the importance of honing your auditory skills to discern subtle nuances in sound, which can dramatically improve the quality of your recordings and mixes. This ability is crucial for identifying issues, making informed decisions during the recording and editing processes, and ultimately creating a polished, professional audio product.

Understanding Audio Characteristics

Listening critically involves more than just paying attention to the sound. It requires an understanding of various audio characteristics, such as:

1. Frequency Response: Learning to identify different frequency ranges and understanding how they affect the sound's warmth, clarity, and presence.
2. Dynamics: Recognizing the range between the softest and loudest parts of an audio signal and understanding how to use dynamic processing tools effectively.
3. Stereo Image: Developing an awareness of how sounds are placed within the stereo field to create a sense of width and depth.

Training Your Ears

Training your ears is a practice that takes time and patience. Here are some ways to improve your listening skills:

1. Critical Listening Exercises: Spend time listening to high-quality recordings in various genres to analyze how different elements are mixed. Focus on individual components like vocals, bass, drums, and how they interact within the mix.

2. Compare and Contrast: Listen to the same piece of music on different playback systems (e.g., studio monitors, headphones, car speakers). Note how the sound changes and which elements become more or less prominent.
3. Use Reference Tracks: When mixing, compare your work to professionally produced tracks that you admire. This can help you gauge your mix's balance, dynamics, and overall sound.

Practical Applications
Mixing Decisions
By developing a keen ear, you'll make more informed decisions when mixing; for example, decisions about balancing levels, equalizing, and applying effects.

Identifying Issues
You'll be better equipped to identify and fix issues such as unwanted noise, clipping, or phase problems.

Communication
Enhanced listening skills will improve your ability to communicate with other audio professionals and articulate your audio vision more effectively.

"Learn to listen" is a principle that highlights the importance of critical listening as a foundational skill in audio production. By developing an acute sense of hearing and a deep understanding of sound, you'll not only be enhancing your production capabilities but also elevating the overall quality of your audio projects. As you progress, remember that listening critically is as much about recognizing what to listen for as it is about the act of listening itself. This skill will serve as a guide through the complex and rewarding journey of audio production.

6 Helpful Apps
In the era of digital audio production, harnessing the power of technology extends beyond hardware and traditional equipment. This section focuses on leveraging software applications to enhance your audio production workflow. These apps can simplify processes, offer

creative solutions, and improve the overall quality of your projects, making them invaluable tools for both beginners and seasoned professionals.

Categories of Helpful Apps

Audio production apps fall into several categories, each serving a specific function within the production process:

1. Digital Audio Workstations (DAWs): These are the central hubs of audio production, offering recording, editing, mixing, and mastering capabilities. Examples include Pro Tools, Ableton Live, Logic Pro, and FL Studio.
2. Tuner and Metronome Apps (Figure 5.11): Essential for musicians, these apps help ensure your instruments are in tune and your performances are in time. They are particularly handy for practice sessions and recording.
3. Mobile Recording Apps: For capturing ideas on the go, mobile recording apps turn your smartphone or tablet into a portable recording studio. Apps like Logic Pro for iOS and BandLab for Android offer multitrack recording features.
4. Virtual Instrument and Synthesizer Apps: These apps (Figure 5.12) provide a wide range of sounds from traditional instruments to electronic synths, expanding your sonic palette without needing physical instruments.

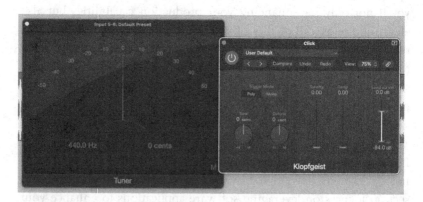

Figure 5.11 Tuner and Metronome

Figure 5.12 Synthesizer App

5. Audio Editing Apps: Specialized apps for editing tasks, such as trimming, noise reduction, and format conversion, can streamline post-
production processes. Audacity and Adobe Audition (see Figure
5.13) are popular choices.
6. Educational Apps: Apps designed to teach music theory, audio engineering principles, and instrument skills can be valuable learning
resources.

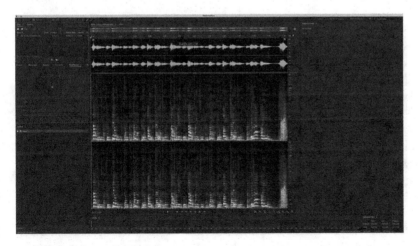

Figure 5.13 Adobe Audition

Integrating Apps into Your Workflow

To effectively incorporate apps into your audio production workflow, consider the following strategies:

1. Identify Your Needs: Evaluate which stages of your production process could benefit from automation or enhancement. Choose apps that address these specific needs.
2. Experiment with Apps: Many apps offer free versions or trials. Experiment with different options to find which ones best fit your workflow and creative style.
3. Integrate with Existing Tools: Look for apps that can integrate seamlessly with your current setup, such as DAWs that offer mobile app companions for remote control or idea capturing.
4. Stay Updated: Keep your apps updated to take advantage of new features and improvements. Developers often release updates that enhance functionality and user experience.

Practical Applications

Songwriting

Use mobile apps to capture musical ideas whenever inspiration strikes. Apps with built-in virtual instruments (see Figure 5.14) can also facilitate the songwriting process.

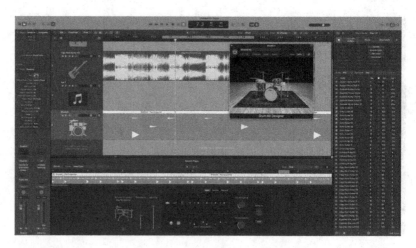

Figure 5.14 Logic Pro Session Player

Figure 5.15 Zoom H3-VR

Field Recording

Mobile recording apps are perfect for capturing natural sounds or interviews in the field, which can be used in podcasts, sound design, or ambient textures in music production. Pairing an app with a portable audio recorder (see Figure 5.15) provides a flexible yet high-quality option for most field-recording situations.

Remote Collaboration

Cloud-based apps enable you to collaborate with other artists or producers remotely, sharing project files and feedback in real time.

This section, "Helpful Apps," underscores the importance of integrating digital applications into the audio production process. By leveraging these tools, you can enhance creativity, efficiency, and collaboration in your projects. Remember, the goal is not to replace traditional methods but to complement and expand your capabilities, allowing you to adapt to the ever-evolving landscape of audio production.

7 Understand Your Voice/Tips

Understanding your voice is a crucial element of audio production, especially for vocalists, podcasters, voice-over artists, and anyone who relies on their voice as a primary tool in their creative endeavors. This section offers tips on how to get to know and make the most of your unique vocal qualities, ensuring that your voice is captured and presented in the best possible light.

1. Know Your Vocal Range: Your vocal range is the span from the lowest to the highest note you can sing or speak comfortably. Knowing your range helps in choosing songs that suit your voice, setting appropriate key signatures for music, and understanding your limits to avoid strain.

2. Practice Proper Breath Control: Good breath control is essential for sustaining notes, maintaining pitch, and delivering powerful performances without fatigue. Practice breathing exercises to strengthen your diaphragm and learn to breathe deeply and evenly.

3. Warm Up Before Recording: Vocal warm-ups are vital to preparing your voice for recording. They reduce the risk of vocal strain and improve your voice's flexibility. Simple exercises like humming, lip trills, and scales can make a significant difference in your vocal performance.

4. Understand Microphone Techniques: Different microphones capture sound in unique ways. Experiment with various microphones and positions to find what best complements your voice. Learn how proximity affects the sound—getting closer to the mic enhances bass frequencies (proximity effect), while backing away produces a more balanced tone.

5. Monitor Your Vocal Health: Your voice is an instrument that needs care. Stay hydrated, avoid excessive shouting or whispering, and rest your voice when needed. If you encounter persistent vocal issues, consult a professional voice coach or a speech therapist.

6. Utilize Technology to Your Advantage: Software and apps can help analyze your voice, providing visual feedback on pitch, tone, and volume. Use this technology to identify areas for improvement and track your progress over time.

7. Learn to Embrace Your Unique Voice: Every voice is unique, with its own texture, color, and character. Rather than trying to mimic others, embrace the qualities that make your voice distinctive. Confidence in your voice comes through in recordings and resonates with listeners.

Practical Applications

Vocalists

Tailor song arrangements to fit your vocal strengths. Use appropriate microphone techniques to capture the nuances of your performance.

Podcasters and Voice-Over Artists

Focus on clear articulation and expressive delivery. Experiment with pacing and intonation to enhance storytelling.

Public Speakers

Practice projection and breath control to maintain energy and clarity in your speeches.

This section, "Understand Your Voice/Tips," emphasizes the importance of getting to know and taking care of your voice. By recognizing your vocal strengths and limitations, practicing proper technique, and embracing your unique sound, you can enhance your audio productions and connect more deeply with your audience. Remember, your voice is a powerful tool for expression—cultivate it with care and respect.

8 Create a Vocal Booth

Creating a vocal booth is an invaluable step for anyone looking to achieve professional-quality audio recordings, especially in environments where controlling external noise and room acoustics is challenging. A vocal booth provides an isolated space that minimizes external noise and room reflections, focusing solely on the clarity and purity of the vocal performance.

Why a Vocal Booth?

1. Isolation: A vocal booth isolates the voice from external sounds such as traffic, appliances, and other disturbances, ensuring a clean recording.

2. Acoustic Treatment: Properly treated, a vocal booth can significantly reduce unwanted echoes and reverberations, allowing for crisper and more controlled vocal tracks.
3. Consistency: A dedicated recording space provides a consistent environment, ensuring reliable sound quality across different recording sessions.

Building a Simple Vocal Booth

You don't necessarily need a professional setup to create an effective vocal booth (Figure 5.16). Here are steps to build a basic, yet effective, booth in your home or studio:

1. Choose the Right Space: Start with a quiet, small room or closet that's away from noise sources. The smaller the space (within reason), the easier it is to control acoustically.
2. Soundproofing: To minimize sound leakage, add density to the walls. This can be as simple as hanging heavy blankets or curtains. For more significant soundproofing, consider using mass-loaded vinyl (MLV) or acoustic panels.

Figure 5.16 Homemade Vocal Booth

3. Acoustic Treatment: Inside the booth, use acoustic foam or DIY panels (made from materials like Rockwool or fiberglass) to absorb sound and prevent reflections. Focus on the walls and the door, and if possible, the ceiling.
4. Ventilation: Ensure there's a way to circulate air without letting in noise. A quiet ventilation fan or a duct that allows air flow without compromising sound isolation can work. If this isn't possible, then keep the recording sessions short and take breaks to keep things cool and fresh.
5. Lighting: A small LED light can provide adequate illumination without taking up too much space or generating heat.
6. Microphone Setup: Inside the booth, set up your microphone on a stand with a shock mount and pop filter. Ensure the cable is long enough to connect to your recording equipment outside the booth.
7. Monitor Your Recording: If possible, have a way to monitor your recording in real time with headphones that can connect back to your recording setup outside the booth.

Tips for Using Your Vocal Booth

Test Different Mic Positions

Experiment with microphone placement within the booth to find the best sound. Moving the mic closer or further from the walls can affect the acoustics.

Stay Comfortable

Make sure the booth is comfortable to use, considering you might be spending extended periods inside. A small stool or chair can help, especially during long sessions.

Regular Breaks

To avoid fatigue and maintain vocal quality, take regular breaks during recording sessions.

Creating a vocal booth is a project that can significantly elevate the quality of your audio productions by providing a controlled environment for vocal recording. Whether you're podcasting, singing, or doing voice-over work, a well-constructed vocal booth can be the difference between an amateur and a professional sound. With some creativity and effort, you can build an effective booth that meets your specific recording needs.

9 Basic Editing

After capturing your audio with the best possible quality, the next step in the production process is editing. Basic editing involves manipulating your audio files to refine the performance, adjust timing, and remove any unwanted sounds or mistakes. This foundational skill set is crucial for creating a polished final product, whether you're working on music, a podcast, voice-over, or any other audio project.

Tools for Basic Editing

Most basic editing tasks can be performed in a DAW, such as Audacity (free), GarageBand (free for macOS and iOS), Adobe Audition, Logic Pro, or Pro Tools. These platforms provide a visual representation of your audio, known as a waveform, which you can manipulate using various tools.

Step-by-Step Guide to Basic Editing

1. Organize Your Session: Import all your recorded audio files into your DAW. Label and organize the tracks for easy navigation.
2. Trimming: Listen to each track and trim away unnecessary parts at the beginning and end, or any long pauses within the clips.
3. Arrangement: Arrange your trimmed clips on the timeline in the desired order. Use separate tracks for different elements (e.g., vocals, background music, effects).
4. Apply Crossfades: Wherever audio clips meet or overlap, apply a short crossfade to ensure a smooth transition.
5. Noise Reduction: Identify any sections with noticeable background noise and apply noise reduction effects as needed. Be careful not to overdo it, as aggressive noise reduction can affect audio quality.
6. Normalize and Adjust Gains: Once your clips are arranged and cleaned, apply normalization to the entire project to ensure consistent volume levels. Adjust the gain of individual clips if there are still volume discrepancies.

7. Final Listen: Listen to your entire project from start to finish in one go. Take notes of any edits or adjustments that are needed and apply them accordingly.

Tips for Effective Editing

Take Breaks

Regular breaks will help keep your ears fresh, preventing fatigue and ensuring you make the best editing decisions.

Use Headphones and Monitors

Listen through both headphones and studio monitors (if available) to get a well-rounded sense of your audio's clarity and balance.

Keep Original Files

Always work with copies of your original recordings, so you can revert to the unedited version if needed.

Back up Everything

Save often and keep backups on separate drives. For long-term, major projects, consider backing up off site.

Basic editing is a critical phase in the audio production process which involves transforming raw recordings into a coherent and engaging piece of audio. By mastering these fundamental skills, you can significantly improve the quality of your projects, making them more enjoyable for your audience. Remember, practice and patience are key to developing your editing abilities.

10 Simple Spectral Improvements

Simple spectral improvements involve adjusting the frequency content of your audio recordings to enhance clarity, balance, and overall sound quality. This process is essential for ensuring that your final product sounds professional and is enjoyable to listen to. By understanding and applying basic equalization (EQ) techniques, you can significantly improve the spectral quality of your recordings.

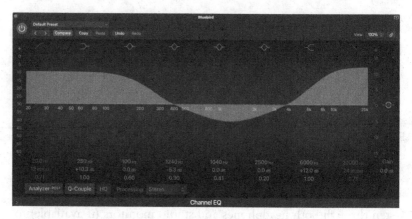

Figure 5.17 Equalizer Example

Understanding the Frequency Spectrum

The frequency spectrum of an audio signal is divided into three main ranges, as seen in Figure 5.17:

1. Low Frequencies (Bass): Ranging from 20 Hz to about 250 Hz, this range includes the bass and the lower end of the midrange. Adjustments here can affect the warmth and fullness of the sound.
2. Mid Frequencies: Spanning from 250 Hz to about 6 kHz, the midrange contains the majority of vocal frequencies and most musical instruments. It's crucial for the clarity and presence of the recording.
3. High Frequencies (Treble): From 6 kHz upwards, this range includes the higher overtones of instruments and the "air" or "brightness" of a recording.

Basic EQ Techniques

1. High-Pass Filter: Applying a high-pass filter (HPF) removes low-frequency rumble and unwanted noise below a certain threshold. This is particularly useful for vocals and instruments that don't require low-end content.
2. Cutting vs. Boosting: Generally, it's better to cut frequencies to reduce muddiness or harshness rather than boosting, which can introduce noise or distortion. Cut narrow to remove unwanted frequencies, and boost wide to enhance desirable qualities.

3. Notch Filtering: If there's a specific frequency that's causing resonance or feedback, a notch filter can remove it without affecting the rest of the frequency spectrum significantly.
4. Shelving EQ: Used to adjust broad areas of the frequency spectrum. A high-shelf EQ can brighten up a recording, while a low-shelf EQ can add warmth or reduce boominess.

Practical Applications

Vocals

Apply an HPF to eliminate low-end rumble. Boost slightly around 3 kHz to enhance clarity and presence. Cut around 500 Hz if the recording sounds muddy (see Figure 5.18).

Acoustic Guitar

Apply an HPF to remove low-end rumble. Boost around 10 kHz for brightness. Cut around 200 Hz if it sounds too boomy (see Figure 5.19).

Podcasts

For voice, clarity is key. Apply an HPF and consider a gentle boost around 4–5 kHz for intelligibility. Cut the low mids slightly if the voice sounds too thick or muffled (see Figure 5.20).

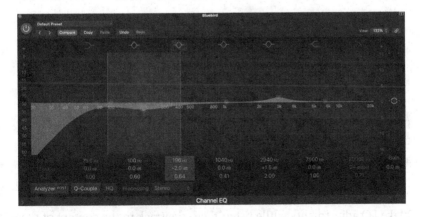

Figure 5.18 Example EQ for Vocals

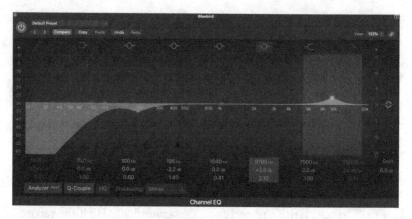

Figure 5.19 Example EQ for Acoustic Guitars

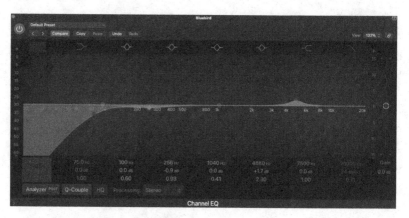

Figure 5.20 Example EQ for Podcasts

Tips for Successful Spectral Improvements

Most DAWs come with built-in EQ plug-ins that are more than capable of making these adjustments. There are also many third-party EQ plug-ins available, offering a variety of interfaces and additional features. Experiment with different tools to find what works best for you and your projects.

Listen in Context

Make EQ adjustments while listening to the track in the context of the full project, as changes can affect how elements blend together.

Frequently switch (A/B test) between the EQ'd and un-EQ'd signal to ensure that your adjustments are improvements, not just changes.

Be Subtle

Subtle adjustments can often have a significant impact. Be wary of making drastic changes unless they're absolutely necessary.

Simple spectral improvements can dramatically enhance the audio quality of your recordings, making them clearer, more balanced, and more professional. By applying basic EQ techniques thoughtfully and judiciously, you can elevate the listening experience for your audience, whether you're producing music, podcasts, or any other audio project. Remember, the goal of EQ is to serve the content and the listener, creating a sound that is not only pleasing but also authentic to the source material.

INTERMEDIATE AUDIO PRODUCTION

This section is all about the tools you will surround yourself with in the audio phase of your projects. There are many of these, and even more opinions on which are the best/most appropriate ones to adopt.

Choosing a Digital Audio Workstation: An Expanded Decision Workflow

Selecting the most suitable Digital Audio Workstation (DAW) is a pivotal choice in setting the foundation for your audio production endeavors. DAWs are integral, offering diverse functionalities for recording, mixing, editing, and mastering. This expanded workflow aims to guide you through the decision-making process with a more detailed examination based on use, cost, operating system compatibility, and popularity, now including five considerations for each category.

By Use

Tailoring your choice to specific applications enhances workflow efficiency and project outcomes.

Music Production

• Ableton Live: Renowned for its session view, which facilitates live performance and improvisation.

Figure 5.21 FL Studio

- FL Studio (Figure 5.21): Popular for beat making and electronic music with an intuitive pattern-based workflow.
- Logic Pro X: Offers a vast library of virtual instruments and loops, ideal for composers and songwriters.
- Cubase: Known for its MIDI editing prowess and comprehensive set of virtual instruments.
- Pro Tools: The standard in professional studios for its advanced editing and mixing capabilities.

Podcasting and Voice-Over

- Adobe Audition: Offers robust multitrack editing and spectral display for precise noise reduction.
- Reaper (Figure 5.22): Flexible and cost-effective, with extensive customization options.
- GarageBand: User-friendly for beginners and Mac users, offering basic podcasting features.
- Audacity: Free and open-source, suitable for simple recording and editing tasks.
- Hindenburg Journalist: Designed specifically for journalists and podcasters, emphasizing ease of use and story-centric tools.

Figure 5.22 Reaper

Film and Video Sound

- Pro Tools (Figure 5.23): Preferred for film scoring and post-production, offering seamless integration with video.
- Nuendo: Steinberg's flagship post-production DAW, offering advanced tools for sound design and film mixing.

Figure 5.23 Pro Tools

- Logic Pro X: Provides strong composition tools, making it suitable for scoring to picture.
- Adobe Audition: Compatible with Adobe Premiere, facilitating workflow between video and audio editing.
- DaVinci Resolve: While primarily a video editor, its Fairlight page offers comprehensive audio post-production tools.

Live Performance

- Ableton Live: The gold standard for live electronic music performance, with extensive MIDI controller support.
- MainStage 3 (Figure 5.24): Offers a vast array of sounds and effects designed for live performance, integrating well with Logic Pro X.
- Traktor Pro: While this is DJ software, it's included here for its live performance capabilities in electronic music sets.
- Bitwig Studio: Offers flexible routing and modulation options, appealing for live performance and improvisation.
- FL Studio: The Performance mode enables the user to trigger samples and sequences live, making it a versatile choice for performers.

Figure 5.24 MainStage

By Cost

Taking into consideration your budget constraints can significantly influence your DAW selection, leading to a balancing of features versus affordability.

Free Options

- Audacity: A straightforward option for basic recording and editing.
- GarageBand: Offers a range of instruments and effects, exclusive to macOS/iOS users.
- Cakewalk by BandLab: A fully-featured DAW for Windows, providing professional-grade tools at no cost.
- Tracktion T7: Offers unlimited audio and MIDI tracks, appealing for its no-frills, single-window interface.
- Ardour: A powerful open-source DAW suitable for recording, editing, and mixing.

Mid-Range

- Reaper: Exceptional value with a fully customizable interface and extensive plugin support.
- Ableton Live Intro/Standard: Provides core functionalities of Live at a reduced price.
- Logic Pro X: An all-in-one production suite for Mac users, priced accessibly for its feature set.
- FL Studio Producer Edition: Offers a balance of features suitable for serious home producers.
- PreSonus Studio One Artist (Figure 5.25): Known for its drag-and-drop workflow and robust feature set.

High-End

- Avid Pro Tools Ultimate: Industry-standard features for professional studios.
- Cubase Pro: Offers a comprehensive set of tools for composition, recording, editing, and mixing.
- Ableton Live Suite: Includes the full range of Ableton's instruments and effects, ideal for electronic music production.

Figure 5.25 Studio One

Figure 5.26 Nuendo

- Logic Pro X: Despite being more affordable, it's included here for its sole attachment to the Mac platform, as the cost of a Mac is significant.
- Steinberg Nuendo (Figure 5.26): Tailored for post-production, game audio, and VR, offering advanced tools beyond Cubase.

By Operating System Type

Your operating system can limit or expand your DAW options, making compatibility a key factor.

MacOS Exclusive

- Logic Pro X: Offers a seamless integration with macOS, providing a stable and powerful production environment.

Figure 5.27 Final Cut

- GarageBand: A free, streamlined version of Logic Pro X, perfect for beginners on Mac.
- Final Cut Pro X (see Figure 5.27): While primarily a video editor, it includes significant audio editing capabilities for macOS users.

Windows Exclusive

- Cakewalk by BandLab: A full-featured, free DAW that continues the legacy of SONAR Platinum.
- FL Studio: Initially Windows-only, its roots and largest user base remain strongly tied to the Windows platform.

Cross-Platform

- Ableton Live: Offers a consistent user experience across macOS and Windows.

- Reaper: Highly customizable and efficient on both macOS and Windows.
- Pro Tools: Provides cross-platform compatibility, ensuring a unified experience in professional environments.
- Cubase: Available and popular among users of both operating systems.
- Bitwig Studio: Designed to be highly flexible across Windows, macOS, and Linux.

By Popularity

Choosing a widely used DAW can provide benefits like a larger community for support and extensive learning resources.

- Avid Pro Tools: The professional studio standard, known for its advanced editing and mixing capabilities.
- Ableton Live: Favored in electronic music and live performance scenes, with a large, active community.
- Logic Pro X: Popular among macOS users, offering deep integration with Apple's ecosystem (see Figure 5.28).
- FL Studio: Has a passionate user base, especially among beat makers and electronic producers.
- GarageBand: Its accessibility and free availability make it a popular starting point for many macOS/iOS users.

Figure 5.28 Fancy Logic Pro Example

- Cubase: Renowned for its MIDI capabilities and comprehensive feature set, appealing to composers and producers alike.
- Reaper: Gaining popularity for its affordability and customizability, with a growing user community.
- Studio One: Known for its modern, streamlined workflow, attracting a broad user base.
- Bitwig Studio: While newer, it's rapidly gaining a following for its innovative approach to music production and performance.
- Audacity: Remains popular for simple recording and editing tasks, thanks to its free and open-source nature.

Choosing the right DAW is a nuanced decision influenced by your specific needs, budget constraints, operating system, and desired features. This expanded guide provides a comprehensive overview to assist in making an informed choice. Ultimately, the best DAW is the one that feels intuitive to you and complements your workflow, enabling you to focus on creativity and production. Consider taking advantage of trial versions to explore firsthand the capabilities and feel of each DAW before committing.

Important Settings in Your DAW

Configuring your DAW with the correct settings is crucial for optimizing performance, ensuring high-quality recordings, and facilitating a smooth production process. This section delves into three fundamental settings that are pivotal for any audio production work: bits and samples, buffer size, and latency. Understanding and adjusting these settings can significantly impact the fidelity and efficiency of your audio projects.

Bits and Samples: Definition and Impact on Audio Quality

Bit Depth

This refers to the number of bits of information in each sample, which determines the resolution of your recording (see Figure 5.29). Common bit depths include 16-bit, 24-bit, and sometimes 32-bit float. Higher bit depths increase the dynamic range, allowing for more detailed recordings with less noise and greater headroom.

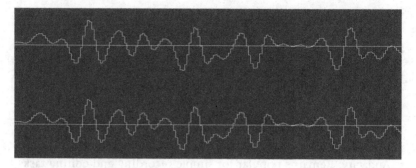

Figure 5.29 Digital Audio Visualization

Sample Rate

This is the number of samples of audio carried per second, measured in Hertz (Hz). Standard sample rates include 44.1 kHz (CD quality), 48 kHz (standard for video production), 96 kHz, and 192 kHz. Higher sample rates capture more frequency content but also require more storage and processing power.

Choosing the Right Settings

1. For most music production, 24-bit/44.1 kHz or 48 kHz is sufficient, balancing quality with file size and system load.
2. For projects requiring the highest fidelity, such as classical music recordings or archival work, higher settings like 24-bit/96 kHz may be preferable.
3. Remember, higher isn't always better. Choose settings that match the final medium of your project to avoid unnecessary processing.

Buffer Size: Balancing Latency and Performance
Buffer Size

This setting determines the amount of time your computer has to process audio before it's sent to your speakers or headphones. It's measured in samples; common sizes range from 32 to 2048 samples.

Low Buffer Size

Setting a lower buffer size reduces latency, which is crucial for recording and monitoring in real-time. However, it demands more from your CPU, increasing the risk of audio dropouts and glitches in complex projects.

High Buffer Size

A higher buffer size gives your CPU more time to process audio, reducing the strain on your system. This is beneficial during mixing and mastering, when low latency is less critical, but can result in noticeable delay when monitoring live inputs.

Optimal Setting Tips

1. Use low buffer sizes (e.g., 128 samples or less) for recording and live performance scenarios where immediate feedback is essential.
2. Switch to higher buffer sizes (512 samples or more) for mixing and mastering to maximize system stability and allow for more plugins and tracks.
3. Adjust based on your system's performance. Faster computers with more RAM can handle lower buffer sizes with less risk of audio dropouts.

Latency: Understanding and Managing Delay

Latency

This refers to the delay between an input being processed (like singing into a microphone) and hearing the output (through speakers or headphones). It's influenced by several factors, including buffer size, sample rate, and the performance of your audio interface and computer.

Reducing Latency

1. Use an audio interface with a dedicated ASIO (Audio Stream Input/Output) driver for Windows or Core Audio for Mac, which is designed to minimize latency.
2. Close unnecessary applications and background processes to free up CPU resources.
3. Consider using Direct Monitoring, if available on your audio interface, which bypasses the DAW for a zero-latency monitoring path.

If you experience high latency, first try lowering the buffer size. If issues persist, check for driver updates for your audio interface or consider optimizing your computer's performance settings.

Some DAWs offer a "Low Latency Mode" for recording, temporarily bypassing plug-ins, which introduce significant delay.

Mastering these settings—Bits and Samples, Buffer Size, and Latency—is essential for a streamlined and efficient workflow in any DAW. By understanding and optimizing these parameters, you can ensure your projects not only sound professional but are enjoyable to work on, minimizing technical distractions and maximizing creative flow.

Recording Techniques in Your DAW

The use of recording techniques within a Digital Audio Workstation (DAW) is pivotal for capturing high-quality audio. The process encompasses several crucial aspects, from managing levels to ensuring synchronization with video, and employing strategies like looping and multiple takes for perfection. Here's a deep dive into effective recording strategies:

Levels

Optimizing input levels is a critical first step in the setup process for recording.

Gain Staging

The process of setting the correct input levels to avoid clipping while maximizing signal-to-noise ratio. Aim for peak levels around -6 dBFS to -12 dBFS on your DAW's meter for most tracks to ensure headroom for mixing.

Use of Meters

Utilize your DAW's metering to monitor input and output levels constantly. Look for peak and RMS (root mean square) levels (see Figure 5.30) to understand both the loudness and the dynamic range of your recordings.

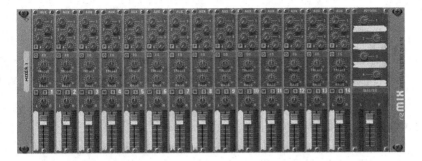

Figure 5.30 Meters

Avoiding Clipping
Clipping occurs when the input level exceeds the maximum recording level of the DAW, resulting in distortion. Always adjust your interface or preamp gain to keep signals below 0 dBFS.

Sync to Video
For projects with visual media, sync is a critical concept to understand and be prepared for in your workflow.

Setting Up
Import the video file into your DAW, ensuring the project's sample rate matches that of the video to avoid synchronization issues.

Timecode
Utilize timecode (see Figure 5.31) to sync audio precisely with video frames. Most DAWs can display timecode, making it easier to align audio cues with visual events.

Frame Rates
Be aware of the video's frame rate and ensure your DAW session matches this setting to maintain sync over time.

Figure 5.31 Timecode in Action

Markers

Use markers to denote important visual cues or changes in the scene, facilitating easier alignment of sound effects, dialogue, or music.

Looping/Takes

Looping is an amazing tool in terms of maximizing performance quality and efficiency.

Loop Recording

Enables recording multiple takes of a section continuously, allowing performers to deliver several attempts without stopping. Ideal for capturing the best performance in music or voice-over work.

Compiling Takes

Many DAWs offer a comping feature, where you can easily splice together the best parts of each take into a single flawless performance.

Efficiency in Workflow

Use loop recording for sections that require perfection, setting the loop points around the desired recording area and letting performers freely take multiple shots at the passage.

File Management

Organizing your sessions is perhaps the most important process of all.

Naming Conventions

Develop a consistent naming scheme for your tracks, takes, and files. Include useful information like the date, the performer's name, and the take number.

Folder Structure: Organize your project files within clearly labeled folders. Most DAWs allow you to set a file path for recording, which can be directed to a specific project folder.

Backup and Archival

Regularly back up your sessions and recordings to an external drive or cloud service. Consider archiving final projects and stems for future use or remixes.

Effective recording in a DAW encompasses careful management of levels to avoid clipping, synchronization with video for multimedia projects, efficient use of looping and takes to capture the perfect performance, and rigorous file management to keep sessions organized and secure. By mastering these techniques, you can ensure your recordings are not only of high quality but also seamlessly integrated into your overall production workflow, whether for music, film, podcasting, or any other audio project.

Editing in Your DAW

Editing is a fundamental phase in audio production, allowing you to refine and enhance your recordings within your Digital Audio Workstation (DAW). Effective editing can significantly improve the clarity, timing, and overall quality of your project. This section covers essential editing techniques, including the use of typical tools, understanding editing modes, and incorporating workflows that can streamline your process.

Typical Tools: Common Editing Tools and Their Uses

- Cut/Copy/Paste: The basics of audio editing—cutting parts of a recording, copying them, and pasting them elsewhere—are crucial for rearranging material, removing errors, or duplicating successful passages.
- Trim: This tool allows you to adjust the start and end points of a clip, removing unwanted portions or extending a clip to fit a specific timing.
- Fade In/Out: Fades are essential as a way of smoothly beginning or ending clips, preventing abrupt starts or finishes that can be jarring to the listener.
- Crossfade: Used between clips to ensure a seamless transition, crossfades blend the end of one clip with the beginning of another, reducing the likelihood of audible pops or clicks.
- Time Stretch: Allows you to lengthen or shorten a clip without altering its pitch; useful for fitting a clip into a specific time slot or matching the tempo of a project.
- Pitch Shift: Adjusts the pitch of a recording without changing its duration; valuable for correcting intonation issues or creatively altering the sound.

- Slip Mode: Allows free movement of clips within a track without affecting adjacent clips. It's ideal for fine-tuning the placement of clips in relation to the timeline.
- Slide Mode: Lets you move a clip while simultaneously pushing adjacent clips forward or backward, maintaining the overall arrangement but adjusting the timing of clips.
- Shuffle Mode: Automatically adjusts the positions of adjacent clips to fill any gaps created by moving or deleting clips, useful for maintaining continuity without leaving empty spaces.
- Grid Mode: Clips snap to a predetermined grid, aligned with musical beats or time increments. This mode is essential for timing precision and is commonly used in music production.
- Spot Mode: For precise placement of clips at specific timecodes or measures; often used in post-production for film and television to align audio precisely with video.

Workflows: Efficient Editing Workflows for Streamlined Production

- Batch Processing: Applying effects or processing to multiple clips at once saves time; this is especially useful for tasks like normalization, compression, or EQ adjustments across several files.
- Templates: Creating project templates (see Figure 5.32) with your most-used tracks, effects, and settings can significantly speed up the setup process for new projects.
- Markers and Regions: Utilize markers to identify important sections or points within your project. Regions can define sections for batch processing or exporting.
- Automation: Use automation for volume, pan, effects, and other parameters to make real-time adjustments during playback. This can add dynamics and interest to your mix without the need to manually editing each clip.
- Hotkeys and Shortcuts: Learning and using keyboard shortcuts for your DAW can dramatically speed up your editing process. Most DAWs allow you to create custom shortcuts, tailored to your workflow.

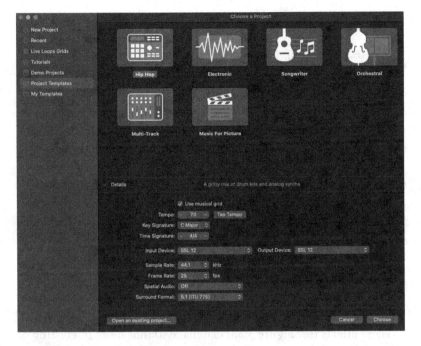

Figure 5.32 Opening a Template

Mastering the editing capabilities of your DAW is essential to producing polished audio content. By understanding and utilizing typical editing tools, selecting appropriate editing modes for specific tasks, and developing efficient workflows, you can enhance the quality and efficiency of your production process. Whether you're working on music, podcasts, or any form of audio content, these editing techniques provide the foundation for creative and technical manipulation of your recordings, leading to professional-quality results.

Mixing in Your DAW

Mixing is a crucial step in the audio production process, where individual tracks are balanced, processed, and blended to create a cohesive final product. This section explores fundamental aspects of mixing within your DAW, covering effects and processing, balancing levels, the use of the spectrum and time, monitoring situations, and the role of automation.

- EQ (Equalization): Adjusts the balance of frequencies within an audio signal. Use EQ to carve out space for each instrument, enhance clarity, and reduce frequency overlap.
- Compression: Reduces the dynamic range of an audio signal, making soft sounds louder and loud sounds softer. Compression is vital for controlling the volume of tracks and adding punch or sustain to instruments.
- Reverb: Adds space and depth to sounds by emulating the natural echoes found in physical spaces. Reverb can place elements within a virtual "space," helping to create a sense of cohesion in the mix.
- Delay: Echoes the audio signal at various time intervals. Use delay to add depth or rhythmic interest to tracks or to thicken vocals and instruments.
- Modulation Effects (Chorus, Flanger, Phaser): Adds movement and texture to sounds by modulating various aspects of the audio signal. These effects (see Figure 5.33) can make sounds more interesting or help them sit better in the mix.

Levels vs. Spectrum vs. Time: Balancing Your Mix Across Dimensions

- Levels: The volume balance between tracks. Start with setting levels to ensure each element can be heard clearly without overpowering others.
- Spectrum: Ensures each instrument occupies its own frequency space. Use EQ to prevent frequency clashes and ensure a full, balanced sound across the frequency spectrum.
- Time: The timing and rhythmic relationship between elements. Adjust timing with quantization or manual alignment, and use delay or reverb to place elements in the mix's foreground or background.

Monitoring Situations: Adapting Your Mix for Different Listening Environments

- Studio Monitors: Provide a flat-ish, accurate representation of your mix. Mixing on studio monitors (see Figure 5.34) in an acoustically treated room is ideal for critical listening.

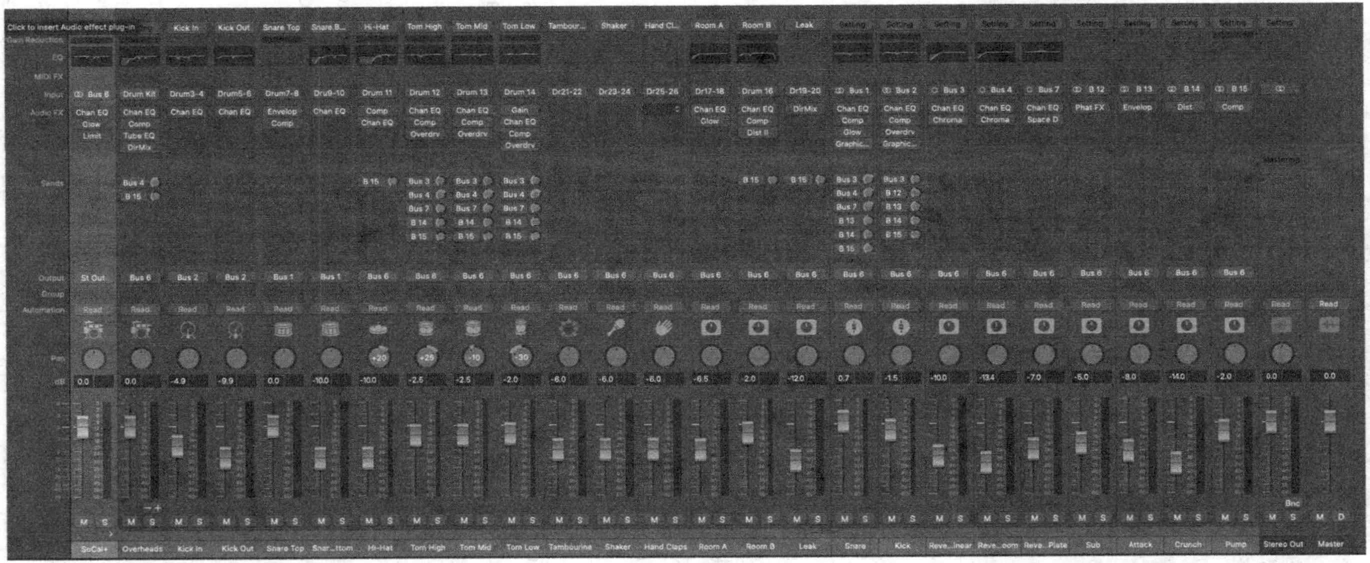

Figure 5.33 The Mixer Loaded with Effects

Figure 5.34 Studio Monitors

- Headphones: Useful for detailed editing and hearing nuances you might miss on monitors. Be aware of the exaggerated stereo field and low-end response in some headphones.
- Consumer Audio Systems: Check your mix on common listening devices like car stereos, earbuds, and Bluetooth speakers to ensure it translates well across different playback systems.
- Mono Compatibility: Ensure your mix sounds good in mono by checking for phase issues and ensuring the core elements of your mix are still clear and balanced.
- Volume Levels: Listen to your mix at various volume levels. Issues that are not apparent at high volumes may become evident at lower levels, and vice versa.

Automation: Dynamic Control for Expressive Mixes

Automation allows for real-time control changes to volume, pan, effects parameters, and more across the timeline of your project. Here are four examples of automation uses:

1. Volume Automation: Smooth out volume discrepancies, create fades, or highlight specific moments.
2. Pan Automation: Move sounds within the stereo field to create dynamic shifts and interest.
3. Effect Parameters: Change reverb depth, delay times, filter sweeps, etc., to add movement and evolve sounds throughout the track.

4. Automate for Interest: Use automation to build tension and release, make choruses bigger, or verses more intimate, adding a dynamic flow to your mix.

Mixing in your DAW is both an art and a science, involving technical know-how and creative decision-making. By effectively applying effects and processing, balancing levels, considering the spectrum and timing, adapting your mix for various monitoring situations, and utilizing automation, you can create mixes that sound professional and engaging across all playback systems. Mastery of these elements allows for the realization of your artistic vision, ensuring your music connects with listeners as intended.

ADVANCED AUDIO PRODUCTION

In this section the advanced, often esoteric tools, are explored to give you an overview of what is possible if you want to take your productions to another level of complexity.

Control Surfaces

Control surfaces (see Figure 5.35) serve as a tangible link between the digital realm of your workstation and the physical world, offering a hands-on approach to mixing, editing, and recording. By integrating a control surface into your workflow, you can enhance efficiency,

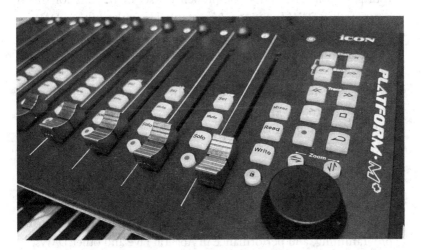

Figure 5.35 A Typical Control Surface

accuracy, and the overall tactile experience of music production. This section explores the various aspects of control surfaces, including apps, physical controllers, and connections.

Apps: Transforming Mobile Devices into Control Surfaces

- TouchOSC: Offers customizable templates and interfaces that can control virtually any aspect of your DAW. It's adaptable for both live performance and studio settings.
- Lemur: Known for its deep customization and flexibility, Lemur can send a wide range of control data (MIDI, OSC, etc.) to your DAW, making it suitable for intricate projects.
- Logic Remote: Designed specifically for Logic Pro X users, this app provides an intuitive way to mix, edit, and navigate sessions directly from an iPad or iPhone.
- Cubasis LE Remote: For Cubase users, this app turns your iPad into a remote control for the Cubase project window, mixer, and transport.
- Avid Control: Works with Pro Tools, Media Composer, and other EUCON-enabled DAWs to offer control over mixing, editing, and transport functions.

Physical Controllers: Enhancing the Tactile Experience

- Mackie Control Universal Pro: A popular choice that offers faders, transport controls, and a comprehensive set of buttons for direct access to key DAW functions. It's compatible with multiple DAWs.
- Avid S3/S6: Offers high-quality motorized faders and rotary encoders in a compact form factor, designed specifically for Pro Tools but compatible with other DAWs through EUCON (see Figure 5.36.)
- Behringer X-Touch: Provides a cost-effective solution with motorized faders, rotary encoders, and LED scribble strips, compatible with a wide range of DAWs.
- PreSonus FaderPort 8: Focuses on fader control with touch-sensitive, motorized faders, transport controls, and integration with PreSonus's own Studio One DAW as well as others.
- Novation Launchpad Pro: While not a traditional control surface with faders, it offers a grid-based input method for clip launching, drum programming, and performance in Ableton Live and other DAWs.

Figure 5.36 An S6 Controller

Connections: Ensuring Seamless Integration

- MIDI: The traditional connection for musical devices, used by many control surfaces to communicate with DAWs. Requires a MIDI interface or USB connection with MIDI support.
- USB: Provides a direct connection to your computer and is the most common type of connection for modern control surfaces. It often carries both data and power.
- EUCON: A high-resolution control protocol developed by Avid, offering deep integration and control over Pro Tools and other EUCON-compatible DAWs. Provides more detailed control than MIDI.
- Ethernet/Network: Used by some advanced control surfaces and apps to connect to the DAW over a network, offering flexibility in placement and potentially lower latency.
- Bluetooth/Wireless: Some controllers and apps use Bluetooth for a cable-free connection, suitable for situations where mobility is key, though it may introduce additional latency.

Control surfaces bridge the gap between tactile interaction and digital precision, offering diverse solutions for every need and budget. Whether through apps that convert your mobile device into a multifunctional controller, physical controllers that bring the studio console experience to your home setup, or seamless connections that integrate these surfaces with your DAW, the right control surface can significantly enhance your production workflow, making it more intuitive, efficient, and enjoyable.

AI Tools in Audio Production

The integration of Artificial Intelligence (AI) in audio production has revolutionized the way music is composed, edited, processed, and even learned. AI tools offer innovative solutions that can streamline workflows, inspire creativity, and enhance the overall production quality. This section delves into the applications of AI in composition, editing and processing, machine learning implications, and a glimpse into the future of AI in the audio industry.

Composition: AI-Assisted Composition Tools

- Suno: An AI music creation tool that allows users to compose and produce music tracks quickly by specifying a few parameters like genre, mood, and length. By the time you are reading this, there will be more just like it and they'll be even better. The floodgates have opened.
- AIVA (Artificial Intelligence Virtual Artist): Focuses on composing emotional soundtrack music using deep learning algorithms, capable of generating compositions in various styles.
- Landr: Uses AI to assist in creating music tracks, offering a range of tools from mastering to music distribution, including AI-driven recommendations for improving your tracks.
- IBM Watson Beat: A cognitive technology that understands music theory and creates music from a user's input, allowing for a collaborative AI–human music composition process.
- Google MusicFX: An experimental lab project exploring the role of AI in the process of creating art and music, providing tools that can generate melodies and rhythms.

- iZotope RX: Renowned for its AI-driven audio repair tools that can intelligently remove noise, clicks, and other unwanted sounds from recordings, significantly speeding up the post-production process.
- Landr Audio Mastering: Provides automated mastering services, using AI to analyze your track and apply processing for a polished, professional sound.
- Descript Overdub: Offers the ability to edit spoken audio content like text in a word processor, including generating new words or phrases in the original speaker's voice using AI.
- Zynaptiq Intensity: Enhances detail, clarity, and loudness of audio recordings or mixes using neural network-based processing.
- Sonible smart:EQ 3: An intelligent equalizer that automatically adjusts frequencies to balance your mix, learning from your input and adapting to your music style.

Machine Learning: Implications of Machine Learning in Audio Production

- Personalized Sound Design: AI algorithms can learn from your production style and preferences to suggest or create sounds tailored to your projects.
- Automated Mixing: Machine learning models can analyze professional mixes and apply similar processing to your tracks, potentially automating routine mixing tasks.
- Voice Manipulation and Synthesis: Advanced models can clone voices or generate singing vocals from text, opening new avenues for vocal production and creative expression.
- Music Recommendation Engines: Machine learning is at the heart of recommendation systems used by streaming platforms, curating personalized playlists based on listening habits.

The Future: Exploring the Potential of AI in Audio Production

- Collaborative AI: Future tools may offer more collaborative experiences, where AI acts as a creative partner, suggesting ideas, generating harmonies, or even proposing changes to compositions.

- Enhanced Learning Tools: AI-driven tutorials and interactive learning platforms could provide personalized training, adapting to the user's progress and focusing on areas needing improvement.
- Intelligent Virtual Performers: AI is already being incorporated into currently available virtual instruments, but is not fully capable of replicating human performance. The next significant steps in AI will certainly lead to the creation of virtual musicians performing complex compositions with human-like expression and dynamics.
- Ethical and Creative Implications: As AI becomes more integrated into creative processes, discussions around copyright, originality, and the role of human creativity in AI-generated content will become increasingly important.AI tools in audio production are not just about automating tasks or analyzing data; they're about opening up new creative possibilities, making sophisticated production techniques more accessible, and enhancing the collaborative interaction between technology and artists. As these tools continue to evolve, they promise to further blur the lines between technology and art, offering exciting opportunities for innovation in music composition, sound design, and production workflows.

Synthesis Tools

Synthesis tools play a pivotal role in sound design and music production, enabling creators to generate a wide array of sounds ranging from realistic instrument simulations to entirely novel timbres. This section explores the capabilities of synthesis tools in terms of creating anything you can imagine, and how they contribute to a deeper understanding of sound.

Create Anything: Expanding Sonic Possibilities with Synthesizers

- Software Synthesizers: Digital counterparts of hardware synths that provide extensive sound-creation possibilities within your DAW. Examples include Native Instruments Massive for rich, complex sounds and Xfer Records Serum for high-quality wavetable synthesis.

- Modular Synthesis: Both physical modular synths and their software equivalents, like VCV Rack, allow for a patch-cable-based approach, offering infinite possibilities by connecting various modules in unique ways to create complex sounds.
- Physical Modeling Synthesis: Techniques that simulate the physical properties of real instruments, such as the vibration of a string or the body of a drum, to create highly realistic sounds. Examples include Logic Pro's Sculpture instrument.
- Granular Synthesis: Manipulates small units of sound, or "grains," to create complex textures and atmospheres. Tools like Output's Portal transform audio in intricate ways, providing a deep level of control over the resulting sound.
- FM (Frequency Modulation) Synthesis: Employs the modulation of one waveform by another to create rich harmonic sounds. Instruments like the Yamaha DX7 (see Figure 5.37) or software equivalents, such as Dexed, offer vast sonic landscapes through FM synthesis.

Deeper Understandings: Enhancing Knowledge and Creativity through Synthesis

- Sound Design Mastery: Exploring various synthesis methods cultivates a deeper understanding of how sounds are generated and manipulated, fostering a more intuitive approach to sound design.
- Innovative Composition: With the ability to create any sound imaginable, composers and producers can push the boundaries of conventional music, incorporating unique sonic elements that define new genres and styles.

Figure 5.37 Classic DX-7

- Educational Value: Learning synthesis principles provides valuable insights into acoustic physics, electronic music history, and the technological evolution behind modern music production.
- Expressive Performance Tools: Advanced synthesizers, equipped with expressive controllers like MPE (MIDI Polyphonic Expression) devices, open up new avenues for performing electronic music with nuanced, expressive control.
- Therapeutic and Experimental Applications: The vast soundscapes achievable through synthesis offer opportunities for therapeutic sound healing practices and avant-garde artistic expressions, challenging our perceptions of music and sound.Synthesis tools are at the forefront of sonic innovation, offering unparalleled flexibility in sound creation and a profound educational journey into the essence of sound itself. Whether through the detailed recreation of acoustic phenomena or the exploration of entirely new auditory realms, these tools empower artists to transcend traditional musical boundaries, inviting both creators and listeners into a world of endless sonic exploration.

MIDI and Loops in Music Production

MIDI (Musical Instrument Digital Interface) and loops are essential tools in the modern music production toolkit, enabling creators to compose, arrange, and produce music efficiently and creatively. This section explores the basics of MIDI and loops, highlighting how they empower social media content creators to craft engaging and dynamic musical content.

Understanding MIDI

What is MIDI?

MIDI is a technical standard that describes a protocol, digital interface, and connectors that enable electronic musical instruments, computers, and other related devices to communicate. It doesn't transmit audio, but rather information about how music is played.

MIDI Messages

MIDI transmits information such as note on/off, velocity (how hard a key is pressed), pitch bend, modulation, and control changes, allowing precise control over musical performance.

MIDI Controllers

These are devices like keyboards, drum pads, and control surfaces that send MIDI data to other devices or software (see Figure 5.38). Popular examples include the Akai MPK Mini and the Novation Launchpad.

Figure 5.38 MIDI Breath Controller

Acoustic Piano MIDI Comparison: By Ann Davison

When considering the quality of sound that a piano is capable of producing, there are many factors that come into play and many adjustments that need to be made in order to have the best outcome. While the size, design and upkeep are important factors, one should look closely at the quality of materials used and the working condition of the instrument, and evaluate the piano action to see that it is properly aligned. Since there are over 100 moving parts in each key that are needed to produce a tone, it is essential that these parts are adjusted properly and are in good working order.

An important part of the piano action is the hammer. The hammers should be adjusted to a consistent strike distance of about 3 mm (1/4 inch) for each key so that the key can be played repeatedly without delay. The hammer is made of felt, which over time has a tendency to become compressed. The result is a tinny or brighter sound on the piano. In order to soften the hammers, they will need to be needled, which is a method of inserting needles repeatedly into the felt of the hammer in order to break down the compressed felt. The hammers can also be moistened or treated chemically to break down any hardening solution that was previously added. In some cases, the hammers create a muffled sound, which could mean the hammers are too soft. A hardening solution can be added or the felt of the hammers can be sanded. The process of sanding hammers is also a technique used to remove the grooves from the strings that have been created after repeated use. Removing these grooves as well as correcting the hammer strike placement on the strings can improve the sound quality of the piano.

Another consideration is the quality of the feedback a player receives as they are playing the instrument. Factors that contribute to this are the type of wood used for the keys. Usually a softer wood is used, as it reacts more to the players' key strikes. The depth of the key dip is also a factor, and there should always be a consistent depth throughout the whole keyboard. It is important that the key height is consistent as well.

Using MIDI in Music Production
Virtual Instruments

MIDI data (just like the hammer action in the side-panel explanation) can trigger virtual instruments in a DAW, enabling creators to play and program a wide variety of sounds from pianos (see Figure 5.39) to synthesizers without needing the physical instruments.

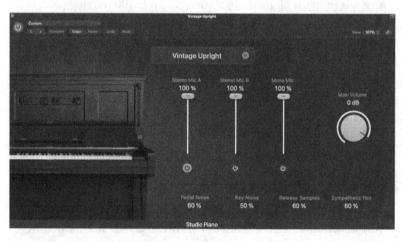

Figure 5.39 Session Piano in Logic Pro

Editing Flexibility

MIDI data is non-destructive and can be edited easily within a DAW. Notes can be moved, lengthened, shortened, or altered in pitch, providing complete control over the performance.

Automation and Control

MIDI can be used to automate parameters in your DAW, such as volume, panning, and effects, allowing dynamic changes throughout a track.

Leveraging Loops

The Basics of Loops

What are loops? Loops are short sections of music that can be repeated seamlessly. They can be audio recordings or MIDI sequences, and serve as building blocks for creating longer sections of music.

- Loop Libraries: Many DAWs and third-party providers offer extensive loop libraries covering various genres and instruments, providing a quick way to start building tracks (see Figure 5.40).
- Creative Arrangements: Loops can be used to build the foundation of a track, such as drum patterns, basslines, or harmonic progressions. Creators can layer loops to develop complex arrangements quickly.
- Customization: Loops can be chopped, rearranged, and processed with effects to create unique variations, allowing for creativity while maintaining a cohesive sound.
- Workflow Efficiency: Using loops can speed up the production process, especially useful for content creators who need to produce music regularly for social media posts, videos, or live streams.

Combining MIDI and Loops

- MIDI Control Over Loops: MIDI controllers can trigger loops in real time, providing a hands-on approach to live performance and improvisation. This is particularly effective for live-streaming or creating engaging video content.
- Integration with DAWs: Most DAWs seamlessly integrate MIDI and loops, allowing creators to use both tools harmoniously. This integration facilitates complex compositions and arrangements that can be easily modified and refined.

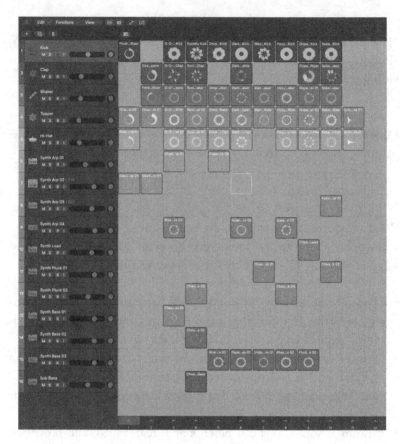

Figure 5.40 Loops in Logic Pro

- Interactive Performances: Combining MIDI with loops enables interactive and responsive performances. Creators can use MIDI controllers to manipulate loops, add effects, and change parameters on the fly, adding an element of spontaneity to their content.

Innovative Content Creation

- Sound Design: Using MIDI to control virtual instruments opens up endless possibilities for sound design, allowing creators to craft unique sounds tailored to their content.
- Genre-Blending: Loops from different genres can be combined and manipulated using MIDI, fostering innovative genre-blending and new musical styles.

- Engagement: High-quality music production enhances the overall appeal of social media content, attracting and retaining a larger audience.MIDI and loops are foundational tools that offer flexibility, creativity, and efficiency in music production. They enable social media content creators to produce high-quality music that enhances their content, engages their audience, and showcases their unique artistic vision. By mastering these tools, creators can push the boundaries of their musical expression and elevate their online presence.

Noise Reduction

Noise reduction technologies are essential in the realm of audio production, allowing creators to enhance the clarity and quality of their recordings by minimizing unwanted ambient noise, hiss, hums, and other audio artifacts. This section explores the standard tools available for noise reduction and their built-in features within DAWs and other audio editing software.

Standard Tools: Key Technologies for Minimizing Unwanted Noise

- Dynamic Noise Reduction (DNR): This technique reduces noise during quieter passages without affecting the louder parts of the audio. It's useful for recordings with variable levels of background noise.
- Spectral Repair: Tools like iZotope RX offer spectral repair features, allowing users to visually identify and eliminate unwanted sounds from a recording's frequency spectrum, perfect for removing specific noises like phone rings or chair squeaks.
- Noise Gates: Noise gates automatically reduce the volume of sections that fall below a set threshold, effectively silencing parts where the intended signal is absent or too quiet. It is commonly used for vocal tracks to eliminate breath sounds or background noise between phrases.
- De-noise Plugins: Many plugins specifically designed for noise reduction analyze a noise profile (a section of audio containing only the unwanted noise) and then remove or reduce this noise across the entire recording. Examples include Waves Z-Noise and the aforementioned iZotope RX's De-noise module.

- De-hum and De-buzz Tools: Target and remove electrical hums and buzzes, often at fixed frequencies like 50/60 Hz and their harmonics. These tools can be invaluable for cleaning up recordings marred by electrical interference.

Built-in Features: Integrated Noise Reduction Capabilities in DAWs and Editing Software

- Audacity: Offers a simple yet effective noise reduction tool where users can select a noise profile and apply the process to the entire track; suitable for basic noise reduction needs.
- Adobe Audition: Features a comprehensive suite of noise reduction effects, including the Adaptive Noise Reduction plugin, which dynamically adjusts to changing noise profiles, and the Spectral Frequency Display for targeted noise elimination.
- Logic Pro X: While primarily a DAW, Logic Pro X includes several plug-ins, such as the Noise Gate and the Expander, that can be used creatively for noise reduction purposes. Its "Remove Silence" feature can also effectively reduce background noise by automatically cutting silence.
- Pro Tools: Provides advanced noise reduction capabilities through its suite of plug-ins and the inclusion of AAX (Avid Audio eXtension) plug-ins like the Waves WNS Noise Suppressor and the Z-Noise, offering professional-grade noise reduction options. Noise reduction plays a critical role in producing clear, professional-sounding audio. With a variety of tools and techniques available, from standard plug-ins to sophisticated spectral repair features, producers can effectively tackle a wide range of noise issues in their recordings. Additionally, the integration of noise reduction features within DAWs and audio editing software makes these technologies accessible to audio professionals and enthusiasts alike, ensuring that achieving high-quality, noise-free recordings is more feasible than ever.

Audio Editing in Video Editors

With the rising demand for multimedia content, video editors increasingly incorporate sophisticated audio editing features. These enhancements enable creators to achieve professional-grade sound within their video projects. This section explores the audio editing capabilities of popular video editing software: Final Cut Pro, Adobe Premiere, and DaVinci Resolve, and introduces capabilities found in screen capture tools like Screenflow, Camtasia, and OBS.

Final Cut Pro: Advanced Audio Features for Mac Users

- Access to Full Effects: Final Cut Pro offers a comprehensive suite of audio effects, including EQ, reverb, and compression, directly within the timeline, allowing for nuanced sound adjustments to be made without needing external audio software.
- Noise Reduction: Integrated noise reduction tools can effectively clean up audio clips, removing unwanted background noise, hum, or hiss with simple controls.
- Keyframes: Audio levels and effects parameters can be automated over time using keyframes, providing precise control over volume fades, panning, and effect intensity.
- Automatic Tools: Features like audio analysis for balancing audio levels and enhancing dialogue quality automatically streamline the post-production process, making it accessible for editors of all skill levels.
- Surround Sound Mixing: Supports 5.1 surround sound mixing and output, enabling the creation of immersive audio landscapes for film and television projects.

Adobe Premiere: Robust Audio Capabilities in a Professional Video Editor

- Effects and Mixing: Premiere Pro includes a full mixer and a wide range of effects, accessible through the Audio Track Mixer panel, mirroring traditional DAW functionality.
- Immersive Audio Features: Supports editing and mixing immersive audio formats, such as Ambisonics for VR content, allowing creators to design sound that envelops the viewer.
- Restoration Features: Tools like DeNoise and DeReverb help clean up recordings directly within Premiere, improving dialogue and on-location audio quality.
- Removing Sounds: The Essential Sound panel offers intuitive controls for common adjustments like repairing, enhancing, or removing specific sounds, making advanced audio editing more accessible.

- Integration with Adobe Audition: For more complex audio post-production, Premiere Pro seamlessly integrates with Adobe Audition, Adobe's dedicated audio editing software, offering round-trip editing capability.

DaVinci Resolve: Combining Professional Video and Audio Editing

- Effects and Mixing: Resolve's Fairlight page offers a digital audio workstation (DAW) environment within the video editor, with a comprehensive range of audio effects, EQ, and dynamics processing.
- Strengths and Weaknesses: Fairlight excels in sound design, dialogue editing, and surround sound mixing, though it may have a steeper learning curve for those new to audio post-production.
- Exporting: Simplifies the audio export process, supporting a wide range of formats and allowing users to bounce out individual tracks or entire mixes for further processing or distribution.
- iPadOS Version: The introduction of DaVinci Resolve for iPadOS brings professional video and audio editing capabilities to a mobile platform, albeit with some limitations compared to the desktop version.

Screenflow, Camtasia, and OBS: Screen Capture and Streaming Tools with Audio Editing Features

- Screenflow and Camtasia: Both offer basic audio editing capabilities, such as noise reduction, EQ, and the ability to add background music or voice-over tracks; they are suitable for creating polished tutorials, presentations, and webinars.
- OBS (Open Broadcaster Software): Primarily a streaming tool, OBS includes features for live audio mixing, noise suppression, and the ability to incorporate multiple audio sources, catering to the needs of live streamers and podcasters.The convergence of video and audio editing tools within video editing software marks a significant advancement in multimedia production, enabling creators to produce content of high quality, both in terms of visuals and of sound. Whether you are working on a film project in Final Cut Pro, a promotional video in Adobe Premiere, a documentary in DaVinci Resolve, or an educational tutorial in Screenflow or Camtasia, these integrated audio features offer the tools necessary to achieve a professional sound, elevating the overall impact of the final content.

Six

The field of audio technology has seen groundbreaking advancements, particularly in the realms of immersive and spatial audio. This chapter delves into the world of immersive audio, exploring its foundational concepts, such as ambisonics, Dolby Atmos (see Figure 6.1), head-tracking, and binaural audio. With a focus on practical applications, it outlines workflows for platforms like YouTube and Facebook, detailing how to capture, edit, mix, and play back 360° video formats integrated with ambisonic audio. It also covers the essential tools and technologies—including microphones, headphone-tracking systems, and speaker configurations,—that are necessary to create an immersive audio experience. This chapter provides insights into the use of

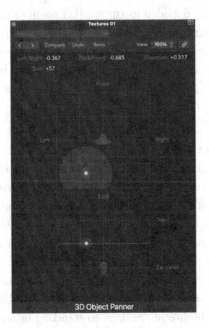

Figure 6.1 Dolby Atmos Panner in Logic Pro

DOI: 10.4324/9781003416180-6

Dolby Atmos in music production and post-production, as well as the emerging role of VR and AR headsets in the music industry, from streaming concerts to enhancing learning and production.

INTRODUCTION TO IMMERSIVE AUDIO

Immersive audio refers to sound technology that creates a 360-degree sound field around the listener, providing a more realistic and engaging auditory experience. Key terms in this field include ambisonics, Dolby Atmos (Figure 6.1), head-tracking, and binaural audio, each of which contributes to the creation and manipulation of spatial sound environments.

Definition of Terms and Practical Theory

Ambisonics

Ambisonics is a full-sphere surround-sound technique that captures and reproduces sound from all directions around the listener. Unlike traditional surround sound, which relies on discrete channels, ambisonics uses spherical harmonics to encode audio signals. This method allows for a highly flexible and accurate representation of a sound field, which can be decoded to any speaker setup or binaural playback. Ambisonics is particularly useful in virtual reality (VR) and 360° video, where a coherent and immersive audio experience is crucial. The technology continues to evolve, with advancements in higher-order ambisonics (HOA) providing even greater spatial resolution.

Dolby Atmos

Dolby Atmos is an advanced audio format that adds height channels to traditional surround sound, creating a three-dimensional soundscape. This format uses object-based audio, where sounds are treated as individual objects that can be placed and moved anywhere in a 3D space. Dolby Atmos is widely used in cinemas and home theaters, as well as in streaming services and video games, to deliver a more immersive audio experience. In addition to enhancing movies and games, Dolby Atmos is increasingly being adopted in music production, allowing artists to create spatially dynamic tracks. Its compatibility with a range of devices, from high-end speakers to standard headphones, makes it accessible to a broad audience.

Head-Tracking

Head-tracking technology allows audio playback to respond to the listener's head movements, maintaining the spatial integrity of the sound field. This technology is crucial for creating realistic and immersive audio experiences in virtual reality (VR) and augmented reality (AR) environments. By continuously adjusting the audio based on the listener's orientation, head-tracking ensures that sounds remain consistent with their virtual sources, enhancing the sense of presence. Various devices, such as VR headsets and specialized headphones, incorporate head-tracking sensors to deliver this experience. The technology is also being explored in applications beyond entertainment, including virtual meetings and remote collaboration.

Binaural Audio

Binaural audio is a method of recording and playback that mimics the natural hearing process, creating a lifelike 3D sound experience through headphones. This technique involves placing two microphones in a configuration that replicates human ears, capturing the time and intensity differences that our brains use to locate sounds. Binaural recordings can produce highly realistic spatial audio, making listeners feel as if they are in the same environment as the sound source. This technology is widely used in VR and AR, audio tours, and immersive storytelling to enhance the listener's experience. Advances in binaural audio continue to improve its realism and application, expanding its use in various fields, from entertainment to therapeutic environments.

IMMERSIVE AUDIO WORKFLOWS

The following represent a snapshot of workflows for the two largest social media platforms that are immersive audio/video compatible. The descriptions are designed in a way to help you understand the principles behind the process without including too many detailed specifics, which are likely to change with each subsequent update.

YouTube Workflow

360° video formats are used to create immersive visual content that surrounds the viewer, allowing them to look in any direction. These formats are essential for platforms like YouTube and Facebook, which support 360° video playback. To produce 360° videos, multiple cameras or specialized rigs capture footage from all angles, which is then stitched together to form a seamless spherical video. Viewers can explore the video by dragging the screen with their mouse, using touch controls on mobile devices, or moving their heads while wearing VR headsets. The integration of 360° video with immersive audio technologies, such as ambisonics, enhances the overall experience, making it more engaging and realistic.

Capturing Ambisonics Audio for 360° Video on YouTube
Capturing ambisonics audio for 360° video on YouTube involves engaging in a detailed process to ensure that the audio quality matches the immersive nature of the visual content. First, it's essential to choose the right ambisonic microphone, such as the Sennheiser AMBEO VR Mic or the Zoom H3-VR (see Figure 6.2), which can capture sound from all directions. These microphones record in a format that can

Figure 6.2 H3VR in Action

later be processed into a 3D soundscape suitable for YouTube's 360° video platform.

Positioning the ambisonic microphone correctly is crucial. It should be placed at the center of the action, ideally at the same height as the 360° camera rig. This ensures that the audio perspective aligns perfectly with the visual experience, creating a cohesive and immersive environment for viewers.

During the recording, monitoring audio levels is vital. Ambisonic microphones capture a wide dynamic range, so it's important to avoid clipping and ensure balanced recordings. Using high-quality headphones and a reliable portable recorder with adequate input channels and preamps helps achieve this balance.

In addition to the primary ambisonic microphone, you may consider using supplementary spot microphones or lavalier mics to capture specific sounds or dialogue. These additional audio sources can be mixed into the ambisonic recording during post-production to enhance clarity and detail, ensuring that important audio elements are not lost in the immersive soundscape.

Environmental considerations are essential to avoid unwanted noise. Wind, traffic, and other background sounds can detract from the immersive experience. Using windshields on microphones and choosing quiet recording locations can significantly reduce these interferences.

Capturing metadata during the recording process is another critical step. This includes details about the microphone setup, orientation, and any relevant head-tracking data. Proper metadata capture ensures accurate processing and synchronization with the 360° video during post-production.

Once the recording is complete, transfer the raw ambisonic audio to a digital audio workstation (DAW) for editing and mixing. Software tools like Reaper, which support ambisonic plugins, or dedicated applications like Noisemakers Ambisonics suite, are ideal for manipulating ambisonic audio.

In the DAW, decode the ambisonic audio into a format compatible with YouTube's 360° video playback. This involves processing the raw ambisonic signals into binaural audio for headphone playback, ensuring the spatial audio effect is accurately reproduced.

Sound design elements such as reverb, spatial effects, and soundscapes can be added to the ambisonic mix to enhance the immersive experience. These elements need to be balanced carefully to avoid overwhelming the listener while maintaining the natural ambiance of the recording environment.

Preview the final mix using the intended playback method, particularly through YouTube's 360° video player (see Figure 6.3), to ensure the spatial audio works as intended. Head-tracking should be tested to confirm that the audio remains consistent and immersive as the viewer's perspective changes.

Quality control is crucial throughout the process. Listen for any artifacts, phase issues, or imbalances in the audio, and address these issues before finalizing the mix. Peer reviews and feedback from other audio professionals can provide additional perspectives and ensure the highest quality.

The completed ambisonic audio track is then encoded and synced with the 360° video. Tools like YouTube's 360 Metadata app ensure the audio and video are properly aligned and that the necessary metadata is correctly embedded for optimal playback on YouTube.

Final testing involves uploading the 360° video with the ambisonic audio to YouTube. Check playback on various devices, including VR headsets, smartphones, and desktops, to ensure compatibility and a consistent immersive experience for all viewers.

Staying updated with the latest tools, techniques, and industry standards is important. Continuous learning and adaptation can significantly

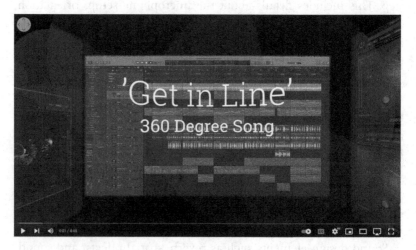

Figure 6.3 360° on YouTube

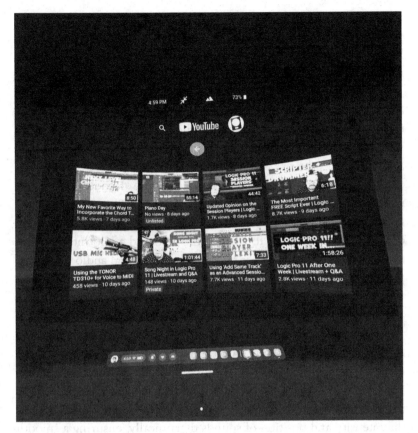

Figure 6.4 Viewing 360° on YouTube in VR

improve the quality of your immersive audio projects, ensuring they meet YouTube's requirements and audience expectations.

By following these steps, content creators can capture high-quality ambisonic audio that enhances the immersive experience of 360° videos on YouTube (see Figure 6.4.) Proper planning, attention to detail, and a thorough understanding of the technology are crucial for creating compelling and engaging immersive content.

Editing and Mixing Ambisonics Audio for 360° Video on YouTube

Editing and mixing ambisonics audio for 360° video on YouTube involves following several detailed steps to create an immersive and high-quality auditory experience. Once the ambisonic audio has been captured, it is transferred to a digital audio workstation (DAW) for editing. Popular DAWs for this purpose include Reaper and Pro Tools, both of which support ambisonic plugins and provide a robust environment for audio manipulation.

The first step in the DAW is to organize and import the ambisonic audio files. It's essential to maintain a structured workflow, labeling tracks clearly and ensuring that all audio sources are correctly synced with the 360° video footage. This helps streamline the editing process and minimizes the risk of errors.

Next, the raw ambisonic audio needs to be decoded into a format suitable for binaural playback on YouTube. This involves using ambisonic decoders, such as the Facebook 360 Spatial Workstation or the IEM Plugin Suite, to convert the recorded audio into binaural audio. This step is crucial for creating the 3D spatial audio effect that provides the immersive experience for listeners. Another useful tool is the RØDE Soundfield plugin, which can be used to covert ambisonic audio into other formats.

Sound design is an integral part of the editing process. Adding reverb, spatial effects, and environmental sounds can enhance the realism and depth of the audio. It's important to use these effects judiciously to avoid overwhelming the listener and to maintain the natural ambiance of the scene. Automation can be employed to adjust the intensity and position of sounds dynamically, ensuring a smooth and engaging auditory experience.

Mixing involves balancing the different elements of the audio track to achieve a cohesive and immersive soundscape. This includes adjusting levels, panning, and equalization to ensure that all sounds are clear and well defined. Special attention should be paid to the spatial positioning of sounds, ensuring that they accurately reflect their locations within the 360° environment.

Monitoring the mix using headphones that support binaural audio playback is essential. This allows the sound engineer to experience the audio as the end user will, ensuring that the spatial effects are correctly rendered. It's also beneficial to test the mix on various devices, including VR headsets and desktop setups, to ensure compatibility and consistency.

Quality control is a vital aspect of the editing and mixing process. Listening for artifacts, phase issues, or any discrepancies in the audio can help identify and resolve potential problems. Peer reviews and feedback from other audio professionals can provide valuable insights and ensure the highest-quality output.

Once the editing and mixing are complete, the final ambisonic audio track needs to be encoded and synced with the 360° video. This involves using software tools like YouTube's 360 Metadata app (see Figure 6.5) to embed the necessary metadata, ensuring that the audio and video are correctly aligned for optimal playback on YouTube.

Before uploading the video to YouTube, it's important to conduct thorough testing. Playback should be checked on multiple devices to ensure that the immersive audio experience is preserved across different platforms. This step helps identify any issues that may arise during playback and allows for necessary adjustments to be made.

Staying updated with the latest developments in ambisonic audio technology and YouTube's 360° video standards is crucial. Continuous learning and adaptation can improve the quality of immersive audio projects and ensure they meet industry requirements and audience expectations.

By following these steps, content creators can effectively edit and mix ambisonic audio for 360° videos, creating a compelling and immersive experience for YouTube viewers. Proper planning, meticulous attention to detail, and a deep understanding of ambisonic audio technology are essential for success in this field.

Figure 6.5 Metadata Injector

Playback of Ambisonics Audio for 360° Video on YouTube

The playback of ambisonics audio for 360° video on YouTube is a critical step that ensures the immersive audio experience is delivered to the viewer as intended. To begin with, once the video with ambisonic audio has been uploaded to YouTube, the platform's built-in support for spatial audio formats, including ambisonics, facilitates the correct playback of the immersive sound.

Viewers typically experience the 360° video through a variety of devices, such as VR headsets, mobile phones, and desktop computers. Each of these devices has different capabilities and requirements for spatial audio playback. VR headsets, like the Meta Quest or Apple's Vision Pro, offer the most immersive experience, as they support head-tracking and can accurately reproduce the 3D audio environment.

For mobile phone users, YouTube's app supports 360° video playback with spatial audio. When a user moves their phone or uses touch gestures to navigate the 360° video, the ambisonic audio dynamically adjusts to reflect the new perspective. This creates a consistent and immersive experience, even without the use of specialized VR hardware.

On desktop computers, viewers can use their mouse to navigate the 360° video. YouTube's spatial audio technology ensures that the ambisonic audio tracks the viewer's orientation within the video, maintaining the immersive effect. It's important for content creators to ensure that the spatial audio encoding is compatible with YouTube's playback system, which typically involves using tools like YouTube's 360 Metadata app to embed the necessary audio metadata.

Testing the playback experience is crucial. Content creators should review the video on various devices to ensure the spatial audio functions correctly across all platforms. This involves checking the head-tracking accuracy on VR headsets, the responsiveness of the spatial audio on mobile devices, and the overall audio quality on desktop systems. Identifying any discrepancies or issues during this testing phase allows adjustments to be made before the video is made publicly available.

Another important aspect is viewer accessibility. Ensuring that the video and its immersive audio can be easily accessed and enjoyed by a wide audience involves providing instructions or tips for optimal playback. This might include recommending specific browsers, app settings, or hardware configurations that enhance the experience.

YouTube's analytics and feedback tools can provide valuable insights into how viewers are engaging with the 360° video and its spatial audio. Monitoring these analytics can help creators understand the effectiveness of their audio implementation and identify areas for improvement in future projects.

Continual updates and improvements to YouTube's platform mean that staying informed about the latest developments in spatial audio playback is essential. This allows creators to leverage new features and technologies to enhance the immersive experience further.

Community feedback is also invaluable. Encouraging viewers to share their experiences and any issues they encounter helps creators refine their techniques and produce better content. Engaging with the audience in comments and forums can foster a better understanding of how spatial audio impacts the viewing experience.

By following these steps, content creators can ensure that the playback of ambisonics audio for 360° videos on YouTube delivers a high-quality, immersive experience. Proper testing, attention to device compatibility, and continuous engagement with new technologies and audience feedback are key to achieving success in this dynamic field.

Metadata Injector for YouTube 360° Videos

The Metadata Injector is a crucial tool for ensuring that 360° videos with ambisonics audio are correctly recognized and played back by YouTube. This process involves taking several detailed steps to embed the necessary metadata into the video file before uploading it to the platform.

First, once the 360° video and its corresponding ambisonics audio track have been edited and mixed, they need to be combined into a single file. This is typically done using a video editing software that supports ambisonics audio tracks, ensuring that the audio is synced correctly with the video footage.

Next, the combined video file is prepared for metadata injection. The Metadata Injector tool, which can be downloaded from YouTube's official resources, is used to embed essential information into the video file. This metadata signals to YouTube that the video contains 360° content and spatial audio, enabling the platform to process and play it back correctly.

The Metadata Injector tool interface allows users to input various details about the video. These include checking options for spherical (360°) video and spatial audio, ensuring that both aspects are flagged for YouTube's playback system. The tool also allows the addition of other metadata, such as video title and description, which can help with content management and searchability on YouTube.

After configuring the metadata settings, the tool processes the video file, embedding the necessary metadata into its header. This step is crucial as it ensures that YouTube's player recognizes the video as 360° content with ambisonics audio. Without this metadata, the video may not display correctly, and the immersive audio experience could be lost.

Once the metadata has been injected, the video file is ready for upload. Content creators log into their YouTube account and upload the video as usual. During the upload process, it's important to double-check the metadata settings on YouTube to confirm that the video is listed as a 360° video with spatial audio. This can be verified in the video's advanced settings.

After uploading, it's essential to test the video playback on various devices to ensure the metadata has been correctly applied and that the 360° video and spatial audio function as intended. This involves viewing the video on VR headsets, mobile devices, and desktop computers to check for any issues with navigation and audio playback.

In addition to verifying playback, monitoring the video's performance using YouTube Analytics can provide insights into how viewers are interacting with the 360° content. This data can help identify any issues with playback on different devices or in different regions, allowing for targeted troubleshooting and optimization.

Keeping the Metadata Injector tool updated is also important, as YouTube periodically updates its specifications and playback capabilities. Staying informed about these updates ensures that content creators can continue to produce high-quality 360° videos with ambisonics audio that meet YouTube's latest standards.

By following these steps, content creators can effectively use the Metadata Injector to ensure their 360° videos with ambisonics audio are properly recognized and played back by YouTube. Proper metadata embedding is essential for delivering an immersive viewing experience and maximizing the impact of 360° video content on the platform.

Best Practices for Capturing and Producing Ambisonics Audio for 360° Video on YouTube

Creating high-quality 360° video content with ambisonics audio for YouTube requires adhering to several best practices throughout the capture, editing, and production processes. These best practices ensure that the final product provides an immersive and engaging experience for viewers.

Planning and Pre-Production

Before beginning the recording process, it's crucial to plan the shoot thoroughly. This includes selecting the right locations, preparing a detailed shot list, and considering how the audio and video will interact within the 360° environment.

Ensure that the environment is suitable for capturing ambisonic audio, with minimal background noise and controlled conditions to avoid interference from unwanted sounds.

Selecting the Right Equipment

Choose high-quality ambisonic microphones, such as the Sennheiser AMBEO VR Mic or the Zoom H3-VR, to capture immersive audio accurately.

Ensure that your 360° camera setup is compatible with your audio equipment, and test all equipment beforehand to avoid technical issues during the shoot.

Microphone Placement and Setup

Position the ambisonic microphone at the center of the action, at the same height as the 360° camera, to ensure that the audio perspective matches the visual experience.

Use additional spot microphones or lavalier mics for capturing specific sounds or dialogue that may not be as clear in the ambisonic recording. These can be mixed in during post-production.

Monitoring and Recording

Continuously monitor audio levels during recording to ensure a balanced capture and avoid clipping. Using high-quality headphones and reliable recording equipment with adequate input channels and preamps is essential.

Capture metadata during the recording process, including microphone setup details and orientation, to ensure accurate processing and synchronization during post-production.

Editing and Mixing

Transfer the raw ambisonic audio to a digital audio workstation (DAW) that supports ambisonic plugins, such as Reaper or Pro Tools.

Playback Testing

Test the video playback on various devices, including VR headsets, mobile phones, and desktop computers, to ensure compatibility and consistency across platforms.

Conduct thorough quality-control checks to identify and resolve any issues with audio synchronization or spatial effects.

Viewer Accessibility and Feedback

Provide clear instructions or tips for viewers on how to optimize their playback experience, including recommended browsers, app settings, and hardware configurations.

Engage with viewers and encourage feedback to understand their experiences and identify areas for improvement.

Continuous Learning and Adaptation

Stay updated with the latest developments in ambisonic audio technology and YouTube's 360° video standards to leverage new features and improve content quality. Monitor YouTube Analytics to gain insights into viewer engagement and performance, using this data to refine future projects.

By following these best practices, content creators can produce high-quality 360° videos with ambisonics audio that deliver a compelling and immersive experience on YouTube. Proper planning, attention to detail, and continuous learning are essential for success in this dynamic field.

Facebook Workflow

Immersive audio on Facebook involves the integration of spatial sound with 360° video content to enhance the viewing experience. While the following is very similar to the above workflows listed for YouTube, there are some minor differences, and it is worth repeating applicable portions. This section explores the unique workflows and tools required to produce high-quality immersive audio for Facebook's 360° video platform. It covers the technical aspects of capturing, editing, and mixing ambisonic audio, as well as best practices for ensuring compatibility and optimal playback on Facebook. Whether you are capturing live events or creating pre-recorded content, understanding these workflows is crucial for delivering an engaging and immersive audio-visual experience to Facebook users.

360° Video Formats on Facebook

Facebook supports a variety of 360° video formats (see Figure 6.6), providing content creators with the flexibility to produce immersive experiences for a wide audience. Monoscopic 360° video is a commonly used format that captures a single image for each frame, which is then projected onto a sphere to create a seamless 360° environment. This format is popular due to its simplicity and lower processing requirements, making it accessible to a broad range of content creators. Despite its simplicity, monoscopic 360° video can deliver a compelling immersive experience, especially when paired with high-quality ambisonic audio.

Figure 6.6 360° Video on Facebook

Stereoscopic 360° video, on the other hand, captures two images (one for each eye), creating a sense of depth and three-dimensionality. This format enhances the immersive experience by providing a more realistic visual representation, although it requires specialized cameras or rigs that can capture dual images simultaneously. As a result, stereoscopic 360° video is often used in professional productions where a heightened sense of depth and realism is desired. This increased sense of depth can be particularly effective when combined with spatial audio, making the viewer feel more present in the virtual environment.

For content that focuses on a specific area or direction, 180° video provides a balance between immersion and simplicity. While it does not offer a full 360° view, 180° video captures a wide field of view in front of the camera, making it easier to produce and edit. This format is useful for applications such as interviews or guided tours, where full 360° coverage is not necessary but an immersive experience is still desired. Additionally, 180° video is more compatible with traditional video production techniques and requires fewer resources compared to full 360° video.

Integrating ambisonic audio is crucial for enhancing the immersive quality of 360° videos on Facebook. Ambisonic microphones capture audio from all directions, which can then be processed and encoded to match the 360° visual environment. This spatial audio provides a coherent and engaging experience, dynamically adjusting itself based on the viewer's perspective to maintain the spatial integrity of the sound field. Ensuring that the ambisonic audio is properly synchronized with the 360° video is essential to creating a seamless immersive experience, and tools like Facebook's Spatial Workstation can aid in the editing and integration process.

Capturing Ambisonics Audio for 360° Video on Facebook

Capturing ambisonics audio for 360° video on Facebook involves taking several steps to ensure high-quality, immersive sound. First, selecting a suitable ambisonic microphone, such as the Sennheiser AMBEO VR Mic or Zoom H3-VR, is essential. These microphones capture sound from all directions, which can be later processed into a 3D soundscape. Proper placement of the microphone is crucial; it should be positioned at the center of the action, ideally at the same height as the 360° camera to align the audio perspective with the visual content. During the recording process, monitoring audio levels is vital to avoid clipping and ensure balanced recordings. Using high-quality headphones and reliable recording equipment helps achieve this balance. Environmental considerations, such as minimizing background noise and choosing quiet locations, are also important to capturing clean and immersive audio. Once the recording is complete, the ambisonic audio is transferred to a digital audio workstation (DAW) for editing and mixing.

Editing and Mixing Ambisonics Audio for 360° Video on Facebook

Editing and mixing ambisonics audio for 360° video on Facebook requires specialized software and a meticulous approach. The raw ambisonic audio is imported into a digital audio workstation (DAW) that supports ambisonic plugins, such as Reaper or Pro Tools. In the DAW, the ambisonic audio is decoded into a format suitable for binaural playback, which is necessary for Facebook's 360° video platform. This involves using tools like the Facebook 360 Spatial Workstation to convert the recorded audio into a spatial audio format. Sound design elements, such as reverb, spatial effects, and environmental sounds, can be added to enhance the immersive experience. It is crucial to balance these elements carefully to avoid overwhelming the listener while maintaining a natural ambiance. The final mix should be monitored using headphones that support binaural audio playback to ensure that the spatial effects are rendered correctly. Regular testing and quality-control checks help identify and resolve any issues with the audio.

Playback of Ambisonics Audio for 360° Video on Facebook

Ensuring proper playback of ambisonics audio for 360° video on Facebook involves several key steps. After editing and mixing, the final audio track needs to be encoded and synchronized with the 360° video. This is done using tools like Facebook's Spatial Workstation, which ensures the audio and video are correctly aligned and that the necessary metadata is embedded. Once uploaded to Facebook, it is essential to test the video playback on various devices, including VR headsets, mobile phones, and desktop computers, to ensure compatibility and a consistent immersive experience. Monitoring playback helps identify any discrepancies or issues with the audio synchronization or spatial effects. Providing clear instructions for viewers on how to optimize their playback experience, such as recommended app settings and hardware configurations, can enhance the overall experience. Continuous engagement with new technologies and updates from Facebook ensures that content creators can leverage the latest features and maintain high-quality immersive content.

Best Practices for Capturing and Producing Ambisonics Audio for 360° Video on Facebook

Creating immersive 360° videos with ambisonics audio for Facebook requires adherence to several best practices throughout the capture, editing, and production processes. These practices ensure the final product offers a high-quality, engaging experience for viewers.

Planning and Pre-production

Thorough planning is essential before starting the recording process. This includes selecting appropriate locations, preparing a detailed shot list, and considering how the audio and video will interact within the 360° environment.

Ensure the recording environment is controlled and free from unwanted background noise to achieve clean audio capture.

Selecting the Right Equipment

Choose high-quality ambisonic microphones, such as the Sennheiser AMBEO VR Mic or Zoom H3-VR, to accurately capture immersive audio.

Ensure compatibility between your 360° camera setup and audio equipment, and test all equipment before the shoot to avoid technical issues.

Microphone Placement and Setup

Position the ambisonic microphone at the center of the action, ideally at the same height as the 360° camera, to ensure the audio perspective aligns with the visual experience.

Use additional spot microphones or lavalier mics to capture specific sounds or dialogue that may not be clear in the ambisonic recording. These can be mixed in during post-production.

Monitoring and Recording

Continuously monitor audio levels during recording to ensure a balanced capture and avoid clipping. Use high-quality headphones and reliable recording equipment with adequate input channels and preamps. Capture metadata during the recording process, including microphone setup details and orientation, to ensure accurate processing and synchronization during post-production.

Editing and Mixing

Transfer the raw ambisonic audio to a digital audio workstation (DAW) that supports ambisonic plugins, such as Reaper or Pro Tools. Decode the ambisonic audio into a format suitable for binaural playback on Facebook, using tools like the Facebook 360 Spatial Workstation or the IEM Plugin Suite. Incorporate sound design elements judiciously, balancing reverb, spatial effects, and environmental sounds to enhance the immersive experience without overwhelming the listener. Regularly test the mix using headphones that support binaural audio playback to ensure the spatial effects are rendered correctly.

Metadata Injection and Upload

Use tools like the Facebook 360 Spatial Workstation to embed the necessary metadata into the video file, signaling to Facebook that the video contains 360° content and spatial audio.

Verify the metadata settings during the upload process on Facebook, ensuring the video is recognized as 360° content with spatial audio.

Playback Testing

Test the video playback on various devices, including VR headsets, mobile phones, and desktop computers, to ensure compatibility and consistency across platforms. Conduct thorough quality-control checks to identify and resolve any issues with audio synchronization or spatial effects.

Viewer Accessibility and Feedback

Provide clear instructions or tips for viewers on how to optimize their playback experience, including recommended app settings and hardware configurations. Engage with viewers and encourage feedback to understand their experiences and identify areas for improvement.

Continuous Learning and Adaptation

Stay updated with the latest developments in ambisonic audio technology and Facebook's 360° video standards to leverage new features and improve content quality. Monitor Facebook's analytics to gain insights into viewer engagement and performance, using this data to refine future projects.

By following these best practices, content creators can produce high-quality 360° videos with ambisonics audio that deliver a compelling and immersive experience on Facebook. Proper planning, meticulous attention to detail, and continuous learning are essential for success in this dynamic field.

IMMERSIVE AUDIO TOOLS

Creating high-quality immersive audio experiences requires the use of specialized tools and technologies. This section explores the essential equipment and software needed to capture, edit, and produce spatial audio. From microphones and headphone-tracking systems to speaker configurations and workstation requirements, each tool plays a crucial role in the immersive audio workflow. Understanding the capabilities and applications of these tools allows content creators to achieve precise and realistic soundscapes, enhancing the overall impact of their audio projects. This section provides an overview of the key tools and their functionalities, ensuring a solid foundation for producing immersive audio content.

Microphones for Immersive Audio

Microphones are a fundamental component in capturing high-quality immersive audio. Different types of microphones are used to achieve various spatial effects and sound qualities, each suited for specific applications in immersive audio production.

Ambisonic microphones are essential for capturing full-sphere surround sound. They record audio from all directions, creating a

3D sound field that can be manipulated during post-production. The Sennheiser AMBEO VR Mic is a popular choice among professionals for its high-quality capture and reliability. It uses four matched capsules arranged in a tetrahedral configuration to capture spatial audio accurately.

The Zoom H3-VR is another versatile ambisonic microphone that integrates recording, decoding, and playback functions in a single device. Its compact and user-friendly design makes it ideal for both field and studio recording. Ambisonic microphones are crucial for applications like VR, AR, and 360° video, where spatial audio enhances the immersive experience.

In addition to ambisonic microphones, binaural microphones are used to create realistic 3D audio experiences. These microphones mimic human hearing by using two microphones placed inside a mannequin head or spaced apart like human ears. The 3Dio Free Space and Neumann KU 100 are well-known binaural microphones that produce lifelike spatial audio.

When using binaural microphones, the captured audio is intended for headphone playback, as it recreates the way sound naturally reaches our ears. This makes binaural recordings perfect for applications like virtual reality, immersive storytelling, and audio tours. They provide an intimate and realistic listening experience, making the listener feel present in the recorded environment.

Shotgun microphones are often used in immersive audio production to capture focused sounds from a specific direction. These microphones have a highly directional pickup pattern, allowing them to isolate sound sources in noisy environments. The Sennheiser MKH 416 and RØDE NTG3 are popular shotgun microphones used in film, TV, and field recording.

Using shotgun microphones in conjunction with ambisonic or binaural microphones can enhance the clarity of specific audio elements, such as dialogue or key sound effects. This combination allows sound engineers to create a balanced and immersive soundscape by blending focused and ambient sounds.

Lavalier microphones, also known as lapel mics, are small and discreet, making them ideal for capturing dialogue in immersive audio productions. They are often used in interviews, film, and theater to capture clear and direct sound from the speaker. The Sennheiser ME 2 and RØDE SmartLav+ are widely used lavalier microphones known for their quality and versatility.

While lavalier microphones are typically used for capturing dialogue, they can also be employed creatively in immersive audio projects. Placing lavalier mics in strategic locations can capture unique perspectives and details, adding depth to the soundscape.

Boundary microphones, or PZM (pressure zone microphones), are another useful tool in immersive audio. These microphones are placed on flat surfaces and capture sound from a wide area. The Shure Beta 91A and Crown PCC-160 are popular boundary microphones used in various recording environments.

Boundary microphones are particularly effective in capturing natural reverb and ambiance in a space. They are commonly used in theater, conference settings, and live performances to provide a sense of the environment. In immersive audio, boundary microphones can add a realistic sense of space and depth to the recording.

Stereo microphones, which capture sound from two distinct channels, are also valuable in immersive audio production. The RØDE NT4 and Audio-Technica AT2022 are examples of stereo microphones that provide a natural and spacious sound. These microphones are useful for capturing environmental sounds and music performances, enhancing the immersive quality of the audio.

When selecting microphones for immersive audio, it's important to consider the recording environment and the desired spatial effect. Each type of microphone has unique characteristics and applications, making it suitable for a different aspect of immersive audio production. Combining multiple types of microphones can create a rich and dynamic soundscape that fully immerses the listener.

Proper placement and usage of microphones are crucial to achieving high-quality immersive audio. Experimenting with different microphone positions and configurations often yields the best results. Monitoring and adjusting audio levels during recording ensures a balanced and clean capture, avoiding issues such as clipping or distortion.

By understanding the various types of microphones and their applications, content creators can effectively capture the intricate details and spatial nuances needed for immersive audio projects. The right choice of microphones and recording techniques plays a pivotal role in delivering a compelling and engaging auditory experience.

Headphone-Tracking

In lieu of having an immersive audio studio setup with extensive speakers and complicated/expensive equipment, another option is to use headphones that can track your head position and give you the illusion of being in an immersive audio monitoring space.

Waves NX

Waves NX (see Figure 6.7) is a pioneering technology that brings immersive 3D audio to headphone listening by using advanced head-tracking capabilities. This software creates a virtual listening environment that mimics the natural acoustic properties of a physical space, providing a more realistic and engaging audio experience. Waves NX can be used with standard headphones, making it accessible to a wide audience without the need for specialized hardware.

The core feature of Waves NX is its head-tracking functionality, which monitors the listener's head movements in real time. This dynamic adjustment ensures that the spatial audio remains consistent with the listener's orientation, much like how we experience sound in the real world. By doing so, Waves NX enhances the sense of immersion and realism in various audio applications, including music production, gaming, and virtual reality.

Waves NX can be integrated into digital audio workstations (DAWs) and other audio playback systems. When used in music production,

Figure 6.7 Waves NX

it allows producers to mix and monitor tracks in a 3D space, ensuring that the final product translates well to immersive listening environments. In gaming, Waves NX provides players with a heightened sense of spatial awareness, improving gameplay and overall experience.

Setting up Waves NX involves installing the software and, optionally, using a head-tracking device, such as the Waves Head Tracker. This small sensor can be attached to headphones or worn as a clip, providing precise tracking of head movements. Alternatively, users can leverage the built-in camera of their device for head-tracking, although the dedicated sensor offers improved accuracy and responsiveness.

Overall, Waves NX is a versatile and powerful tool for anyone looking to enhance their audio experience with realistic 3D spatial sound. Its head-tracking capabilities and compatibility with standard headphones make it an accessible solution for a wide range of applications, from professional audio production to everyday listening.

Apple AirPods

Apple AirPods, particularly the AirPods Pro and AirPods Max (Figure 6.8), have incorporated advanced spatial audio features that provide an immersive listening experience. Spatial audio with dynamic head-tracking delivers a theater-like sound experience, making audio seem as though it is coming from all around the listener.

Figure 6.8 AirPods Max

The spatial audio technology in Apple AirPods utilizes built-in gyroscopes and accelerometers to track the listener's head movements. By adjusting the audio output in real time based on these movements, AirPods ensure that sounds remain fixed in the virtual space relative to the listener's position. This creates a more natural and immersive auditory environment, enhancing the experience of watching movies, playing games, or listening to music.

Apple's spatial audio works seamlessly with content from supported apps, such as Apple TV+, Disney+, and other streaming services that offer Dolby Atmos or 5.1, 7.1 surround-sound tracks. When watching a movie or TV show with spatial audio, users will feel as though the sound is coming from specific locations around them, corresponding to the action on screen.

Setting up spatial audio on Apple AirPods involves a straightforward process. Users need to ensure that their AirPods are connected to a compatible Apple device running the latest software. In the settings menu, spatial audio can be enabled and customized, allowing users to test and adjust the spatial audio effect to their preference.

In addition to enhancing entertainment experiences, Apple AirPods' spatial audio can be beneficial in other applications, such as virtual meetings and augmented reality (AR). The ability to spatially position audio sources can make virtual interactions feel more natural and intuitive, improving communication and engagement.

Overall, Apple AirPods with spatial audio provide a cutting-edge listening experience that leverages advanced head-tracking and audio-processing technologies. This makes them a valuable tool for immersive audio applications, offering users a heightened sense of realism and presence in their auditory experiences.

Speaker Configurations

Speaker configurations play a critical role in delivering immersive audio experiences. They determine how sound is distributed within a space, creating a multidimensional auditory environment that can enhance the realism and impact of the audio content. Different setups are used based on the application, whether it's for home theaters, professional studios, or large-scale installations.

Stereo Speaker Configuration

The simplest and most common setup, stereo configurations use two speakers placed to the left and right of the listener. This setup is ideal for music playback, providing a sense of width and directionality. Stereo speakers can create a basic spatial audio effect, but they are limited in providing a full 3D sound experience. They are often used as a starting point for more complex configurations.

Surround Sound

A popular configuration for home theaters, 5.1 surround sound includes five speakers and one subwoofer. The speakers are arranged with a center channel, left and right front channels, and left and right rear channels, along with the subwoofer for low-frequency effects. This setup enhances the immersive experience by enveloping the listener in sound from multiple directions, making it suitable for movies, games, and TV shows. Expanding on the 5.1 setup, 7.1 surround sound adds two additional speakers to the side of the listener, creating an even more immersive environment. The additional channels provide more precise audio placement and movement. This configuration is commonly used in high-end home theaters and professional audio production, offering a richer and more detailed soundscape.

Dolby Atmos and Object-Based Audio

Dolby Atmos (see Figure 6.9) takes surround sound to the next level by introducing height channels. This setup can include speakers placed

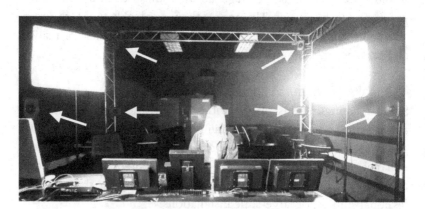

Figure 6.9 Atmos Speaker Setup

on the ceiling or upward-firing speakers that reflect sound off the ceiling. Atmos setups can range from 5.1.2 (five surround speakers, one subwoofer, and two height speakers) to more complex arrangements like 7.1.4. The "object-based" nature of Dolby Atmos allows sounds to move freely in a 3D space, creating a highly immersive experience.

Ambisonic Speaker Arrays

Ambisonic configurations use multiple speakers arranged in a sphere or dome around the listener to create a full 3D sound field. This setup captures and reproduces sound from all directions, providing a true immersive audio experience.

Ambisonic arrays are commonly used in VR installations, research, and specialized audio environments where accurate spatial audio reproduction is crucial.

Professional Studio Configurations

In professional audio studios, speaker configurations can be customized to fit the specific needs of the space and the type of audio work being performed. This often includes multiple near-field monitors, subwoofers, and reference speakers placed strategically to ensure accurate sound reproduction. Studios may also use immersive audio setups like Dolby Atmos or ambisonic arrays to mix and master content intended for these formats.

Large-Scale Installations

For large venues such as concert halls, theaters, and theme parks, speaker configurations are designed to cover wide areas and provide consistent audio quality across the space. This involves complex arrays of speakers, including line arrays, subwoofers, and surround speakers, all carefully positioned and tuned. These setups often use advanced sound reinforcement techniques and digital signal processing (DSP) to ensure clarity and impact, regardless of the listener's location in the venue.

Hybrid Configurations

Hybrid setups combine elements from different configurations to suit specific needs. For example, a home theater might use a 5.1 surround-sound system with additional height speakers for a Dolby Atmos experience, or a professional studio might incorporate both near-field monitors and an ambisonic array for versatile audio production.

Calibration and Tuning

Proper calibration and tuning are essential for any speaker configuration to ensure optimal performance. This involves adjusting speaker placement, levels, and equalization to match the acoustics of the space and achieve a balanced and accurate sound. Tools like room calibration software and acoustic treatments help optimize the listening environment, enhancing the immersive audio experience. By understanding and implementing the appropriate speaker configurations, content creators and audio professionals can deliver powerful and immersive audio experiences that captivate and engage listeners. Whether for personal enjoyment, professional production, or large-scale installations, the right setup can make all the difference in achieving high-quality spatial audio.

Workstation Requirements for Immersive Audio

Creating immersive audio requires a robust and well-equipped workstation capable of handling the complex processes involved in capturing, editing, mixing, and rendering spatial sound. The following outlines the key components and considerations for setting up an effective immersive audio workstation.

High-Performance Computer

A powerful computer is essential for processing the intensive tasks associated with immersive audio. It should have a multicore processor to handle multiple audio tracks and real-time processing. Ample RAM ensures smooth operation when running demanding DAWs and plugins.

Digital Audio Workstation (DAW)

A DAW is the core software for audio production. Popular DAWs for immersive audio include Reaper, Pro Tools, Logic Pro, and Nuendo, which offer extensive support for spatial audio plugins and formats. The DAW should support ambisonics, binaural, and other immersive audio formats. Plugins like Facebook 360 Spatial Workstation, IEM

Plugin Suite, and Waves NX are essential for editing and rendering spatial audio.

High-Quality Audio Interface

An audio interface with multiple inputs and outputs is necessary to connect microphones, monitors, and other audio equipment. It should support high-resolution audio (at least 24-bit/96 kHz) for professional-quality recordings. Interfaces from brands like Focusrite, Universal Audio, and RME are known for their reliability and audio fidelity.

Ambisonic Microphones and Headphones

Ambisonic microphones, such as the Sennheiser AMBEO VR Mic or the Zoom H3-VR, are essential for capturing spatial audio. They should be paired with high-quality headphones for accurate monitoring. Headphones with head-tracking capabilities, like those compatible with Waves NX or Apple's spatial audio, provide an immersive monitoring experience.

Monitor Speakers

Accurate monitor speakers are crucial for mixing and mastering immersive audio. Near-field monitors, such as those from Genelec, KRK, or Yamaha, are commonly used in professional studios. For spatial audio, additional speakers or an ambisonic speaker array may be required to accurately reproduce the 3D sound field.

Acoustic Treatment

Proper acoustic treatment of the workstation environment is essential to ensure accurate sound reproduction. This includes using bass traps, diffusers, and absorbers to manage reflections, standing waves, and other acoustic issues. Acoustic treatment helps create a neutral listening environment, allowing for precise mixing and editing of spatial audio.

External Storage

High-capacity and fast external storage solutions, such as SSDs or RAID arrays, are necessary for managing large audio files and project data.

This ensures quick access and efficient workflow during production. Regular backups are important to safeguard project files and ensure data integrity.

Control Surfaces and MIDI Controllers

Control surfaces and MIDI controllers enhance the workflow by providing tactile control over DAW parameters, mixing levels, and plugin settings. Devices like the Avid S1 or the PreSonus FaderPort can improve efficiency and precision. MIDI controllers are also useful for sound design and creating musical elements within immersive audio projects.

DOLBY ATMOS

The music industry loves buzzwords and at the time of writing, Atmos is the flavor of the month. We'll see how long it lasts as the immersive format of choice for the music streaming services.

Apple Music

Dolby Atmos on Apple Music brings an advanced level of immersive audio to streaming music. It allows listeners to experience music in a 3D sound field, where sounds can be placed all around the listener, including above and below. This creates a more dynamic and engaging listening experience compared to traditional stereo audio.

Apple Music supports Dolby Atmos for a growing catalog of tracks, making it accessible to a wide audience. To take full advantage of Dolby Atmos on Apple Music, listeners need compatible devices, such as the latest iPhone, iPad, Mac, or Apple TV, along with supported headphones or speakers. Apple's spatial audio technology further enhances this experience by using dynamic head-tracking to adjust the sound field based on the listener's movements.

For music producers, mixing in Dolby Atmos involves using a DAW that supports object-based audio and spatial mixing. Tools like Logic Pro offer integrated Dolby Atmos support, enabling producers to create and export tracks in this immersive format. Producers can place individual audio elements precisely in the 3D space, giving them creative control over the listener's experience.

Listening to music in Dolby Atmos on Apple Music is seamless, as the service automatically plays available tracks in this format if the listener's device supports it. Users can also manually enable or disable Dolby Atmos in the settings of the Apple Music app. This feature provides an enhanced audio experience that brings out new dimensions in music, making it feel more lifelike and enveloping.

Overall, Dolby Atmos on Apple Music represents a significant advancement in how music is experienced, offering artists and listeners alike a new way to enjoy and appreciate the intricacies of musical compositions.

Apple Renderer Workflow

The Apple Renderer Workflow for Dolby Atmos is a streamlined process designed to facilitate the production of immersive audio content. It integrates seamlessly with Apple's software and hardware ecosystem, providing a cohesive and efficient workflow for creators.

Producers can import their multitrack sessions and begin arranging them in a 3D sound space using the DAW's built-in tools and plugins. Logic Pro's Dolby Atmos tools allow for precise placement of audio objects, dynamic movement, and spatial effects, enabling detailed and immersive sound design.

Once the mix is complete, the DAW renders the audio into a Dolby Atmos format. This involves encoding the spatial information and audio channels into a file that can be played back on compatible devices. The rendered file retains all the spatial characteristics defined during the mixing process, ensuring an accurate representation of the immersive audio experience.

The next step involves testing and playback. Using Apple's ecosystem, creators can easily transfer their Dolby Atmos mixes to an Apple TV or other compatible device to evaluate the final product. This step is crucial to ensure that the mix translates well across different playback systems, from high-end home theater setups to personal headphones.

Apple's integration of Dolby Atmos extends to distribution as well. Once the mix is finalized and approved, it can be uploaded directly to platforms like Apple Music, where it will be available to listeners in its immersive format. Apple provides detailed guidelines and support to ensure that the upload and distribution process is smooth and that the content meets quality standards.

By following the Apple Renderer Workflow, producers can efficiently create, test, and distribute high-quality Dolby Atmos content.

This workflow leverages Apple's robust tools and platforms to deliver an unparalleled immersive audio experience to audiences worldwide.

Dolby Tools for Post-Production vs. Music

Dolby Atmos tools for post-production and music production cater to the specific needs of each industry, providing tailored solutions for creating immersive audio content. While both fields benefit from the advanced spatial audio capabilities of Dolby Atmos, the tools and workflows differ to address their unique requirements.

Post-Production

In post-production for film and television, Dolby Atmos is used to create immersive soundscapes that enhance the storytelling experience. Tools like Avid Pro Tools and Nuendo are commonly used in this industry, offering robust support for Dolby Atmos mixing. These DAWs provide features for handling complex audio sessions, including dialogue, sound effects, foley, and music, all within a 3D space.

Sound designers and mixers can use object-based audio techniques to place sounds precisely in the environment, creating realistic and dynamic audio experiences. The ability to move audio objects fluidly around the listener enhances scenes by adding depth and directionality to sound effects and ambient noises. In addition, the integration of Dolby Atmos in post-production workflows includes tools for encoding and decoding, ensuring that the final mix can be accurately reproduced in cinemas, home theaters, and streaming platforms.

Music Production

Creative Exploration: Dolby Atmos opens up new creative possibilities for musicians and producers. By leveraging spatial audio, artists can experiment with placing sounds in unconventional positions, creating unique and immersive musical experiences that stand out from traditional stereo mixes.

Workflow Integration: Music production tools like Logic Pro and Ableton Live integrate Dolby Atmos capabilities seamlessly into the existing workflow. This allows producers to work with familiar tools and processes while incorporating spatial audio elements, reducing the learning curve and enhancing productivity.

Distribution and Playback: With the rise of streaming platforms that support Dolby Atmos, music producers can reach a wider audience with their immersive mixes. Dolby provides guidelines and support to ensure that tracks are properly encoded and optimized for playback on services like Apple Music, Tidal, and Amazon Music HD.

The distinction between post-production and music production tools for Dolby Atmos highlights the versatility and adaptability of the technology. While post-production tools focus on creating realistic and dynamic soundscapes for film and television, music production tools emphasize creative expression and emotional impact. Both fields benefit from the advanced spatial audio capabilities of Dolby Atmos, enabling creators to push the boundaries of audio production and deliver captivating experiences to audiences worldwide. By providing tailored solutions for each industry, Dolby ensures that professionals have the tools they need to excel in their respective fields, whether they are crafting the next blockbuster film or producing an innovative music album.

Atmos in Logic Pro

One of the most integrated platforms for mixing audio in the Dolby Atmos format is Logic Pro. As has been mentioned a few times in this chapter, Logic has Atmos included in its tools, but it is worth exploring it a little deeper to help you understand exactly what is offered. Apple has included all of the tools necessary, including native access to the Apple Rendering toolkit.

Importing/Exporting

Logic Pro offers robust support for Dolby Atmos, enabling seamless importing and exporting of immersive audio projects. When starting a new project, users can easily import existing multitrack sessions or audio stems. Logic Pro supports a wide range of audio file formats, ensuring compatibility with various sources.

Once the project is ready for export, Logic Pro allows users to render their mix into a Dolby Atmos format (see Figure 6.10.) This involves encoding the spatial audio information into an ADM (Audio Definition Model) file, which retains all the spatial characteristics defined during the mixing process. The exported ADM file can be used for playback on Dolby Atmos-compatible devices or for distribution on platforms like Apple Music and Tidal.

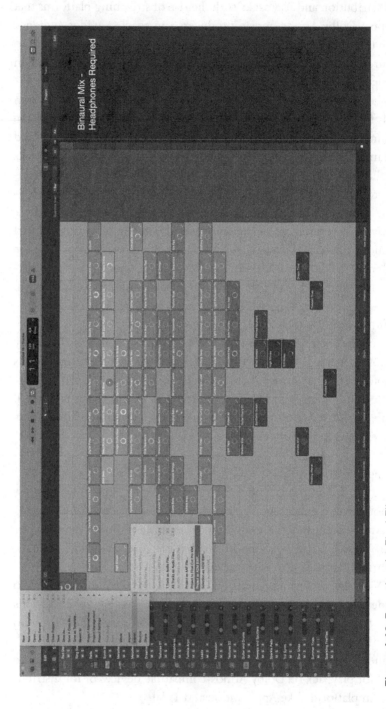

Figure 6.10 Exporting the Final File

Logic Pro also provides options for exporting traditional stereo or surround mixes alongside the Dolby Atmos version, ensuring versatility in distribution and playback.

Object Tools

Logic Pro's object tools are integral to creating immersive audio mixes in Dolby Atmos. These tools allow users to designate audio tracks as objects, which can then be positioned and moved within a 3D sound field. This object-based approach provides precise control over the placement and movement of sounds, enhancing the spatial experience.

Users can assign objects to specific audio tracks and manipulate their position using an intuitive 3D panner. The panner interface in Logic Pro enables users to place objects anywhere in the sound field (see Figure 6.11), including above and below the listener. Automation features allow for dynamic movement of objects, creating immersive effects that follow the action in the audio content.

Logic Pro also includes tools for managing object metadata, ensuring that spatial information is accurately preserved during the export process. This object-based approach is essential to producing high-quality Dolby Atmos mixes that provide a truly immersive listening experience.

Monitoring Options

Monitoring is a critical aspect of creating immersive audio, and Logic Pro offers several options to ensure accurate playback of Dolby Atmos mixes. Users can monitor their projects in real time using binaural rendering, which simulates the 3D sound field over headphones. This allows producers to experience the spatial characteristics of their mix without the need for a full speaker setup.

For those with access to a Dolby Atmos speaker system, Logic Pro supports multichannel monitoring configurations. This includes setups ranging from 5.1.2 to more complex arrangements like 7.1.4, allowing for precise playback of the spatial audio content. Logic Pro's monitoring tools also support downmixing, enabling users to hear how their Dolby Atmos mix will sound in traditional stereo or surround formats.

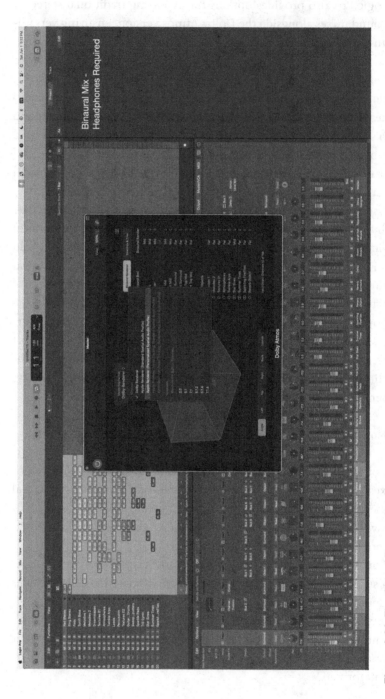

Figure 6.11 The Object Panner Setup

Additionally, Logic Pro provides visualization tools that display the spatial positioning of audio objects, helping users ensure that their mix translates well across different playback environments.

Personalized Spatial Audio

Logic Pro's support for personalized spatial audio takes immersive mixing to the next level by allowing users to tailor the listening experience to individual preferences. This feature leverages dynamic head-tracking technology, available in devices like the Apple AirPods Pro and AirPods Max, to adjust the audio based on the listener's head movements (see Figure 6.12.)

Producers can create mixes that respond to the listener's orientation, ensuring that sounds remain consistent and immersive regardless of how the listener moves. This personalized approach enhances the sense of presence and realism, making the audio experience more engaging.

Setting up personalized spatial audio in Logic Pro involves configuring the head-tracking settings and ensuring compatibility with supported devices. Once enabled, producers can monitor and adjust their mixes in real time, experiencing the same dynamic audio effects that end users will hear.

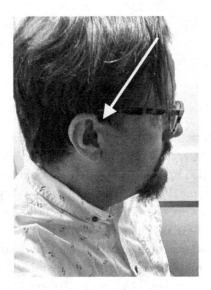

Figure 6.12 Personalizing Spatial Audio

By leveraging these tools in Logic Pro, content creators can produce high-quality Dolby Atmos mixes that deliver an unparalleled immersive audio experience. From precise object positioning to personalized spatial audio, Logic Pro provides the comprehensive capabilities needed to bring immersive audio projects to life.

VR/AR HEADSETS

The integration of virtual reality (VR) and augmented reality (AR) headsets into the music industry is revolutionizing how artists create, perform, and share their work, as well as how fans experience music. These amazing headsets offer immersive and interactive experiences, transforming concerts, rehearsals, and music education. From enabling virtual concerts to be staged that reach global audiences to providing realistic virtual rehearsal spaces and innovative learning tools, VR and AR technologies are expanding the boundaries of musical creativity and engagement. This section explores the common headset brands, the diverse content they support, their use in musicians' toolkits, and the promising future of these technologies in the music industry.

Common Headset Brands

The following represent the most common headsets available at the time of writing. Given the fast-paced nature of this technology niche, it is expected that readers will have a slew of additional options at their fingertips.

Meta Quest

The Meta Quest series, including the Quest 2 and the upcoming Quest 3 (see Figure 6.13), are among the most popular VR headsets available today. Developed by Meta (formerly Facebook), these headsets are known for their standalone capabilities, meaning they do not require a PC or console to operate. This makes them highly accessible and user-friendly, ideal for a wide range of immersive audio applications.

Meta Quest headsets come equipped with integrated spatial audio, enhancing the immersive experience by providing 3D sound directly from the headset's speakers. This feature allows users to experience spatial audio content naturally, whether they are gaming, watching 360° videos, or using VR applications.

Figure 6.13 Meta Quest 3

Apple Vision Pro

The Apple Vision Pro is Apple's highly anticipated entry into the VR/ AR headset market, known for its advanced features and seamless integration with Apple's ecosystem. Launched in 2024, the Vision Pro has high-resolution displays and powerful processing capabilities and offers a user-friendly experience. Apple's Vision Pro headset is designed to offer superior immersive audio experiences, leveraging Apple's spatial audio technology. This includes dynamic head-tracking, which adjusts the audio based on the listener's head movements, ensuring that sounds stay anchored in their virtual positions. This creates a more realistic and engaging auditory experience, enhancing overall immersion in VR and AR applications.

The Vision Pro integrates tightly with Apple's suite of services and devices, including Apple Music, Apple TV+, and the broader iOS ecosystem. This integration allows users to access a vast library of spatial audio content and enjoy a cohesive experience across their Apple devices. Apple's focus on user comfort and design is expected to be a significant aspect of the Vision Pro, making it not only powerful but also comfortable to wear for extended periods. This headset is poised to set a new standard in the VR/AR market, combining cutting-edge technology with Apple's signature ease of use and quality.

Other

Beyond Meta Quest and Apple Vision Pro, several other VR headsets offer immersive audio experiences, catering to various needs and preferences.

HTC Vive

The HTC Vive series, including the Vive Pro and Vive Cosmos, are known for their high-quality displays and precise tracking systems. These headsets are often used in professional and gaming environments, offering robust performance and extensive compatibility with VR content. The Vive Pro features integrated headphones with spatial audio capabilities, providing an immersive sound experience that complements its visual performance. HTC's focus on modularity and expandability allows users to customize their VR setups with additional trackers and accessories, enhancing both audio and visual immersion.

Sony PlayStation VR

The PlayStation VR (PSVR) is designed specifically for use with the PlayStation console, providing an accessible entry point to VR for gamers. The PSVR includes integrated headphones that support 3D audio, offering an immersive sound experience for games and media. Sony's strong library of VR titles and the upcoming PSVR2, with improved resolution and tracking, continue to make it a popular choice for console gamers seeking immersive experiences.

Valve Index

The Valve Index is a high-end VR headset known for its impressive display quality, wide field of view, and precise tracking system. It features built-in speakers that deliver high-fidelity audio, creating an immersive soundscape that enhances the VR experience. The Valve Index's adjustable comfort settings and ergonomic design make it suitable for extended use, appealing to both gamers and VR enthusiasts.

Pico Neo

The Pico Neo series, including the Pico Neo 3, are standalone VR headsets that offer competitive features at an affordable price. They include integrated spatial audio and a variety of applications, making them a versatile option for both consumers and enterprises. Pico's focus on ease of use and accessibility has made it a popular choice in educational and training environments, where immersive audio and visual experiences can enhance learning outcomes.

These headsets represent a diverse range of options in the VR market, each offering unique features and capabilities that cater to different user needs. Whether for gaming, professional use, or entertainment, these VR headsets contribute to the growing landscape of immersive audio and visual experiences.

Common Content for Headsets

The following represent examples of the content one would typically find on AR/VR headsets.

360° Videos

Immersive Visuals: 360° videos provide a complete panoramic view, allowing viewers to look in any direction for a fully immersive experience.

Applications: Popular in virtual tours, documentaries, and storytelling where viewers can explore environments freely.

Platforms: Widely supported on platforms like YouTube and Facebook, which provide specific support for 360° video content.

Production: Requires special 360° cameras to capture footage from all angles, followed by stitching software to create a seamless video.

Engagement: Enhances viewer engagement by allowing interaction with the content through VR headsets or compatible mobile devices.

180° Videos

Focused Immersion: Captures a wide field of view in front of the camera, offering a balance between traditional video and full 360° immersion.

Uses: Ideal for scenarios where the action is predominantly in front of the viewer, such as concerts, interviews, and presentations.

Advantages: Easier to produce and edit compared to 360° videos, requiring fewer cameras and less complex stitching. Is typically 3D as well.

Compatibility: Supported by major VR platforms and can be viewed on VR headsets or standard screens with panning controls.

Accessibility: Provides an immersive experience while being less resource intensive, making it accessible for a broader range of productions.

Gaming

Interactive Experiences: VR gaming offers highly interactive and immersive experiences, with players able to move and interact within a virtual environment.

Popular Titles: Includes games like Beat Saber, Half-Life: Alyx, and VR adaptations of popular franchises.

Platforms: Available on various VR platforms such as Oculus, PlayStation VR, and SteamVR.

Equipment: Often requires VR controllers and motion sensors to track movements and provide a fully immersive gaming experience.

Future Trends: Continual advancements in VR technology promise even more realistic graphics, better motion tracking, and more immersive gameplay experiences.

Experiences

Virtual Travel: Allows users to explore new locations and landmarks from the comfort of their home, providing an immersive travel experience.

Education and Training: Used for educational purposes, such as virtual classrooms, historical recreations, and hands-on training simulations.

Entertainment: Includes virtual concerts, theater performances, and interactive storytelling, offering unique ways to enjoy entertainment.

Healthcare: Utilized in therapeutic settings for treatments like exposure therapy and relaxation exercises, providing immersive and controlled environments.

Social VR: Platforms like VRChat and AltspaceVR enable social interactions in virtual environments, creating communities and shared experiences.

The Metaverse

Virtual Worlds: Encompasses vast, interconnected virtual spaces where users can interact, socialize, and create within a shared digital environment.

Interoperability: Aims to integrate various VR platforms and experiences, allowing seamless transitions between different virtual worlds and applications.

Economy: Features its own virtual economy with opportunities for commerce, such as virtual real estate, digital art, and in-game purchases.

Customization: Users can create and customize their avatars, virtual spaces, and experiences, contributing to the growth and diversity of the metaverse.

Future Vision: Envisioned as the next evolution of the internet, providing a persistent, immersive digital universe that parallels real-world activities and interactions.

These common content types for VR headsets highlight the diverse applications and experiences available, from interactive gaming and educational experiences to the expansive possibilities of the metaverse. Each type leverages the immersive capabilities of VR technology to provide unique and engaging experiences for users.

Examples of Headsets in the Musician's Toolkit

While AR/VR technology is quickly growing and expanding, it is useful to explore what these tools can potentially do for musicians now and in the near future.

Streaming Concerts

Immersive Experience: VR headsets provide an immersive experience, allowing fans to feel as though they are attending a live concert from the comfort of their homes.

Enhanced Engagement: Viewers can look around the venue, choose different vantage points, and feel closer to the performers.

Platforms: Services like MelodyVR and Oculus Venues specialize in streaming live music events in VR, offering a wide range of concerts and performances.

Interactivity: Some platforms allow users to interact with other virtual concertgoers, enhancing the social aspect of the experience.

Accessibility: Makes live music accessible to fans who cannot attend in person due to geographical or physical limitations.

Experiences

Virtual Rehearsals: Musicians can use VR to rehearse in virtual spaces, collaborating with bandmates from different locations as if they were in the same room.

Soundscapes: VR allows musicians to create and explore custom soundscapes, experimenting with different acoustics and environments for their music.

Music Videos: Artists can create immersive music videos that fans can experience in VR, adding a new dimension to their storytelling and artistic expression.

Educational Tools: VR applications can provide interactive music lessons, tutorials, and practice environments, making learning more engaging and effective.

Fan Interaction: Virtual meet-and-greets and backstage experiences can be offered to fans, enhancing the connection between artists and their audience.

Learning Music with Headsets

In addition to experiencing music, AR/VR can also be used as a tool to aid in the process of learning how to create and produce music.

Apps to Learn Music

Interactive Lessons: VR music apps offer interactive lessons that provide a hands-on learning experience. Users can practice playing instruments, reading music, and understanding theory in an engaging and immersive environment.

Gamified Learning: Many apps incorporate game-like elements to make learning music fun and motivating. Features such as scoring, challenges, and virtual rewards encourage consistent practice and skill development.

Apps to Enhance Learning Audio Production

Virtual Studios: VR apps for audio production simulate professional studio environments, allowing users to learn and practice production techniques. Users can interact with virtual equipment and software, gaining practical experience in a realistic setting.

Real-Time Feedback: These apps often provide real-time feedback and tutorials, guiding users through the process of mixing, mastering, and editing audio. This immediate guidance helps users quickly identify and correct mistakes, accelerating their learning curve.

The Future of Headsets in the Music Industry

The integration of VR and AR headsets in the music industry is set to revolutionize the way we experience music, blending cutting-edge technology with artistic creativity to open up new realms of possibility. As these technologies continue to evolve, they promise to transform not only how music is consumed but also how it is created, performed, and shared.

Imagine a future where attending a concert no longer means being physically present at a venue. Instead, fans around the world can don their VR headsets and be transported to a virtual concert hall, standing shoulder to shoulder with other avatars, feeling the energy of the crowd, and seeing the performers up close as if they were on stage themselves. These virtual concerts will not be limited by geography or venue capacity, allowing artists to reach a global audience instantaneously. Enhanced by spatial audio, these experiences will deliver sound that moves around the listener, mimicking the acoustics of real-world venues and providing an unprecedented level of immersion.

Beyond live performances, VR and AR headsets will offer new ways for musicians to engage with their fans. Virtual meet-and-greets, backstage tours, and interactive Q&A sessions can be held in immersive environments, creating intimate and personalized experiences. Fans could explore digital replicas of iconic studios or even participate in the creative process by virtually sitting in on recording sessions. This level of access and interactivity will deepen the connection between artists and their audience, fostering a more engaged and loyal fan base.

In the realm of music education, VR and AR headsets will revolutionize learning. Aspiring musicians will be able to take virtual lessons from renowned teachers, regardless of their physical location. These lessons can be highly interactive, with real-time feedback and visualizations that demonstrate proper technique and theory. AR headsets, in particular, can overlay instructional content onto the real world, allowing students to see notes and chords superimposed on their instruments. This blend of physical and digital learning will make music education more accessible and effective.

For music producers, VR and AR will bring the studio environment into the digital realm. Virtual studios will replicate the acoustics and equipment of professional recording spaces, enabling producers to mix and master tracks with a high degree of accuracy. They will be able to manipulate virtual mixing boards and effect racks as if they were tangible objects, offering a more intuitive and immersive workflow. Collaboration will also become easier, as multiple producers can work together in a shared virtual space, regardless of their physical location.

Looking further into the future, the concept of the metaverse, a fully immersive, interconnected digital universe, will play a significant role in the music industry. Artists will have the opportunity to create entire virtual worlds for their fans to explore, complete with interactive elements, exclusive content, and unique experiences. Concerts in the metaverse will be more than just performances; they will be multimedia events with stunning visuals, interactive storytelling, and real-time audience participation. These experiences will blur the lines between music, gaming, and social media, offering fans new ways to engage with their favorite artists.

In conclusion, the future of headsets in the music industry is incredibly promising, with the potential to transform every aspect of how music is experienced and produced. As VR and AR technologies advance, they will bring about new trends and possibilities, making music more immersive, interactive, and accessible. The fusion of technology and creativity will open up unprecedented opportunities for artists and fans alike, shaping the next era of the music industry.

Seven

Live-streaming technology allows users to broadcast video content in real time to audiences worldwide. This form of media has transformed how people interact with content online, offering unique opportunities and challenges for creators and viewers alike.

THE PHILOSOPHY OF LIVE-STREAMING

In order to understand the context of streaming and how it might benefit the career of those in the music industry, the following pro/con lists help illuminate what streaming is capable of doing.

10 Benefits of Streaming

1 Real-Time Engagement

- Immediate Feedback: Streamers receive comments and reactions in real time, allowing for instant adjustments and interactions.
- Audience Participation: Viewers can influence the content of the stream through live polls, choices, and suggestions.
- Dynamic Content Creation: The interaction often leads to spontaneous content that keeps the stream lively and engaging.
- Community Feel: Continuous interaction fosters a sense of community among viewers, which can enhance loyalty and regular viewership.
- Event-Style Experience: Live streams can mimic the atmosphere of live events, making viewers feel like they are part of an exclusive happening.

2 Authenticity

- Trust Building: Genuine interactions and reactions help build trust between the streamer and their audience.
- Unique Content: Each stream is unique, which can differentiate a creator from others who post more polished, edited content.

DOI: 10.4324/9781003416180-7

- Personal Connection: Streamers often share live reactions and personal stories, creating a strong personal connection with their audience.
- Unscripted Content: The lack of a script makes the content feel more "real" and relatable to viewers.
- Transparency: Demonstrating processes, decisions, and reactions transparently can increase credibility and viewer trust.

3 Global Reach

- Access to International Viewers: Streamers can reach viewers around the world without physical or geographical barriers.
- Cross-Cultural Exchange: Streams can attract a culturally diverse audience, allowing for exchange and broader perspectives.
- 24/7 Potential Audience: No matter the time of the broadcast, global accessibility means there's always someone awake to tune in.
- Viral Potential: The global nature of the internet can help content go viral, reaching exponentially more viewers.
- Language and Localization: Streams can be done in multiple languages or tailored to specific cultural contexts, broadening the potential audience base.

4 Diverse Content Opportunities

- Variety of Genres: Live-streaming supports a wide range of content from gaming, cooking, music performances to tutorials.
- Niche Markets: Creators can find and cultivate niche markets that are specifically interested in their content style or subject matter.
- Interactive Formats: Incorporation of interactive elements like live tutorials, workshops, or Q&A sessions.
- Collaborations: Live interactions with other creators or experts can be arranged to diversify content.
- Special Events: Hosting special event streams, such as charity events or anniversaries, can draw larger audiences.

5 Monetization Opportunities

- Direct Donations: Viewers can send money directly to creators during live streams through features like Super Chat on YouTube.
- Subscriptions: Platforms often offer subscription options that provide steady monthly income from dedicated fans.

- Sponsored Streams: Companies pay creators to promote products or services directly during their broadcasts.
- Ad Revenues: Ads played during live streams can generate significant revenue, especially with large audiences.
- Exclusive Content: Offering pay-per-view content or members-only streams as part of a subscription model.

6 Community Building

- Regular Schedules: Establishing regular streaming times helps build a routine for viewers.
- Engagement Tools: Using tools like chat, polls, and games to foster interaction and strengthen community ties.
- Viewer Recognition: Acknowledging regular viewers and contributors can enhance community loyalty.
- Shared Experiences: Community members share experiences and support each other during live streams.
- Feedback Loop: Ongoing feedback from the community helps shape the stream's content and direction.

7 Marketing and Promotion

- Product Launches: Companies can use live streams to launch new products, reaching a large audience instantly.
- Brand Humanization: Live streams allow companies to humanize their brands by showing the people behind the products.
- Real-Time Promotion: Offers and promotions can be shared in real time, with instant viewer reactions.
- Engagement Analytics: Real-time data on viewer engagement helps refine marketing strategies.
- Lead Generation: Interactive elements and direct calls to action during streams can serve as effective lead-generation tools.

8 Immediate Feedback

- Product Improvement: Immediate reactions to product demos can guide development and improvement.
- Content Tailoring: Real-time feedback allows creators to tailor their content to audience preferences.

- Performance Enhancement: Instant feedback helps performers adjust their delivery to better engage the audience.
- Learning and Growth: Creators learn quickly what works and what doesn't, helping them improve their skills.
- Audience Insight: Direct insights into audience demographics and preferences guide future content and strategies.

9 Educational Impact

- Interactive Learning: Live streams offer interactive learning opportunities that can be more engaging than traditional methods.
- Broad Accessibility: Students from anywhere in the world can access educational content without physical constraints.
- Expert Access: Students can interact with experts they wouldn't typically have access to, asking questions and gaining insights in real time.
- Supplemental Education: Live streams can supplement traditional education with real-world applications and discussions.
- Customized Learning: Streams can be tailored to different learning styles and speeds, accommodating a diverse student body.

10 Event Accessibility

- Inclusive Participation: People with disabilities or those who are geographically isolated can participate in events they otherwise couldn't attend.
- Reduced Costs: Attending virtual events can significantly reduce costs for both organizers and participants.
- Archived Events: Live events can be recorded and archived for later access, extending the life and reach of the event.
- Environmental Impact: Reduces the carbon footprint associated with traveling to events.
- Flexible Viewing: Viewers can join part of the live event and revisit the rest at their convenience.

These expanded points provide a thorough understanding of the multifaceted benefits of live-streaming, illustrating why it's such a powerful tool in modern digital communication.

Figure 7.1 Typical Streaming Software

10 Drawbacks of Live-Streaming

1 Technical Issues

- Connectivity Problems: Poor internet connections can lead to frequent buffering, low-quality streams, and interruptions.
- Hardware Dependence: Quality streaming requires good hardware, which can be expensive and needs regular updates.
- Software Glitches: Live-streaming software (see Figure 7.1) may encounter bugs or crashes, potentially disrupting broadcasts.
- Platform Limitations: Each streaming platform has different limitations on stream quality, duration, and features, which can restrict what creators can do.
- Complex Setup: Setting up a professional-quality stream involves managing multiple software and hardware components, which can be daunting for beginners.

2 Moderation Difficulties

- Scale of Viewership: Large audiences can make it nearly impossible to effectively moderate chat and interactions in real time.
- Inappropriate Content: Live chats may include spam, offensive language, or harmful content that can deter viewers and harm the streamer's reputation.

- Delayed Response: Even with moderation tools, there is often a delay in addressing problematic content, which may already have impacted viewers.
- Resource Intensive: Effective moderation requires either sophisticated software or a team of human moderators, both of which can be costly.
- Legal and Policy Compliance: Streamers must ensure their content and user interactions comply with platform policies and legal standards, adding complexity.

3 Privacy Concerns

- Accidental Sharing: Streamers might inadvertently share personal information or sensitive data during a live broadcast.
- Hacking Risks: High-profile streams are attractive targets for hacking, leading to potential data breaches.
- Viewer Data: Collecting and managing viewer data for interactive features can pose privacy risks if not handled properly.
- Location Exposure: Streaming in public or even from home can accidentally reveal a streamer's location.
- Recording and Distribution: Live streams can be recorded and shared without consent, spreading content beyond the intended audience.

4 High Pressure on Creators

- Consistency Requirement: To build and maintain an audience, streamers need to broadcast regularly, which can be stressful.
- Audience Expectations: The need to meet or exceed audience expectations consistently can create significant pressure.
- Creative Burnout: Constantly generating new, engaging content can lead to burnout, especially without breaks.
- Public Scrutiny: Live streamers are under constant scrutiny from their audience, which can be psychologically taxing.
- Financial Stress: For those who rely on streaming for income, fluctuations in viewer numbers and donations can create financial instability.

5 Negative Interactions

- Trolling: Live streams can attract trolls who engage in disruptive or abusive behavior.
- Harassment: Streamers, especially women and minorities, may face harassment both during and outside of their streams.
- Conflict Among Viewers: Differences among viewers can lead to conflicts in the chat, creating a hostile environment.
- Pressure to Respond: Streamers might feel compelled to respond to negative comments, which can escalate conflicts or detract from the quality of the stream.
- Mental Health Impact: Regular exposure to negative interactions can have a serious impact on a streamer's mental health.

6 Unpredictability

- Variable Viewer Numbers: Audience size can fluctuate widely without clear reasons for this, making planning and monetization challenging.
- Dependence on Platform Algorithms: Changes to platform algorithms can unpredictably affect stream visibility and viewer engagement.
- Market Saturation: With more people streaming, it becomes increasingly difficult to predict what will capture viewers' interest.
- Technical Failures: Unexpected technical issues can disrupt even the most well-planned streams.
- Real-Time Mistakes: Mistakes made live cannot be edited out, leading to potential reputational damage.

7 Resource Intensive

- Investment Costs: Upfront costs for high-quality streaming gear can be prohibitive.
- Ongoing Expenses: Regular upgrades and maintenance of equipment, as well as software subscriptions, add to expenditures.
- Time Commitment: Preparing, executing, and following up on live streams requires a significant time investment.

- Energy Consumption: Live-streaming, especially with advanced setups, can consume a lot of electrical power.
- Space Requirements: Creating a dedicated streaming space that is quiet and well equipped can require significant physical space.

8 Legal Risks

- Copyright Issues: Playing copyrighted music, showing videos, or streaming games without permission can lead to legal action.
- Defamation and Liability: Comments made during a live stream can lead to defamation claims if they harm someone's reputation.
- Regulatory Compliance: Different countries have varying regulations regarding broadcasting, which can complicate international streams.
- Contract Violations: Streamers with partnerships or sponsorships may face legal issues if they don't adhere to contract terms during streams.
- Age Restrictions: Managing age-appropriate content and complying with laws regarding minors can be challenging.

9 Skill Requirements

- Technical Proficiency: Understanding and managing streaming software and hardware requires technical skills.
- Content Creation: Developing engaging and original content consistently requires creative skills.
- Communication Abilities: Effective live-streaming requires good on-camera communication and interaction skills.
- Adaptability: Streamers must be able to adapt to new technologies, viewer preferences, and platform changes.
- Problem-Solving: Handling issues that arise during live broadcasts requires quick thinking and problem-solving.

10 Market Saturation

- High Competition: The increasing number of streamers makes it difficult to stand out and attract viewers.
- Reduced Visibility: More content can dilute individual visibility, making it harder for new streamers to gain traction.

- Audience Fragmentation: With more options, viewers are spread thinner across streams, potentially reducing the number of consistent viewers per stream.
- Pressure to Innovate: The need to continuously innovate to keep content fresh and engage viewers can be demanding.
- Dependency on Trends: Streamers may feel compelled to follow trends rather than create original content, which can stifle creativity.

This expanded examination of live-streaming's advantages and disadvantages equips creators with a comprehensive understanding of the medium's impact. With this knowledge, they can better navigate the challenges and leverage the opportunities that live-streaming presents in various fields, from entertainment to education. Moving forward, the next sections will explore specific features and workflows of popular live-streaming platforms, providing practical insights for effective streaming strategies.

WORKFLOWS FOR VARIOUS PLATFORMS

Keep in mind that platforms are ever-changing, and so it is not possible to include detailed instructions without the risk of its becoming outdated almost immediately. The following reflects a snapshot in time and is intended to be a reference place where you can get started, but please view content on the following playlist for more recent information:

https://www.youtube.com/playlist?list=PLIezNGtdLioi9MKcvPwq ZyOk9WKsDMIK7

Instagram
Quick Start Guide

- Setting Up: Download the Instagram app, create an account, and navigate to your profile. Tap the camera icon on the top left or swipe right from anywhere in the feed.
- Going Live: Swipe to the "Live" option (see Figure 7.2) under the record button, then tap the button to start streaming. A ring will appear around your profile picture in stories to indicate you are live.

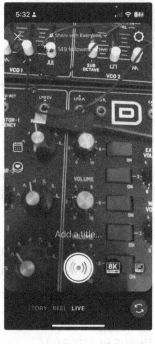

Figure 7.2 Streaming Page

- Interface Overview: The screen displays the number of viewers, the comments, and a field to write comments in. You can pin a comment for all viewers to see by tapping on it.
- Tools and Features: Use features like filters and face effects. You can also invite a friend to join your live video, turning it into a split-screen session.
- Ending the Stream: You can end your live stream at any time by tapping "End" in the top right corner. Once the live stream is over, you can choose to share a replay to your story, save it to your camera roll, or discard it.

Audience Engagement

- Interactivity: Encourage viewer interaction by asking questions and prompting responses to create a conversational atmosphere.
- Use of Polls and Q & A: Utilize Instagram's Q & A feature or create polls to gather viewer opinions and questions, increasing engagement.

- Shoutouts and Acknowledgments: Mention viewers by name as they join the stream or comment, which personalizes the experience and can increase loyalty and the number of return viewers.
- Consistent Scheduling: Hold streams at regular intervals, which can help build a routine for viewers and increase anticipation for your broadcasts.
- Content Variety: Mix up the content of your live streams to keep them fresh and engaging. This could include behind-the-scenes tours, live performances, tutorials, or guest appearances.

Audio/Video Guide

- Optimal Lighting: Ensure you are well lit from the front; use natural light or soft artificial lighting to improve video quality.
- Sound Quality: Use a good external microphone if possible. Avoid background noise by streaming from a quiet environment.
- Camera Stability: Use a tripod or steady surface to keep your device stable. Avoid handheld streaming unless necessary for dynamic movement.
- Framing and Composition: Frame yourself centrally and use the rule of thirds to make the stream visually appealing. Make sure the background is tidy and not distracting.
- Connection Quality: Ensure a strong and stable internet connection before going live to avoid interruptions and quality degradation.

Requirements

- Instagram Account: You must have a verified account or at least meet minimum follower thresholds in some cases to access certain streaming features.
- Age Requirement: You must be over the age of 13 to create an Instagram account, and certain features may be restricted to older users.
- Appropriate Content: Follow Instagram's community guidelines to avoid having your live stream interrupted or banned for inappropriate content.
- Device Specifications: Use a device with a good camera and processing power to handle the demands of live-streaming.
- Software Updates: Keep the Instagram app updated to the latest version to ensure access to all features and maintain stream stability.

This structured breakdown of Instagram's live-streaming workflow provides a clear starting point for freshmen to explore live broadcasting, ensuring they have the knowledge and tools needed to engage effectively with their audience.

TikTok
QuickStart Guide

- Setting Up: Download TikTok from your app store, sign up for an account, and complete your profile. Navigate to the home screen.
- Going Live: To start a live stream, press the "+" icon at the bottom of the screen, swipe to the "Live" option among the camera modes, and then tap "Go Live." Note that you need at least 1,000 followers to unlock the live feature.
- Interface Overview: The live interface displays viewer count, comments, and live reactions. Tools for filters, effects, and flipping the camera are also available.
- Tools and Features: Enhance your stream with various beauty effects, filters, and interactive features like co-hosting with other users.
- Ending the Stream: You can end your live session by swiping down and tapping "End Live." You'll then see a summary of your live performance, including viewer statistics and interactions.

Audience Engagement

- Interactive Content: Utilize TikTok's interactive features like live polls, Q & A sessions, and duet/live reactions to maintain viewer engagement.
- Viewer Incentives: Encourage participation and longer viewership by hosting giveaways, contests, or exclusive reveals during your live streams.
- Real-Time Interaction: Engage with viewers by responding to comments in real time, acknowledging viewers by name, and answering questions during the broadcast.
- Scheduled Events: Promote scheduled live events ahead of time using your TikTok posts or other social media platforms to build anticipation and gather a larger audience.
- Community Building: Foster a community by regularly interacting with your audience, hosting collaborative streams, and creating content based on viewer feedback.

- Good Lighting: Ensure your streaming area is well lit, ideally with natural light facing you; or use ring lights, which eliminate shadows and enhance video quality.
- Clear Audio: Invest in a good external microphone to improve audio clarity. Minimize background noise by choosing a quiet location for your streams.
- Stable Camera Setup: Use a tripod or other stabilizing equipment to keep your smartphone or camera steady during live broadcasts.
- Visual Appeal: Arrange a visually appealing background and consider your on-screen appearance. Dress in bright, solid colors, as these stand out and help you maintain a professional yet approachable look.
- Reliable Internet Connection: Ensure a strong Wi-Fi or cellular data connection to maintain high video quality without interruptions.

Requirements

- Follower Count: TikTok requires users to have at least 1,000 followers to access the live-streaming feature.
- Age Restrictions: You must be at least 16 years old to access live-streaming. If you want to send virtual gifts, you need to be 18 or older.
- Content Guidelines: Adhere to TikTok's community guidelines to avoid content strikes or bans. This includes avoiding the broadcast of prohibited activities, hate speech, and explicit content.
- Device Compatibility: Ensure your device is capable of supporting the TikTok app, especially focusing on camera quality and processing speed for a smooth streaming experience.
- App Updates: Regularly update the TikTok app to access the latest features and maintain compatibility with new operating system updates.

This overview provides the essential steps and considerations for freshmen who are interested in exploring TikTok for live-streaming. It offers a solid foundation for engaging effectively with a growing and dynamic audience on one of the most popular social media platforms today.

Facebook Live
QuickStart Guide

- Setting Up: Ensure you have a Facebook account. Navigate to your news feed and click on "Live" under the "Create" menu at the top of the page.
- Going Live: Choose between going live now or scheduling a live event for later (see Figure 7.3.) Select your privacy settings (public, friends, or private), and if you're on a page you manage, decide which audience to target.

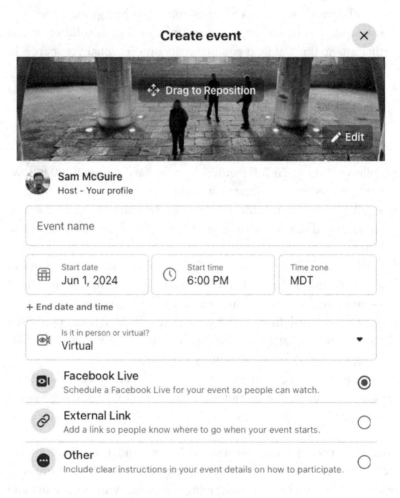

Figure 7.3 Setting up a Facebook Stream

- Interface Overview: The live-streaming dashboard on Facebook provides options for managing your stream's description, adding titles, and setting audience restrictions. It displays real-time interaction data such as viewer counts, comments, and reactions.
- Tools and Features: Facebook offers features like screen sharing, adding guests to your stream, and various broadcast tools through its Live Producer.
- Ending the Stream: Conclude your broadcast by clicking the "End Live Video" button. After ending, you can choose to publish the video to your page or delete it if you do not want to keep the recording.

Audience Engagement

- Direct Interaction: Respond to viewer comments live. Acknowledging viewers by name and answering their questions can foster a more personal connection.
- Use of Real-Time Polls and Q & A: Incorporate polls and Q & A sessions to gather viewer opinions and keep the content interactive.
- Announcements and Reminders: Regularly remind viewers about upcoming streams and important announcements at the beginning and end of each session.
- Viewer Challenges and Calls to Action: Encourage viewer participation with challenges, calls to action, or prompts that require viewer input, enhancing engagement.
- Regular Scheduling: Maintain a consistent streaming schedule to build a regular audience. Announce upcoming streams to keep your audience informed.

Audio/Video Guide

- Professional Setup: Invest in high-quality cameras and microphones to enhance the audio and video quality of your streams.
- Environment Considerations: Choose a quiet, well-lit environment for streaming. Good lighting and minimal background noise can significantly improve the quality of the video.
- Camera Framing: Position the camera at eye level and frame the shot appropriately to engage directly with your audience.
- Test Your Setup: Before going live, conduct test streams to troubleshoot any issues with sound or video quality.

- Backup Equipment: Have backup audio and video equipment ready in case of technical failures.

Requirements

- Platform Guidelines: Familiarize yourself with Facebook's community guidelines and terms of service to ensure your content remains compliant.
- Technical Specifications: Ensure your broadcasting setup meets Facebook's technical requirements, including supported browsers and internet bandwidth recommendations.
- Age Restrictions: You must be 13 years or older to create a Facebook account, and certain features are restricted to adults.
- Account Status: Your account must be in good standing with Facebook to use the live-streaming feature without restrictions.
- Viewer Permissions: Be aware of who can see your live stream based on the privacy settings you select (e.g., public, friends, or specific groups).

Web/App Interface vs Third-Party Streaming Software

- Web/App Interface: Facebook's native interface is straightforward and designed for basic streaming needs. It is ideal for users who prefer simplicity and do not require advanced broadcasting features.
- Third-Party Software: For more professional broadcasts, using software like OBS Studio or Streamlabs (see Figure 7.4) can enhance your stream with features like overlays, multi-camera setups, and more in-depth audio management. These tools integrate directly with Facebook for a seamless streaming experience.

Immersive Audio/Video-Streaming

- 360-Degree Video: Facebook supports 360-degree video-streaming, allowing for a more immersive viewer experience. Viewers can interact with the video to explore different angles.
- Virtual Reality: Leverage Facebook's VR capabilities to offer unique experiences like virtual events or tours.
- High-Definition Streaming: Ensure you stream in the highest possible definition supported by your equipment and internet connection to provide a clear, engaging viewing experience.

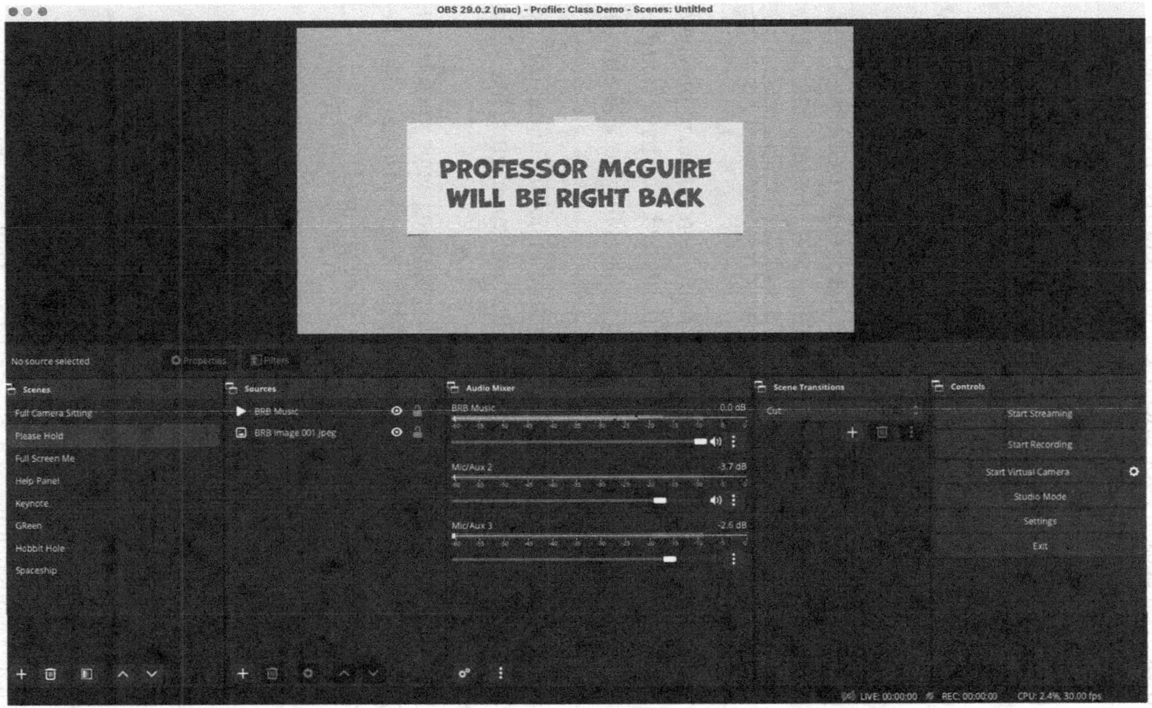

Figure 7.4 OBS Interface

This comprehensive guide outlines the critical aspects of utilizing Facebook Live for streaming, from basic setup and engagement strategies to more advanced broadcasting techniques. It provides the tools and knowledge necessary for effective and interactive live broadcasts on one of the world's largest social platforms.

YouTube Live
Quick Start Guide

- Setting Up: Sign in to your YouTube account and verify it if you haven't already to enable live-streaming capabilities. Navigate to YouTube Studio, and select the "Create" button then "Go Live."
- Going Live: Once in the YouTube Live dashboard (see Figure 7.5), you can choose to start streaming immediately or schedule a live event for later. Set your stream's title, description, and privacy settings (public, unlisted, or private).
- Interface Overview: The live control room offers a stream preview, chat interface, and analytics all in one dashboard. You have controls for stream health, stream settings, and the ability to add stream markers.
- Tools and Features: Utilize features such as enabling monetization (if eligible), adding stream thumbnails, and managing live chat settings.
- Ending the Stream: End your stream by stopping your encoder or using the "End Stream" button in YouTube. Your video can then be saved as a VOD (video on demand) on your channel.

Audience Engagement

- Live Chat Interaction: Engage with your viewers via the live chat. Prompt responses and interactions can help maintain viewer interest and build community.
- Polls and Viewer Q&A: Use YouTube's built-in features for live polls and Q&A sessions to interact and gather feedback from your audience in real time.
- Channel Memberships and Super Chat: Leverage monetization features like Super Chat and Channel Memberships to encourage financial support while increasing engagement.

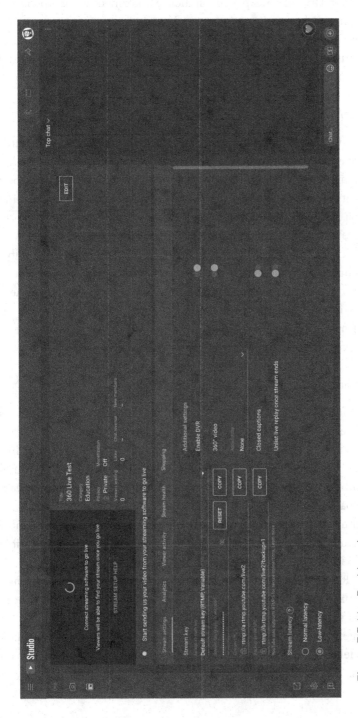

Figure 7.5 Live Dashboard

- Regular Updates: Keep your audience informed about upcoming streams with community posts and reminders.
- Interactive Content: Plan interactive content such as live tutorials, gaming, or real-time discussions to keep the audience engaged and returning for more.

Audio/Video Guide

- High-Quality Equipment: Use a high-quality camera and microphone to ensure your audio and video are clear and professional.
- Optimal Streaming Settings: Configure your encoder for the best quality settings that your internet bandwidth can support, aiming for at least 720p or 1080p.
- Stable Internet Connection: A wired connection is preferable to Wi-Fi in order to reduce the risk of interruptions and maintain a stable stream.
- Environment Setup: Stream in a quiet and controlled environment to minimize background noise and distractions.
- Testing and Previews: Utilize YouTube's stream preview feature to check your setup and make adjustments before going live.

Requirements

- Platform Compliance: Adhere to YouTube's Community Guidelines and terms of service to avoid restrictions or bans.
- Subscriber and View Hours Requirements: For certain features like Super Chat and monetization, you will need to meet the required number of subscribers (1,000) and public watch hours (4,000 in the past 12 months).
- Technical Specifications: Ensure your equipment and software meet YouTube's requirements for live-streaming, including compatible encoders.
- Age Restrictions: You must be at least 13 years old (with parental permission) to create a YouTube account. To live-stream without adult supervision, you must be 18 or older.
- Content Ratings: Manage content ratings according to YouTube's guidelines, especially if your content might not be suitable for all ages.

- Native Interface: YouTube's web and app interfaces provide basic live-streaming capabilities and are suitable for straightforward broadcasts.
- Advanced Software: For more complex streams, use third-party software like OBS Studio, Streamlabs, or XSplit. These tools offer advanced features such as multi-camera setups, graphic overlays, and more detailed audio controls.

Immersive Audio/Video-Streaming

- 4K Streaming: YouTube supports streaming in 4K resolution, offering an incredibly detailed viewing experience for audiences with capable devices.
- 360-Degree and VR: Engage your audience with 360-degree videos and VR content, providing a more immersive experience that allows viewers to control their perspective.
- Enhanced Audio: Implement spatial audio for 360-degree and VR streams, which enhances the realism of the sound as it corresponds to video playback.

This comprehensive guide on using YouTube Live for streaming covers all aspects necessary for a successful broadcast, from basic setup and viewer engagement to advanced techniques for professional-quality streams. This information is crucial for college freshmen looking to explore or enhance their live-streaming capabilities on one of the most popular video platforms globally.

EQUIPMENT

The following section explores the tools available for use in supporting streams. These include software and hardware options, and the section also takes a look at various workflows.

Software

There are a variety of software tools you can use for streaming; sometimes you will find that there is more than one that works for you. Some of these can simultaneously stream to multiple platforms.

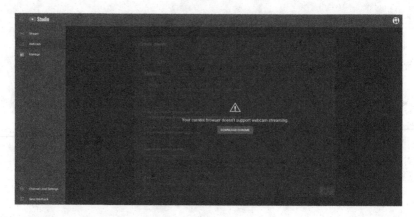

Figure 7.6 Stream for YouTube Webpage

Native Tools
Platform-Specific Apps

Many streaming platforms offer built-in streaming functionalities directly through their apps (see Figure 7.6), such as Instagram Live, Facebook Live, or TikTok.

Basic Features

These native tools typically include basic live-streaming features such as camera access, microphone use, simple graphics, and chat functionalities.

Ease of Use

The tools are designed for simplicity and integrated directly with social media features, making them accessible even to beginners.

Limitations

These apps generally lack advanced features like multi-camera inputs, extensive graphic overlays, or detailed audio controls.

Ideal Use

Best for casual streamers or those just starting out who do not require complex setups.

Streaming Software
OBS Studio (Open Broadcaster Software)

Free and open-source software that supports streaming and recording in high definition without limitations on the duration.

Streamlabs

Based on OBS but with additional features tailored for streamers, such as integrated alerts, widgets, and built-in donation processing.

XSplit

Offers both a free and a premium version, providing powerful live-streaming and recording capabilities with an intuitive interface.

vMix

A comprehensive live production software solution that includes features like live mixing, switching, recording, and live to stream of HD and 4K video sources.

Wirecast

Professional live video-streaming production tool that allows for broadcasting of live or recorded video to multiple destinations simultaneously.

Connecting Options

RTMP (Real-Time Messaging Protocol)

Universal standard for the delivery of audio, video, and data from the media encoder to the streaming server.

SRT (Secure Reliable Transport)

Designed to transport high-quality video over even the most unreliable networks, such as public internet.

WebRTC (Web Real-Time Communication)

Enables real-time communication directly in web browsers through simple APIs, useful for guest appearances and multi-user streams.

Real-Time Effects

Graphic Overlays

Add logos, lower thirds, scoreboards, and other graphics in real-time during the broadcast (see example in Figure 7.7).

Video Transitions

Smooth transitions between different scenes or camera angles enhance the professional quality of the stream.

Figure 7.7 Overlay Example

Audio Mixers
Software-based audio mixers allow for the adjustment of sound levels, application of effects, and balancing of various audio sources.

Green Screens and Lights
Virtual Backgrounds
Using a green-screen setup, streamers can superimpose themselves onto virtual backgrounds or graphical environments (see Figure 7.8).

Lighting Requirements
Proper lighting is crucial for green-screen effectiveness: ensure that the green is evenly lit for easy keying out in the software.

Software Integration
Most advanced streaming software supports chroma keying, allowing for easy setup and integration.

Layering Content
Multiple-Source Inputs
Combine various video sources such as cameras, screen captures, and pre-recorded videos into a single stream (see Figure 7.9).

Scene Composition
Create scenes with layered inputs like text, images, and live video for dynamic and engaging content.

Source Transitions
Utilize different transitions for switching between sources smoothly during a broadcast.

Branding
Custom Graphics
Incorporate custom graphics like logos, banners, and other brand identifiers to maintain brand consistency and recognition.

Branded Content
Tailor content to reflect brand messaging and values to enhance your brand identity and viewer loyalty.

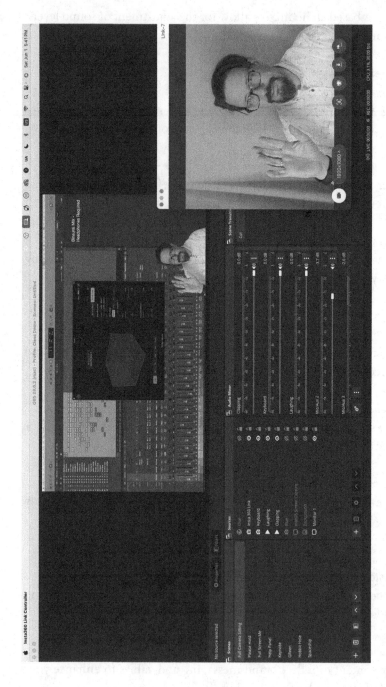

Figure 7.8 Green-Screen Demo

Figure 7.9 Multiple Inputs

271   **Introduction to Live-Streaming**

Figure 7.10 Recording Option in OBS

Templates and Themes
Use software that supports templates and themes to easily maintain a consistent visual style.

Recording Streams
Local Recording
Most streaming software provides options to record a local copy of the live stream for archiving, editing, or on-demand playback (Figure 7.10).

High-Quality Archives
Ensure recordings are in high resolution to serve as quality content for later use.

MultiTrack Recording
Advanced options include recording different audio and video tracks separately for more flexibility in post-production editing.

This comprehensive overview of software tools for live-streaming equips music professionals with the necessary knowledge to choose the right tools and technologies for their specific streaming needs. Whether for simple personal broadcasts or more complex productions, understanding these options will help you effectively manage and enhance their live-streaming capabilities.

Hardware
From using your phone to larger turn-key systems, hardware plays an important role in streaming.

Streaming Systems

For those looking into serious live-streaming, custom-built PCs equipped with high-performance processors, along with powerful graphics cards, are recommended for their ability to handle intensive video-processing tasks. Alternatively, all-in-one live production systems like the YoloBox Pro or Roland V-1HD, which combine switching, graphics, and streaming capabilities, offer a portable and simplified solution. The workflow involves setting up the system with necessary software installations, connecting multiple input sources, and managing live production directly from the integrated interface.

Phones/Tablet

Utilizing high-end smartphones like the newest iPhone Pro or Samsung Galaxy can be an effective mobile streaming solution due to their advanced camera systems and robust processing capabilities. Streamers can install dedicated streaming apps such as Streamlabs Mobile or Larix Broadcaster to enhance control over their broadcasts. The setup process includes ensuring devices are fully charged, mounting them on tripods or stabilizers for stable video, and configuring stream settings within the app before going live.

Microphones

Audio quality is crucial, and options range from USB microphones like the Blue Yeti or Audio-Technica AT2020USB+ for easy setup, to more professional XLR microphones like the Shure SM7B, which provide superior sound quality but require an audio interface. Streamers should conduct sound checks to adjust levels for clarity and volume, monitor audio input during the stream for real-time adjustments, and may use software for additional audio processing to ensure professional-grade audio output.

Cameras

For visual setup, webcams such as those from Logitech offer a good balance between quality and ease of use, making them suitable for entry-level streamers. More advanced streamers might opt for DSLRs or mirrorless cameras like those from Canon or Sony, which provide higher video quality but need an HDMI capture card for connectivity. PTZ cameras like the Panasonic AW-UE4 are ideal for event spaces, offering remote control capabilities for dynamic filming. The

Figure 7.11 Camera Setup

workflow includes mounting the camera securely (Figure 7.11), connecting it to the streaming device, and adjusting settings like exposure and focus to optimize video quality. During live streams, camera angles and settings can be managed through streaming software, with live previews used to ensure the best output.

This section has presented a detailed overview of the essential hardware components for live-streaming, guiding students through the selection and setup of systems, mobile devices, microphones, and cameras to achieve a professional streaming setup. Each component is vital for ensuring the stream runs smoothly and appears professional, enhancing both the viewer's experience and the streamer's performance.

7 Live-Stream Workflow Examples

Concert Streaming: A 15-Step Process

1. Create the Plan: Define the goals of the concert stream, such as audience reach, engagement metrics, or revenue targets.

2. Team Assembly: Gather a team with varied expertise, including audio engineers, camera operators, a director, and a streaming technician.
3. Budget Planning: Establish a budget that covers all necessary equipment, personnel, and other logistical needs.
4. Venue Selection: Choose a venue that supports live-streaming with adequate space for equipment and good acoustics.
5. Equipment Procurement: Secure all necessary streaming gear, such as cameras, microphones, mixing boards, and lighting.
6. Streaming Platform Selection: Decide on the streaming platform (e.g., YouTube, Twitch) and understand its specific requirements and capabilities.
7. Internet Access Check: Ensure the venue has a robust and reliable internet connection capable of handling high-quality live video.
8. Stage Design: Plan the stage layout to optimize both live and streaming audience experiences.
9. Sound Check: Perform a detailed sound check to adjust levels and settings for optimal audio quality.
10. Camera Placement: Strategically place cameras to capture various angles, ensuring dynamic visual content.
11. Rehearsal: Conduct a full rehearsal to troubleshoot any issues with sound, lighting, or camera work.
12. Streaming Setup: Set up the streaming station, configure the encoder, and test the stream to the selected platform.
13. Audience Engagement Plan: Develop a plan for engaging with the online audience, including moderating comments and adding interactive elements like polls or Q & A.
14. Go Live: Start the stream, closely monitor all technical aspects, and communicate regularly with the team to address any issues.
15. Post-Event Analysis: After the concert, analyze performance against goals, gather feedback from viewers, and review any recorded footage to assess areas for improvement.

By following these steps, you can ensure a well-organized and professionally executed live concert stream, maximizing audience engagement and achieving the set objectives. This structured approach not only enhances the viewer's experience but also helps in building a reliable workflow for future streaming events.

1. Conceptualize the Podcast: Define the theme, target audience, and main objectives of your live podcast.
2. Select Co-Hosts and Guests: Choose engaging and knowledgeable co-hosts and guests who can contribute valuable insights and discussions to the podcast.
3. Script Planning: While maintaining a degree of spontaneity, plan the main segments and talking points to ensure a structured flow of conversation.
4. Technical Setup: Assemble the necessary equipment, including microphones, headphones, a sound mixer, and computers with streaming software.
5. Streaming Platform Choice: Decide which platform (e.g., YouTube Live, Twitch, Facebook Live) best suits the podcast's audience and format.
6. Visual Elements: Prepare any visual elements if the podcast will feature video components, such as background settings, lighting, and camera setup.
7. Internet Reliability Check: Confirm that the internet connection is stable and fast enough to support live-streaming without interruptions.
8. Audio Configuration: Set up and test all audio equipment to ensure clear sound quality. This includes checking microphone levels and the mix between hosts and guests.
9. Camera Angles: If video is involved, set up multiple camera angles to keep the visual dynamic and engaging.
10. Rehearsal: Conduct a dry run with all hosts and guests to iron out any technical glitches and finalize the show's structure.
11. Promotion: Announce the live podcast on social media and other channels ahead of time to build an audience.
12. Engagement Strategies: Plan how to interact with the live audience, such as taking live questions or using polls.
13. Broadcast: Go live, sticking as closely as possible to the planned script but also adapting as needed based on audience interaction.
14. Monitor Feedback: Keep an eye on audience responses and technical performance throughout the stream to make adjustments on the fly.

15. Post-Stream Debrief: After the podcast, review the stream's performance, gather feedback, and discuss what worked and what could be improved for future episodes.

By adhering to these steps, students can effectively manage a live podcast stream, from initial planning to post-event analysis. This comprehensive approach ensures that the podcast not only reaches its intended audience but also engages them effectively, making the live-streaming experience enjoyable and informative for all participants.

Live-Streaming Tutorial Content: A 15-Step Process

1. Identify the Topic: Select a clear and focused topic that is educational and valuable to your target audience.
2. Research Thoroughly: Gather all necessary information, data, and resources that will make the tutorial comprehensive and authoritative.
3. Outline the Session: Plan the structure of the tutorial, including an introduction, main content sections, and a conclusion with key takeaways.
4. Prepare Visual Aids: Create slides, diagrams, or other visual aids that will help illustrate key points and make the content more engaging and easier to understand.
5. Select Appropriate Tools: Choose software and tools that are best suited for demonstrating the tutorial content, such as coding environments, design software, or practical demonstrations.
6. Set Up Equipment: Ensure all necessary equipment, such as cameras, microphones, and lighting, is set up and tested to produce high-quality video and audio.
7. Choose a Streaming Platform: Decide on a platform (e.g., YouTube, Twitch, or LinkedIn Learning) that supports the type of tutorial content and reaches the intended audience.
8. Prepare Interactive Elements: Plan to include interactive elements such as Q & A sessions, live polls, or exercises that viewers can follow along with.
9. Test Internet Connection: Verify that the internet connection is stable and robust enough to handle a live stream without disruptions.

10. Rehearse the Presentation: Run through the tutorial at least once to practice the delivery and use of tools and visual aids.

11. Promote the Stream: Market the tutorial session on social media, forums, and other channels to attract viewers who would benefit from the content.

12. Engage with Viewers: During the stream, actively engage with the audience by encouraging questions and comments and responding in real time.

13. Record the Session: Make sure to record the live session so it can be accessed later for on-demand viewing.

14. Monitor and Adjust: Keep an eye on the stream's performance and viewer feedback throughout the session to make any necessary adjustments.

15. Follow-Up: After the stream, provide additional resources, answer follow-up questions, and gather feedback to improve future tutorial streams.

By following these steps, you can effectively plan, execute, and review educational live streams that are informative and engaging. This methodical approach ensures that the content delivered is not only relevant but is also presented in a manner that maximizes learning and interaction.

Live-Streaming Update Videos: A 15-Step Process

1. Define the Purpose: Clearly establish the purpose of the update video. Determine what specific information needs to be conveyed and what the audience should take away from it.

2. Gather Content: Collect all relevant data, updates, and news items that need to be included in the live stream.

3. Script Outline: Draft a concise script or outline to structure the flow of information. Make sure it includes an introduction, main points, and a conclusion.

4. Select Visual Aids: Prepare any visual aids that will support your updates, such as charts, graphs, or images that illustrate key points or data.

5. Design Presentation Slides: Create engaging slides if necessary, which can be shown during the stream to help convey information visually.

6. Set Up Equipment: Ensure that all the necessary broadcasting equipment, including camera, microphone, and lighting, is set up and functioning properly.

7. Choose a Streaming Platform: Select an appropriate platform (e.g., Facebook Live, YouTube, or a corporate intranet) that suits the target audience for the update.

8. Schedule the Stream: Announce the date and time of the live stream in advance to ensure maximum viewership. Consider time zones if addressing a geographically diverse audience.

9. Promote the Stream: Use social media, email newsletters, and other communication tools to promote the upcoming live stream.

10. Rehearse the Delivery: Practice the entire presentation to smooth out any rough edges in the delivery and to ensure all technology works seamlessly.

11. Engage Viewers: Plan to actively engage with the audience during the stream through Q & A sessions, live polls, or inviting comments.

12. Go Live: Start the live stream, sticking closely to the script but also adapting as needed based on live audience feedback and interaction.

13. Monitor Feedback: Keep an eye on viewer responses and technical issues during the stream. Be prepared to adjust the flow or troubleshoot as needed.

14. Record the Session: Make sure to record the live stream so it can be accessed later for those who missed the broadcast or want to revisit the information.

15. Post-Stream Follow-Up: After the live stream, provide additional materials or answers to questions that could not be addressed during the session. Gather feedback to improve future updates.

By following this detailed process, you can ensure your live update videos are well prepared and professionally delivered, effectively communicating important information while engaging their audience. This structured approach not only facilitates the smooth execution of the live stream but also enhances viewer retention and satisfaction.

Live-Streaming Educational Experience: A 15-Step Process

1. Identify Educational Goals: Define clear learning objectives and outcomes for your audience in order to ensure the content is purposeful and measurable.

2. Select the Subject Matter: Choose a topic that is relevant and appealing to your target audience, ensuring it aligns with their educational needs and interests.

3. Develop a Curriculum: Plan the structure of the content, including introductory material, key concepts, examples, and summaries to ensure comprehensive coverage of the topic.

4. Gather Resources: Compile necessary educational materials such as textbooks, articles, slides, and multimedia elements that will support the live presentation.

5. Plan Interactive Elements: Integrate interactive elements like quizzes, polls, and problem-solving exercises to engage the audience actively in the learning process.

6. Choose Appropriate Tools: Select tools and software that facilitate online learning effectively, such as virtual whiteboards, screen-sharing apps, and interactive platforms like Kahoot or Quizlet.

7. Set Up the Streaming Environment: Prepare your streaming environment to be conducive to learning, ensuring it is quiet, well lit, and free from distractions.

8. Test Technology Setup: Check all technical equipment including cameras, microphones, and internet connections to prevent disruptions during the live stream.

9. Promote the Session: Use social media, educational forums, and email campaigns to advertise the live session to attract the maximum number of learners.

10. Conduct a Dry Run: Perform a rehearsal to practice the delivery of the material and use of interactive tools to ensure smooth execution during the actual session.

11. Engage the Audience Early: Start the stream with an icebreaker or an interesting question to capture the audience's interest and encourage participation right from the beginning.

12. Deliver Content Methodically: Present the educational material in a logical, engaging manner, pausing frequently to ask questions and encourage feedback.

13. Facilitate Live Interactions: Actively moderate the session, responding to viewer questions and comments to maintain an interactive learning environment.

14. Wrap Up with Key Takeaways: Conclude the session with a summary of key points and takeaways, reinforcing the learning objectives and providing closure.

15. Follow-Up: After the session, provide additional resources, answer any outstanding questions, and solicit feedback for future improvements. Consider making the recorded session available for on-demand viewing.

This 15-step process ensures that educational live streams are not only informative but also engaging and interactive, enhancing the learning experience for viewers. By methodically planning and executing these steps, streamers can deliver educational content that is both impactful and memorable.

Live-Streaming Tour Guide: A 15-Step Process

1. Select the Location: Choose a location that is applicable to your musical goals.
2. Research Thoroughly: Gather detailed information about the site, including its history, significance, and interesting anecdotes to share with your audience.
3. Plan Your Route: Map out a logical and efficient route that covers all significant aspects of the location, ensuring a smooth flow from one point of interest to another.
4. Obtain Necessary Permissions: If required, get permission to stream live from the location, especially if it's a protected or privately owned site.
5. Check Connectivity: Verify that you have a reliable internet connection throughout the route to maintain a stable live stream.
6. Prepare Your Script: While spontaneity is valuable, having a prepared script or bullet points on key facts and stories will help keep the tour structured and informative.
7. Gather Visual Aids: Collect maps, old photographs, or other visual aids to show during the tour, enhancing the storytelling with visual context.
8. Select Appropriate Equipment: Choose portable, high-quality streaming equipment that can handle outdoor conditions if necessary, including stabilizers for smooth walking shots.
9. Promote the Tour: Advertise your live tour on social media, websites, and local forums to attract viewers who are interested in the location or subject matter.
10. Rehearse the Tour: Do a dry run to practice your commentary and check the feasibility of the walking route and timing.

11. Engage with Your Audience: Encourage viewer interaction by asking questions, inviting comments, and responding to viewer feedback in real time during the tour.

12. Highlight Unique Features: Focus on unique details and lesser-known facts that viewers wouldn't easily find elsewhere, adding value to your tour.

13. Manage Time Effectively: Keep track of time to ensure you cover all points of interest within the allotted time without rushing.

14. Conclude with a Q & A Session: End the tour with a Q & A session, giving viewers the chance to ask questions about the site, which can further engage and inform the audience.

15. Follow-Up After the Tour: Post the recorded video for those who missed the live stream, and provide additional resources or answers to questions that arose during the tour. Solicit feedback for future improvements.

Following this comprehensive 15-step process will ensure that you can effectively plan, execute, and review a live-streamed tour, providing a rich, engaging, and educational experience for viewers. By thoroughly preparing and focusing on interaction, the virtual tour becomes an interactive and enjoyable learning opportunity for all participants.

SUMMARY

Live-streaming is a dynamic method of digital communication that allows real-time interaction between broadcasters and viewers. It has transformed various sectors, including entertainment, education, and marketing, by allowing content creators and businesses to reach a global audience instantaneously. The philosophy behind live-streaming emphasizes authenticity, audience engagement, and the democratization of content creation.

The core philosophy of live-streaming integrates the principles of real-time engagement and audience participation. It supports a variety of content, from educational webinars to live concerts, making it a versatile tool across disciplines. Platforms like Twitch, YouTube Live, and Facebook Live offer unique features that cater to different streaming requirements: real-time interaction tools, monetization options, and various content management functionalities.

Live-streaming is a powerful tool that offers vast potential for those who understand and navigate its complexities effectively. By mastering the technical aspects and engaging creatively with the audience, streamers can enhance their digital presence and achieve various personal and professional goals. As technology evolves, so too will the strategies and tools available for live-streaming, promising even greater opportunities and challenges for content creators worldwide.

Eight

This chapter contains your blueprint to embarking on the thrilling journey of building your own online presence, whether it's to share your music, showcase your talents, or simply be your authentic self online. Imagine stepping into a vast, bustling city for the first time. That's what venturing into the digital world feels like. Building on all of the skills covered so far in this book, we finally take the plunge into the subject of how to take your first steps towards success.

STARTING FROM SCRATCH

In this section we will follow the process in three different timelines: day one, month one, and year one. Pay attention to the practical steps you can take during each period and make note that this only works if you proactively take action.

Day One: Laying the Foundation

The most important step is the very first one. Make it count.

1 Pick Your Name

This is like choosing your superhero alias. Your name should reso-nate with what you do and be memorable enough to stick in people's minds. Think of it as your first handshake with the world.

Choosing your social media name (see Figure 8.1) is a crucial step in carving out your digital identity. It's the first piece of yourself you share with the world, and it sets the tone for everything that follows. Your name is not just a label; it's a reflection of your person-ality, your brand, and your mission online. Think of it as selecting a title for your autobiography: it needs to be catchy, meaningful, and memorable.

When brainstorming for the perfect name, consider incorporating elements that reflect the essence of your content or personality. If you're

DOI: 10.4324/9781003416180-8

Figure 8.1 My YouTube Name

into gaming, for instance, a name like "PixelPioneer" could resonate well. For a food blogger, something appetizing like "SavorTheFlavor" might make mouths water. Since this is a book about music, it makes sense to keep it music related. The key is to blend relevance with creativity. Use puns, alliterations, or clever wordplay to make your name stand out. However, ensure it's easy to spell and pronounce; your name should roll off the tongue and be easily searchable.

Another technique is to check the availability of your chosen name across all platforms you plan to use. Consistency in your social media handle makes it easier for your audience to find you everywhere. Tools like Namechk or KnowEm can help you verify the availability of your name across numerous sites. If your preferred name is taken, don't fret. Try variations by adding underscores, numbers, or abbreviations that make sense. For example, if "MusicQueen" is taken, "Music_Queen" or "MusicQueen101" might still keep your brand's essence alive. Remember, picking the right name is like laying the foundation of a house—it supports everything you build on top of it, so take your time and choose wisely.

2 Decide on the Platform(s)

Where do you think your voice or talent will shine the most? Is it the visual storytelling of Instagram, the conversational nature of Twitter, or perhaps the creative showcase of YouTube? Choose wisely; where you speak influences who listens.

Deciding on the right platforms to share your content is like picking the perfect stage for a play. Each platform has its own audience, culture, and expectations, making some more suited to your style and goals than others. Imagine trying to perform a Shakespearean drama at a comedy club; it might not resonate as well as it would in a traditional theater. Similarly, the platform you choose must align with the type of content you create and the audience you wish to engage.

Begin by researching the demographics and primary user base of each platform. For example, Instagram and TikTok thrive on visual content and cater to a younger, more dynamic audience that loves quick, engaging, and visually appealing posts. If you're a concert photographer, a travel vlogger, or someone who loves creating short, impactful musical videos, these platforms can be your digital canvas. On the other hand, LinkedIn is the go-to for professional content, ideal for sharing industry insights, career tips, or professional development content. For long-form content creators, such as writers or analysts, a blog or Medium could be the perfect platform, offering the space to delve deep into topics and share detailed insights.

After identifying which platforms best suit your content, consider how much time and effort you can realistically commit to each. Managing multiple social media accounts can be time-consuming and may dilute the quality of your content if spread too thin. It's often more effective to focus on one or two platforms where your content has the strongest impact.

Engage with the community on these platforms, learn from others, and refine your approach based on feedback and performance. Remember, the goal is not just to broadcast but to build relationships and create a community around your content. Choose your platforms wisely, as they will become the ecosystems where your digital identity flourishes and evolves.

3 Identify an Initial Brand Profile

What colors, fonts, and vibes scream "you"? This step is like choosing your outfit for your first concert. You want to make an impression that's truly you.

Identifying an initial brand profile (see Figure 8.2) is like sketching your character before bringing it to life in a story. It's a comprehensive blueprint that includes your aesthetics, tone, values, and the unique traits that set you apart. This profile isn't just about choosing your favorite colors or fonts; it's about crafting a coherent identity that resonates with your target audience and reflects the essence of your content.

Banner image

This image will appear across the top of your channel

For the best results on all devices, use an image that's at least 2048 x 1152 pixels and 6MB or less. (?)

CHANGE   REMOVE

Figure 8.2 The Brand My Channel Started With

Start with defining your brand's personality. Ask yourself, if your brand were a person, what kind of characteristics would it have? Would it be fun and quirky, professional and informative, or inspiring and motivational? This personality will guide the tone of your content, the style of your visuals, and the way you interact with your audience. For example, a travel blogger aiming to inspire adventure might choose vibrant colors, dynamic images, and an enthusiastic tone, while a tech reviewer might opt for a sleek, minimalist design with a straightforward, informative tone.

Next, consider your visual identity. This includes your logo, color scheme, typography, and any recurring motifs or imagery that will appear across your content. These elements should be consistent across all platforms to make your brand instantly recognizable. Your visual identity is like your wardrobe; it should match your personality, fit the occasion (platform), and appeal to those you're trying to impress (your audience). Additionally, think about your values and what you stand for. This could range from sustainability in travel, transparency in tech reviews, or authenticity in lifestyle blogging. Your values should resonate through your content, influencing topics, collaborations, and how you engage with followers.

Lastly, understand that your brand profile will evolve. As you grow and receive feedback, you'll refine your identity. However, having a clear initial brand profile sets a strong direction, making it easier for people to connect with you, follow your journey, and become loyal fans. It's about laying down the roots from which your online presence will flourish, ensuring that every piece of content you create contributes to a larger, cohesive narrative.

What tools do you already have in your arsenal? A smartphone, a laptop (Figure 8.3), or maybe a microphone? Knowing what you have can help you start strong without breaking the bank.

Listing your existing equipment assets before diving into content creation is akin to taking stock of your tools before embarking on a crafting project. It's about knowing what you have at your disposal and understanding how to make the most of these resources. This step not only sets the stage for the quality of your content but also helps you budget for future investments in your brand.

Firstly, evaluate the essentials. For most digital creators, a computer or a smartphone with a good camera is the cornerstone of content creation. Assess the quality of your devices. Can your smartphone capture high-resolution videos for YouTube or clear, vibrant photos for Instagram? Does your computer have the necessary processing power to edit videos or run content management software efficiently? It's crucial to understand the capabilities and limitations of your devices, as they directly impact the quality and variety of content you can produce.

Next, consider auxiliary equipment that enhances content quality. This includes microphones for clear audio in podcasts or videos, tripods or stabilizers for steady shots, and lighting equipment for well-lit

Figure 8.3 | Started With a Laptop

visuals. Even basic accessories, like a pop filter for microphones or a ring light can significantly elevate your production value. Remember, you don't need to have a studio full of equipment to start. Many successful content creators began with just a smartphone and a passion for their craft.

Finally, inventory any software or apps that could assist in content creation and management. This could be editing software like Adobe Premiere Pro or Final Cut Pro for video editing, Canva for graphic design, or Hootsuite for managing social media posts. Free or trial versions of these tools can be incredibly useful when you're just starting out. Knowing what software is at your disposal allows you to plan your content production process more effectively, from initial creation to final edits and publication.

Understanding your equipment assets is not just about making a list; it's about strategizing how to use these tools creatively and efficiently. It encourages you to think critically about your content production process and plan for upgrades or investments that align with your growth and aspirations. Remember, the goal is to maximize the potential of what you have, gradually building your toolkit as your audience and resources grow.

5 Create a Plan

Dream big, but start small. What's your main gig? Is it your captivating personality, your soothing voice, or your production skills? Pin down why people would tune into your content.

Creating a plan (Figure 8.4) for your content creation journey is like drawing a map before embarking on a treasure hunt. It provides direction, sets goals, and prepares you for the adventure ahead. This plan isn't just a schedule of posts; it's a comprehensive strategy that includes understanding your primary product, defining your audience, and determining how to engage that audience in a meaningful way.

A Identifying Your Primary Product

Firstly, pinpoint what you're offering to your audience. Is it the unique insights you share through your blog posts, the captivating stories you tell through your videos, or perhaps the infectious energy you bring

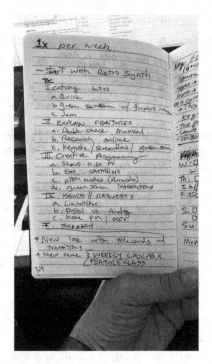

Figure 8.4 The Plan I Wrote in a Journal

to live streams? Your primary product could also be a physical product or service you're promoting through your content. Understanding what you're offering is crucial because it shapes your content strategy, from the types of content you produce to the platforms you prioritize. For example, if your primary product is visual, platforms like Instagram and Pinterest might be your main focus, showcasing your creations through high-quality images and engaging stories about your creative process.

B Why Would People Consume Your Content?

This question gets to the heart of your value proposition. Are people tuning in for your expertise on a subject, the entertainment value of your personality, or the practical skills you teach? Knowing why people would consume your content helps you to refine your messaging and ensure that every piece of content you create delivers on that promise. It's about understanding the intersection between your passions and what your audience craves. For instance, if you're a talented musician, people might follow you both for the enjoyment of your music and for the insights into your creative process.

C Crafting a Strategy

Once you have a clear understanding of your primary product and its appeal, the next step is to craft a strategy that encompasses content themes, production schedules, and engagement tactics. This involves setting short-term and long-term goals, such as reaching a certain number of followers or launching a new series. It also includes planning the types of content you will create, whether these are tutorials, reviews, or behind-the-scenes looks, and determining how often you can realistically produce and share this content without compromising on quality.

A well-thought-out plan also accounts for interaction with your audience. Engagement strategies could include responding to comments, running contests, or collaborating with other creators. Moreover, it's essential to be flexible and willing to adjust your plan based on feedback and performance metrics. Keeping an eye on analytics will tell you what's working and what isn't, allowing you to pivot as needed to keep your content fresh and your audience engaged.

Summary

Creating a plan is about laying down a roadmap for your content creation journey. It provides clarity and focus, helping you to navigate the challenges of building an online presence. Remember, the key to a successful plan is not just in its creation but in its execution and the willingness to adapt as you grow and learn more about your audience and yourself as a creator.

Month One: Finding Your Groove

1 Posting Schedule

Consistency is key. Sketch out a schedule that's realistic, yet keeps you in your audience's thoughts.

As you step into the first month of your content creation journey, establishing a posting schedule (Figure 8.5) is like setting a rhythm for your newfound digital life. This rhythm not only keeps you on

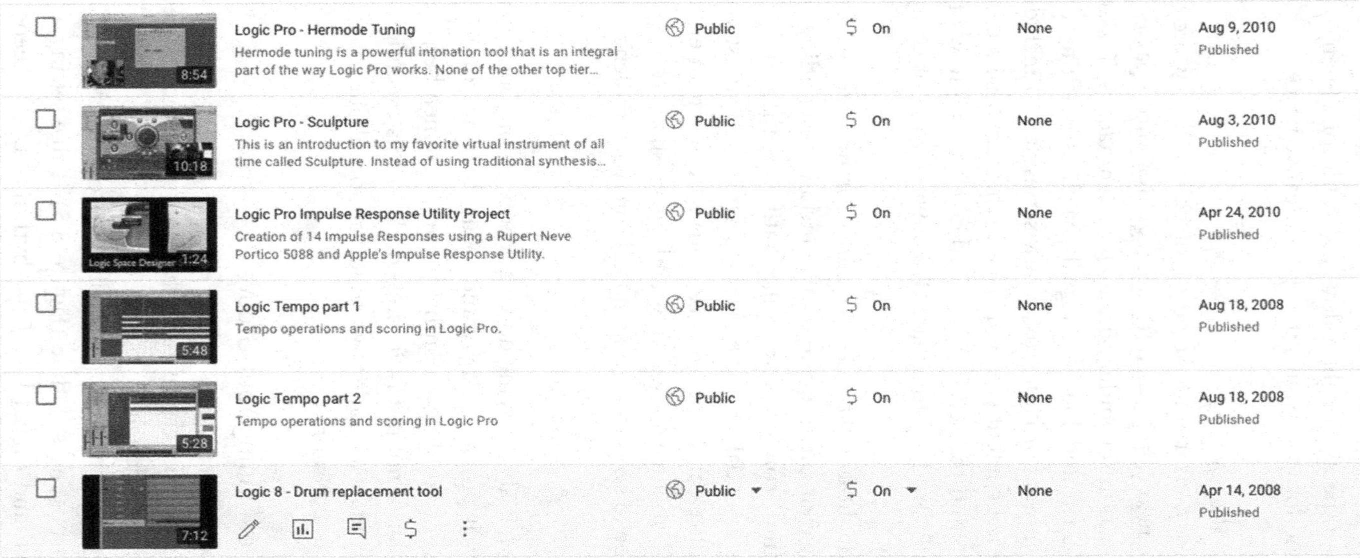

8:54
Logic Pro - Hermode Tuning
Hermode tuning is a powerful intonation tool that is an integral part of the way Logic Pro works. None of the other top tier...
Public
On
None
Aug 9, 2010
Published
10:18
Logic Pro - Sculpture
This is an introduction to my favorite virtual instrument of all time called Sculpture. Instead of using traditional synthesis...
Public
On
None
Aug 3, 2010
Published
Logic Space Designer 1:24
Logic Pro Impulse Response Utility Project
Creation of 14 Impulse Responses using a Rupert Neve Portico 5088 and Apple's Impulse Response Utility.
Public
On
None
Apr 24, 2010
Published
5:48
Logic Tempo part 1
Tempo operations and scoring in Logic Pro.
Public
On
None
Aug 18, 2008
Published
5:28
Logic Tempo part 2
Tempo operations and scoring in Logic Pro
Public
On
None
Aug 18, 2008
Published
7:12
Logic 8 - Drum replacement tool
Public
On
None
Apr 14, 2008
Published

Figure 8.5 My Initial Posting Schedule

track but also lets your audience know when to tune in for your latest masterpiece. A well-planned schedule can be the heartbeat of your online presence, driving consistency, building anticipation, and fostering a loyal community.

Why Consistency Matters

Consistency is your secret weapon in the crowded world of online content. It helps in building a habit among your audience, making your posts a part of their daily or weekly routines. Imagine your favorite TV show airing at a different time each week; it would be frustrating and easy to miss episodes. Similarly, if your followers know they can expect new content from you at specific times, they're more likely to keep coming back for more. Consistency also signals to social media algorithms that you're a regular contributor, which can improve your content's visibility.

Crafting Your Schedule

When devising your posting schedule, consider the nature of your content and the lifestyle of your target audience. Are your followers most active in the evenings or on weekends? Use insights and analytics tools provided by social media platforms to determine when your audience is online. Start with a manageable frequency that aligns with your ability to produce quality content without burning out. For instance, a daily vlog might be too ambitious at the start, but one well-crafted video per week or bi-weekly blog posts could be perfect for keeping your audience engaged without overextending yourself.

Flexibility and Adaptation

While consistency is key, flexibility is equally important. Life happens, and there may be times when sticking to your schedule isn't feasible. It's okay to adjust as needed, but communicate any changes with your audience to keep them in the loop. Pay attention to which posts get the most engagement and consider adjusting your schedule to capitalize on these trends. Perhaps your Wednesday wisdom posts are a hit, or your weekend DIY projects garner the most comments. Use this feedback to refine your posting schedule, always aiming to serve your audience's preferences while staying true to your creative vision.

A thoughtful posting schedule is a cornerstone of successful content creation. It balances your creative process with audience expectations, setting the stage for a vibrant and engaged online community. Remember, the goal is to create a consistent presence that your followers can rely on, making your content a regular and anticipated part of their digital experience.

2 Leverage Your Existing Networks

Don't be too shy to tell your friends and family about your new adventure. Their support can be the wind beneath your wings (Figure 8.6).

Leveraging your existing networks during the first month of your content creation journey is akin to planting seeds in a garden you've already cultivated. Your personal and professional connections are fertile ground for growing your audience, offering a supportive base from which to expand. By reaching out to friends, family, and acquaintances, you're not just seeking immediate viewership; you're

Figure 8.6 A Message From My Mom

building a foundation of genuine supporters who can help spread the word about your new venture. If you find yourself hesitant to talk about this new adventure with family and friends, then a reevaluation of your entire plan is a good idea.

The Power of Personal Networks

Your personal network is your first line of support. These are the people who already know and trust you, making them more likely to engage with your content and share it within their circles. Don't underestimate the impact of a friend sharing your post or a family member praising your work on their social media. It's organic, heartfelt promotion that can reach potential followers in a way that feels personal and authentic. Begin by sharing your content with them directly through messaging apps, emails, or even in-person conversations. Let them know why you're passionate about this project and how they can help support you.

Professional and Academic Networks

Beyond your personal circles, your professional and academic networks can also be invaluable. Colleagues, classmates, and industry contacts may offer a different kind of engagement, one that's perhaps more critical or insightful, offering feedback that can help refine your content. Additionally, these networks often have a wider reach into communities that share your professional or academic interests, opening doors to audiences you may not have accessed otherwise. Sharing your content in relevant groups, forums, or mailing lists (where appropriate) can help attract viewers with specific interests aligned with your content.

Engaging Authentically

As you leverage your networks, remember the importance of authentic engagement. This isn't just about broadcasting your content; it's about inviting conversation and building relationships. Respond to comments, thank people for sharing your posts, and show genuine interest in their feedback. This two-way interaction not only strengthens your existing relationships but also fosters a sense of community around your content. Additionally, consider collaborating with peers who are also creating content. These collaborations can introduce you to their followers and vice versa, creating a symbiotic growth for both parties involved.

Tapping into your existing networks in the early stages of your content creation journey offers a dual benefit: it provides immediate engagement that can boost your confidence and visibility, and it lays the groundwork for organic growth through word of mouth. Approach this process with gratitude and authenticity, acknowledging the support of your personal and professional circles. By nurturing these initial connections, you're planting the seeds for a thriving online community that will grow alongside your content.

3 Tracking Analytics

Keep an eye on what works and what doesn't. It's like checking the weather before heading out. Adjust your plans accordingly.

In the first month of your content creation journey, tracking analytics emerges as a vital tool for understanding and refining your strategy. Think of analytics as your GPS, guiding you through the vast landscape of social media by providing real-time feedback on your journey's progress. It offers a clear view of what resonates with your audience, which paths are worth pursuing further, and where adjustments are needed.

Understanding Analytics

Analytics can initially seem overwhelming with its array of metrics, but focusing on key indicators can simplify this complexity. Engagement rates (likes, comments, shares), reach, views, and follower growth are primary metrics that offer insight into how your content is performing. For instance, high engagement rates typically indicate that your content is resonating well with your audience, prompting interaction. Conversely, if your reach is high but engagement is low, it might be time to reassess the relevance or appeal of your content.

Most social media platforms provide built-in analytics tools. Familiarize yourself with these tools, exploring the kinds of data they offer and how you can access them. Regularly check these metrics to gauge the performance of individual posts and overall content strategy over time.

Applying Insights from Analytics

The true power of analytics lies in how you apply the insights gathered. For example, if you notice that posts featuring behind-the-scenes content generate more engagement, consider producing more of this content type. Or, if analytics reveal that your audience is most active at specific times, adjust your posting schedule accordingly to maximize visibility.

It's also worthwhile to track which types of content are not performing as expected. This doesn't mean you should immediately abandon these formats or themes, but rather that you should experiment with different presentation styles, captions, or posting times to see if changes yield better results.

Adapting and Experimenting

Analytics should inform an ongoing cycle of adaptation and experimentation in your content strategy. It's about finding the sweet spot between what you love to create and what your audience loves to consume. Be open to testing new ideas, formats, or themes based on analytics insights, and use this information to fine-tune your approach.

Remember, the goal of tracking analytics is not just to chase numbers but to deepen your understanding of your audience and how they interact with your content. This knowledge empowers you to make informed decisions, tailor your content more effectively, and, ultimately, grow your online presence in a way that feels authentic and engaging.

As you navigate through the initial month and beyond, let analytics be your guide, but don't lose sight of your creative instincts and the passion that drove you to start this journey. Balancing data-driven decisions with genuine creativity is the key to building a meaningful and sustainable connection with your audience.

4 Improvement/Adjustment Cycle

Refine your content based on feedback and analytics. Think of it as a solo in a jazz performance, adapting and changing based on what the other musicians in the group are doing.

Entering the fourth week of your content creation journey, the concept of an improvement/adjustment cycle becomes increasingly important. This period is a time for reflection, learning, and recalibration, in which you focus on refining your content based on the feedback and analytics you've gathered thus far. Implementing a cycle of continuous improvement ensures that your content remains dynamic, engaging, and aligned with your audience's interests and needs.

Embracing Feedback

Feedback from your audience, whether it comes in the form of comments, direct messages, or engagement metrics, is a gold mine of insights. It provides direct input on what your audience appreciates and what could be improved. Positive feedback highlights your strengths, encouraging you to double down on what works. Constructive criticism, though sometimes hard to hear, is invaluable for pinpointing areas for enhancement. Embrace both with an open mind and consider them as opportunities for growth rather than as critiques of your worth or effort.

The Cycle of Improvement

Integrate a routine of reviewing your content's performance, incorporating feedback, and making adjustments. This could mean tweaking your content's tone, experimenting with different content formats, or adjusting your posting schedule. For example, if analytics show that tutorial videos have higher engagement than other types of content, you might decide to produce more tutorial videos while experimenting with their length or style to see what resonates best.

Moreover, it's crucial to recognize that not all content will perform equally, and that's okay. Failure is part of the process. What's important is learning from what didn't work and using that knowledge to inform future content creation. This iterative process (create, measure, learn, adjust) keeps your content fresh and your audience engaged.

Investing Time Wisely

One of the most significant insights during this adjustment phase is understanding how your time investment correlates with content performance. You might discover that certain types of content require a disproportionate amount of time compared to the engagement they receive. This realization allows you to reallocate your efforts more efficiently, focusing on content that not only performs well but also is sustainable for you to produce.

Remember, the goal of the improvement/adjustment cycle is not to chase perfection but to foster a mindset of continuous learning and adaptation. Content creation is an evolving journey, with each piece of content serving as a stepping stone toward understanding your audience better and refining your craft.

As you conclude the first month and look ahead, keep this cycle of reflection and adaptation at the core of your content strategy. It will ensure that your content stays relevant, engaging, and true to your unique voice and vision. The path of content creation is one of discovery and growth, both for you as a creator and for the community you're building around your content.

5 Put in the Right Amount of Time

Starting a channel is like nurturing a plant: give your project the time it needs to grow, but remember, just as a plant can have too much sunlight, your channel can also have too much of a good thing, so don't overthink it.

As you navigate through the first month of your content creation journey, understanding the significance of dedicating the right amount of time to your project is crucial. This is not merely about allocating hours in a day; it's about striking a balance between consistency in content creation and the other responsibilities and passions in your life. Recognizing and respecting this balance is key to sustainable growth and personal well-being.

Quality Over Quantity

One common pitfall for new creators is the belief that more content equals more growth. While consistency is important, the quality of your content holds more weight. It's better to publish fewer pieces of high-quality content that truly resonate with your audience than to churn out daily posts that lack substance or value. Consider the time you can realistically dedicate to content creation without compromising on quality or your personal life. This might mean starting with one well-thought-out post per week and gradually increasing as you find your rhythm and streamline your production process.

Time Management and Productivity

Effective time management plays a pivotal role in content creation. Utilize tools and techniques to maximize productivity within the time you've allocated for content creation. This could include setting specific work hours, using content calendars to plan ahead, or employing batching (producing multiple pieces of content in one sitting) to streamline your workflow. Remember, the goal is to make the most of the time you have available, ensuring each session of content creation is focused and productive.

Listening to Feedback and Watching for Burnout

Paying attention to how your audience responds to the frequency and quality of your content (Figure 8.7) can offer valuable insights into how much time you should be investing. If you notice increased engagement and positive feedback on your posts, you're likely striking the right balance. Conversely, if you find yourself feeling overwhelmed or notice a drop in content quality or audience engagement, it may be a sign that you're overextending yourself.

Burnout is a real challenge in the content creation world. It's essential to recognize the signs early and take steps to address them. This

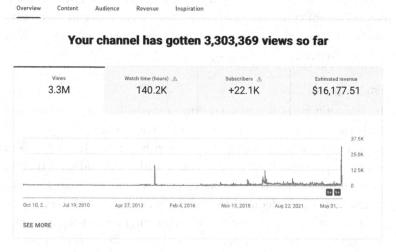

Figure 8.7 My YouTube Analytics

might involve taking a step back to reassess your content strategy, allowing for more flexibility in your schedule, or even taking a short break to recharge. Your well-being is paramount; your ability to create and engage with your audience depends on it.

Adapting Your Time Investment

As you progress, you'll likely become more efficient at content creation, and your audience's preferences will become clearer. This evolving understanding allows you to adapt the amount of time you invest in content creation, optimizing it to support both growth and personal fulfillment. The right amount of time to put into your project is not a static figure—it will change as you grow as a creator and as your circumstances evolve.

In conclusion, finding the right balance in the time you dedicate to content creation is a dynamic and personal journey. It requires a conscious effort to manage your time effectively, produce quality content, listen to your audience, and most importantly, take care of yourself. As you move forward, remember that the sustainability of your content creation journey is just as important as its initial growth.

Year One: Reflecting on Your Journey

As the first year progresses, you'll begin to realize that this is a full-time job and isn't always glamorous. It is sometimes difficult but hopefully it is also rewarding. If things aren't growing and progressing, then take some time to figure out why. Return to day one or month one if needed.

1 How Much Have Things Grown?

Look back and marvel at how far you've come. Every follower gained is a victory.

Reflecting on the first year of your content creation journey offers a pivotal moment to celebrate your growth, assess your achievements, and recalibrate your goals. This milestone is not just about quantifying your progress with metrics but also about understanding the qualitative changes in your relationship with your audience and your content.

Figure 8.8 The Number of Videos I've Posted

Celebrating Growth

The first step in your annual reflection should be recognizing how much you've achieved. Growth can be measured in various ways—increased numbers of followers, enhanced engagement rates, or even the number of posts you've managed to publish consistently (Figure 8.8). Each of these metrics tells a story of perseverance, learning, and connection. Remember, even modest growth is a testament to the effort you've invested and the resilience you've shown. It's important to celebrate these achievements, no matter the scale, acknowledging that every milestone is a step forward in your journey.

Assessing Achievements

Beyond the numbers, consider the broader achievements you've unlocked over the year. Perhaps you've refined your content strategy, honed your unique voice, or established meaningful collaborations with fellow creators. Reflect on the feedback you've received, the skills you've developed, and the confidence you've built in sharing your ideas and creations with the world. These accomplishments are as significant as any metric, reflecting the depth and impact of your journey.

Recalibrating Goals

After celebrating your successes and assessing your progress, it's crucial to look ahead. Consider what goals you set at the beginning of your journey and how they align with where you find yourself now. Some goals might have been met or exceeded, while others may no longer reflect your current interests or the evolving landscape of your niche. This reflection offers an opportunity to recalibrate your objectives for the coming year.

Think about what you want to achieve next, whether it's expanding your audience, diving deeper into a specific content area, or enhancing your production quality. Set new milestones that are challenging yet attainable, keeping in mind the lessons learned from the past year. It's also a time to consider any strategic shifts that may be necessary,

The Music Producer's Guide to Social Media Content

whether that's exploring new platforms, experimenting with different content formats, or investing in better equipment to enhance your content quality.

The first year of your content creation journey is a significant period of growth, learning, and connection. Taking the time to reflect on this year not only celebrates your hard work and achievements but also sets the stage for future success. As you move forward, carry with you the insights and experiences gained, allowing them to inform and inspire your next steps in the ever-evolving journey of content creation.

2 What Has Worked and What Hasn't?

Analyze your strategies. It's okay to drop what doesn't work. Keep experimenting.

After a year of content creation, taking stock of what has worked and what hasn't is essential for shaping your future strategy. This reflective process is not just about recognizing successes and failures; it's an opportunity to dive deep into the reasons behind them, fostering a mindset of continuous improvement and strategic adaptation.

Analyzing Successes

Begin by identifying the content that resonated most with your audience. Look at the posts that generated the highest engagement, the videos that were viewed the most, or the blog entries that sparked the most discussion. What common elements do these successes share? Is it the topic, the format, the storytelling style, or perhaps the way you engaged with your audience in the comments? Understanding the drivers behind your most successful content can help you double down on what your audience loves, ensuring that your future content aligns with these preferences.

Learning from Challenges

Equally important is examining the content that didn't perform as expected. Analyzing these instances provides invaluable insights into your audience's preferences and content consumption habits. Ask yourself tough questions: Was the topic not as relevant to your audience as you had thought? Was the content quality not up to par? Or was it a matter of timing or poor promotion? Identifying the root causes of these less successful endeavors is crucial for avoiding similar pitfalls in the future.

Remember, every piece of content is a learning opportunity. Embrace these lessons with an open mind and a commitment to growth.

Engagement and Feedback

Engagement metrics and direct feedback from your audience are gold mines of information. Pay close attention to the comments, messages, and feedback you've received over the year. What are your followers praising, and what are they critiquing? This direct line of communication can offer more nuanced insights into your audience's needs and preferences than quantitative metrics alone.

Strategic Adjustment

Armed with the knowledge of what's worked and what hasn't, the next step is to adjust your content strategy accordingly. This might mean refining your content themes, experimenting with new formats, or adjusting your posting schedule to better match your audience's active times. It could also signal a need for investment in areas like equipment, marketing, or education to enhance your content's quality and reach.

Reflecting on your content's performance over the past year is a powerful exercise that can significantly influence your future direction. It encourages a strategic approach to content creation, where decisions are driven by data, feedback, and a deep understanding of your audience. As you prepare for the next year, keep these insights at the forefront of your planning process, allowing them to guide your content strategy, goals, and aspirations. This process of continuous reflection and adaptation is what will keep your content fresh, relevant, and engaging, ensuring sustained growth and success in your content creation journey.

3 Are People Engaging?

Interaction is the soul of your online presence. Cherish the comments, the likes, and even the constructive criticism.

As you mark the end of your first year in content creation, evaluating audience engagement is key to understanding the depth of your impact and connection. This assessment goes beyond surface-level metrics to delve into the quality of interactions and the community you've built around your content. It's a moment to reflect on the conversations, relationships, and overall engagement that have defined your journey thus far.

Measuring Engagement
Start by examining the nature and frequency of interactions with your audience. Are people commenting, sharing, and participating in discussions on your platforms? Engagement can manifest itself in many ways, from lively debates in the comment sections to shares and reposts that extend your content's reach. High engagement levels often indicate that your content is resonating with your audience, sparking interest, and encouraging participation.

Understanding the Quality of Interactions
Beyond the numbers, the quality of these interactions is equally important. Positive, meaningful exchanges between you and your followers or among the followers themselves suggest a strong community bond. Look for signs of a supportive and engaged community, such as followers responding to each other's comments, sharing personal stories related to your content, or expressing anticipation for your next post. These indicators reveal an invested audience that values your content beyond mere consumption.

Addressing Feedback and Criticism
Reflect on how you've engaged with both positive feedback and criticism over the year. Constructive criticism is a valuable tool for improvement, which offers insights into your audience's expectations and areas where your content could be enhanced. Consider how you've incorporated this feedback into your content strategy. Engaging with your audience's input demonstrates respect for their opinions and a commitment to evolving your content in alignment with their preferences.

Fostering Engagement Moving Forward
Based on your reflections, identify strategies to further cultivate audience engagement in the coming year. This might involve more direct

interactions through Q & A sessions, polls to gauge their interests, or even community challenges that encourage participation. Consider also how you can leverage analytics to identify content that drives the most engagement, enabling you to produce more of what your audience loves.

Reflecting on audience engagement after a year of content creation offers insights into the strengths of your community and areas for growth. This evaluation is not just about applauding your successes but about understanding the dynamics of your audience relationship. It's an opportunity to deepen your connection with your followers and ensuring that your content continues to engage, inspire, and resonate. As you move into the next year, keep fostering this engagement, as it's the cornerstone of a thriving and vibrant online community.

4 What Has Changed and/or Remained the Same?

Reflect on your growth and the journey. It's important to stay true to your roots while embracing the winds of change.

Starting from scratch is daunting, but it's also a canvas full of possibilities. Every great journey begins with a single step, and yours starts here. Keep learning, stay adaptable, and most importantly, enjoy the ride. Your audience is out there waiting to discover you; all you need to do is take that first leap.

Concluding the first year of your content creation journey, evaluating what has changed and/or remained the same since you began provides a comprehensive view of your evolution as a creator and the shifts within your audience. This reflective exercise helps in recognizing the adaptability of your strategies, the persistence of your core values, and the ongoing relevance of your content amidst the dynamic digital landscape.

Identifying Changes

Reflect on the transformations that have taken place over the year. These could range from shifts in your content focus or style or adaptations in your engagement methods to changes in the platforms you prioritize. Perhaps you've noticed a shift in your audience demographic or their preferences, prompting a pivot in your content strategy. Technology and platform algorithms evolve, influencing content visibility and engagement; staying agile and responsive to these changes is crucial for sustained growth.

Evaluating the tools, techniques, and technologies you've adopted over the year also falls under this analysis. The introduction of new equipment, software, or platforms can significantly affect the production quality and distribution of your content, reflecting a commitment to improvement and innovation.

Acknowledging Consistencies

Equally important is acknowledging what has remained consistent. These are the core elements of your brand and content that have stood the test of time, serving as the backbone of your online presence. These could include your unique voice, your commitment to certain values, or the specific niche you cater to. These constants not only define your brand identity but also foster a sense of trust and familiarity among your audience.

Consistency in your mission and the quality of your content reassures your audience of your authenticity and dedication. It's these elements that likely contributed to building a loyal following in the first place. Recognizing and honoring these aspects of your content creation journey underscores the importance of staying true to your vision while navigating the evolving digital environment.

Planning for the Future

Armed with insights from your reflections on changes and consistencies, you can strategically plan for the future. Consider how you can leverage the changes you've successfully navigated to explore new opportunities or address challenges more effectively. Simultaneously, think about how the elements you've maintained can continue to serve as your foundation or perhaps be refreshed to stay relevant and engaging.

Planning for the next phase of your journey involves balancing innovation with authenticity, ensuring that your content continues to evolve without losing the essence of what makes it uniquely yours. This may include setting new goals, experimenting with emerging trends and technologies, or deepening your engagement with your community.

Reflecting on the past year's journey of change and consistency offers valuable lessons that can guide your future direction. It highlights your ability to adapt and grow in response to the shifting landscape of content creation while maintaining the core attributes that define your brand. As you step into the next year, carry forward the resilience, creativity, and authenticity that have brought you this far, ready to embrace new challenges and opportunities with confidence and strategic foresight.

RESEARCHING CONTENT IDEAS

When planning social media post ideas, utilizing analytics is a powerful strategy to use to ensure your content resonates with your audience and meets your engagement goals. Analytics tools, provided by most social media platforms, offer a wealth of data about your audience's behavior, preferences, and interaction patterns with your content. By analyzing this data, you can tailor your post ideas to better align with what your audience enjoys and engages with the most.

Analytics

Here are three examples of how you can use analytics to plan your social media posts.

Example 1: Identifying High-Performance Content

Dive into your analytics to identify which types of posts have historically performed the best in terms of engagement, reach, and conversions. For instance, you might find that tutorial videos on your channel generate more comments and shares compared to other post types. Or perhaps posts that include user-generated content (UGC) have a higher engagement rate. Use this insight to plan more content that mirrors these successful formats, themes, or topics. If tutorial videos are a hit, consider creating a series that covers different aspects of your niche, encouraging viewers to tune in regularly.

Example 2: Analyzing Audience Activity Times

Analytics tools can show you when your audience is most active on social media. This information is invaluable for planning not only what you post but also when you post it. If your data indicates that your audience is most engaged on weekday evenings, schedule your most important posts during these peak times to maximize visibility and interaction. Tailoring your posting schedule based on audience activity can lead to higher engagement rates and ensure your content reaches your followers when they're most likely to see it and interact.

Example 3: Leveraging Demographic Insights

Understanding the demographic composition of your audience—such as their ages, locations, and interests—can also inform your social media planning. For example, if analytics reveal that a significant portion of your audience is interested in sustainable living, you might plan posts that highlight eco-friendly practices within your niche. Or, if you notice a large number of your followers are from a particular geographic area, consider creating content that resonates with cultural, seasonal, or regional interests. This tailored approach ensures your content is relevant to your audience and engaging in terms of their specific needs and preferences.

By leveraging analytics in these ways, you can make data-driven decisions that enhance the relevance and appeal of your social media content. This strategic approach not only increases your content's chances of success but also helps in building a deeper connection with your audience by consistently delivering the value and engagement they seek.

Search Trends

Researching search trends is an indispensable method of planning your social media post ideas so as to ensure that your content stays relevant and captures the attention of your audience at the right moment. By keeping an eye on trending topics, seasonal interests, and emerging conversations, you can craft posts that resonate with the current cultural or social zeitgeist.

Here are three examples of how you can use search trends to inform your social media content planning:

Example 1: Capitalizing on Seasonal Trends

Seasonal trends offer a wealth of inspiration for timely and relevant content. Whether it's holiday-related posts, summer wellness tips, or back-to-school hacks, aligning your content with the seasons can significantly boost engagement. For instance, if you're in the fashion industry, showcasing your fall collection with styling tips and trends as summer winds down can capture your audience's interest as they look to update their wardrobes. Tools like Google Trends can help you identify when certain seasonal topics start to gain popularity, allowing you to schedule your posts for maximum impact.

Example 2: Engaging with Current Events

Staying abreast of current events and weaving them into your content can also increase relevancy and engagement. This doesn't mean jumping on every news story, but rather selectively engaging with events that align with your brand's values and audience's interests. For example, if there's a significant environmental summit or an international day of awareness that pertains to your niche, creating content that contributes to the conversation can show your audience that you're informed and engaged with global issues. This approach not only boosts visibility when these topics trend but also positions your brand as socially conscious and connected to wider community concerns.

Example 3: Riding the Wave of Viral Topics

Viral topics and memes can spread like wildfire across social media, and tactfully engaging with them can provide a significant engagement boost. Monitoring platforms like Twitter, TikTok, or Instagram can help you catch these trends early. Suppose a particular challenge, hashtag, or meme format is gaining traction. In that case, consider how you might put a unique spin on it that fits your brand and appeals to your audience. For example, if a dance challenge goes viral on TikTok, a musician brand could adapt it into a tutorial, making the trend relevant to its niche while engaging with a broader audience.

By integrating search trends into your content planning, you not only ensure your posts are timely and relevant but also demonstrate your brand's awareness of and responsiveness to the world around it. This strategy can help attract new followers, engage your existing audience, and foster a sense of community and relevance that keeps people coming back for more.

Keywords

Incorporating keywords into your social media content strategy, especially for music-related topics, is a methodical way of boosting your visibility and engagement on platforms where potential fans are searching for new tunes or music insights. Keywords can be thought of as the bridge connecting your content with your target audience's interests. By understanding and using the right keywords, you can optimize your posts to appear more frequently in search results and on the feeds of users interested in music.

Here are three examples of how to effectively use keywords for planning music-related social media posts:

Example 1: Utilizing Music Genre Keywords
Identify the most popular and relevant keywords associated with your music genre. Whether you produce indie rock, classical music, or hip-hop, incorporating these genre-specific keywords into your posts can help attract listeners who are specifically interested in that type of music. For instance, if you're releasing a new jazz album, using keywords like "jazz music," "smooth jazz," "new jazz album," and "jazz saxophone" in your posts can help jazz enthusiasts discover your music more easily. Tools like Google Keyword Planner or SEMrush can offer insights into which keywords are most searched for within your genre.

Example 2: Targeting Music-Related Event Keywords
Music festivals, concerts, and other events often generate a lot of search traffic and social media buzz. By including event-related keywords in your posts, you can tap into the audience looking forward to these events. If you're performing at a music festival, for example, use the festival's name, related hashtags, and genre-specific keywords in your content. This approach not only makes your posts more discoverable to attendees but also to those following the event online. Sharing behind-the-scenes content, rehearsal snippets, or your thoughts on the event using these keywords can further engage your audience and build excitement.

Example 3: Leveraging Keywords from Trending Music Topics
Stay updated on trending topics in the music industry, such as new technology in music production, emerging artists, or significant awards announcements. By creating content that includes keywords related to these trending topics, you can engage users who are exploring current

music trends. For example, if a particular music production software becomes popular, sharing tips, tutorials, or your own music created with that software, and including specific keywords related to it, can attract an audience interested in music production technologies.

In each of these examples, the strategic use of keywords is aimed at enhancing the discoverability and relevance of your content among music enthusiasts on social media. It's important to naturally integrate these keywords into your posts, ensuring they add value and context rather than just serving as Search Engine Optimization (SEO) tools. This thoughtful approach to keyword usage can significantly impact your ability to reach and engage with your target audience, helping to grow your presence and influence in the music community.

Search Gaps

Exploring search gaps (Figure 8.9) is a strategic approach to identifying content opportunities that haven't been fully addressed or are underserved in the music niche on social media. By focusing on these areas, you can attract an audience looking for specific music-related

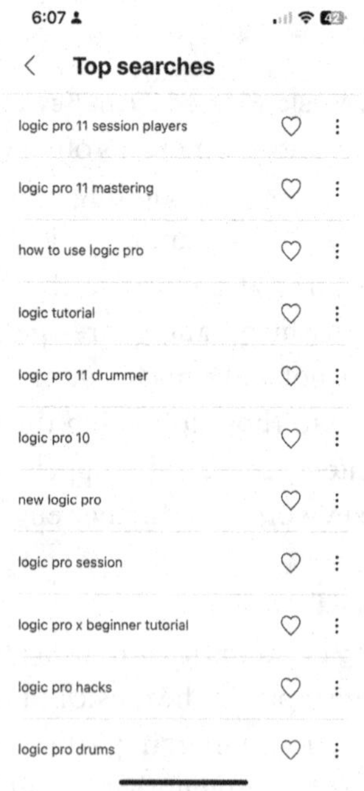

Figure 8.9 Research Tab in YouTube Studio

content that they haven't been able to find elsewhere. This method requires a bit of detective work and creativity but can lead to high engagement and niche authority building.

Here are three examples of how to identify and utilize search gaps for music-related social media content:

Example 1: Underserved Music Genres or Subgenres
One effective strategy is to look for genres or subgenres that have passionate fan bases but not enough quality content catering to them. For example, while there's a plethora of content for mainstream genres like pop or hip-hop, niches like neo-soul, math rock, or traditional folk music from various cultures might be underserved. By creating in-depth content around these genres—such as spotlighting emerging artists, sharing playlists, or discussing genre-specific production techniques—you can tap into an eager and underserved audience.

Example 2: Music Education and Tutorials for Beginners
Another area often overlooked is beginner-level content for those just starting their musical journey. There might be a gap in content that breaks down music theory, instrument tutorials, or production tips in a way that's accessible to novices. By identifying these gaps and creating content that addresses them, you become a go-to resource for newcomers. For instance, simple tutorials on reading music, beginner guitar chords, or how to set up a home recording studio can fulfill a need for educational content in the music community.

Example 3: Behind-the-Scenes Insights into the Music Industry
While there's a lot of content focused on music itself, there may be less covering the behind-the-scenes aspects of the music industry. This could include topics like the process of music production or day-to-day life of touring musicians, or insights into music marketing and promotion. Fans and aspiring musicians alike are often curious about these aspects but may find there is a lack of accessible, engaging content. Providing a peek behind the curtain can satisfy this curiosity and build a dedicated following interested in the intricacies of the music world.

To identify these search gaps, start by browsing music forums, social media comments, and Q & A sites like Quora to see what questions people are asking and what topics are being discussed but not adequately covered. Tools like Answer the Public can also help you discover what people are searching for in relation to music. Once you've identified potential gaps, create content that fills these needs, ensuring it's informative, engaging, and shareable.

Filling search gaps with your music-related content not only serves an underserved audience but also positions you as an authority in your niche. This approach requires keeping your finger on the pulse of the music community and being responsive to its evolving interests and needs. By doing so, you can build a loyal audience that turns to you for unique insights and content they can't find elsewhere.

Mimicking Posts

Mimicking established posts is a strategy that involves analyzing and drawing inspiration from successful content within the music niche on social media. This approach doesn't mean copying content verbatim but rather understanding the elements that contributed to its success and applying those principles to your own unique creations. By observing trends, styles, and formats that resonate with audiences, you can craft posts that engage and attract viewers.

Here are three examples of how to apply this strategy to music-related social media content:

Example 1: Cover Versions with a Twist

One of the most engaging types of content in the music world is cover versions of popular songs. Look for cover videos that have garnered significant attention and analyze what made them successful. It could be the artist's unique vocal style, an unexpected genre crossover, or a creative video concept. Create your own cover versions by adding a personal twist that aligns with your brand and musical identity. For instance, if you're a classical musician, consider covering a popular rock song with classical instruments, or if you're a producer, remix a current pop hit with an entirely different beat or tempo.

Example 2: Educational Content with Engaging Formats

Music theory tutorials, instrument lessons, and production tips often perform well on social media. Identify popular educational posts and videos in your niche, noting how they're structured and what makes them appealing. Is it the simplicity and clarity of the explanation, the use of engaging visuals, or perhaps the interactive element where viewers can ask questions or submit requests? Apply these observations to your educational content by using clear, concise language, incorporating visual aids or animations, and encouraging viewer interaction to make learning music more accessible and enjoyable.

Example 3: Behind-the-Scenes and Personal Stories

Posts that offer a glimpse into the life of a musician or producer, including behind-the-scenes content and personal stories, tend to create a strong connection with audiences. Look for successful examples of this content type, paying attention to storytelling techniques, the authenticity of the message, and the balance between professional and personal insights. Share your own experiences in the music industry, including those around the creative process, challenges faced, and milestones achieved, ensuring your narrative is genuine and relatable. These stories can inspire and engage fans, making them feel like a part of your musical journey.

By analyzing and drawing inspiration from established posts, you're not just replicating what works; you're learning from the best and adapting those lessons to your unique context. This strategy requires a keen eye for detail and an understanding of your audience's preferences. Mimicking the format, tone, and approach of successful content—while infusing it with your originality—can help you create posts that resonate with your followers and enhance your presence in the music community on social media.

DISTRIBUTION

Media distribution is a key element in getting your content into the hands of your audience. In this section let's explore tips to help with the distribution of various media types.

Music Distribution

Music distribution in the digital age is crucial to getting your music heard by a wider audience and maximizing your potential in the industry. Here are 10 tips to help you navigate the complexities of music distribution effectively:

1 Choose the Right Distribution Service

Select a distribution service that aligns with your goals and reaches your desired audience. Platforms like DistroKid, TuneCore, and CD Baby offer different features, pricing models, and reach. Some services might have better coverage in certain geographical areas, or specific music stores and streaming platforms that are more aligned with your target audience. Research and compare these services to find the best fit for your music distribution needs.

2 Understand the Fee Structure

Each distribution platform has its unique fee structure, including annual fees, percentage cuts of royalties, or a combination of both. Some platforms charge per release, while others offer unlimited releases for a yearly fee. Understanding these costs upfront can help you budget effectively and choose a service that offers the best value for your specific needs.

3 Optimize Your Metadata

Metadata—information like your track's title, artist name, album name, genre, and release date—is crucial for discoverability and ensuring you get paid when your music is played. Accurate and complete metadata helps your music appear in the right searches and playlists. Take the time to correctly tag your music and double-check for errors before submitting your tracks for distribution.

4 Choose Your Release Date Wisely

Timing your release can impact its success. Avoid releasing music during overcrowded periods, like major holidays, when major artists typically drop new music. Look for a release date that gives you enough time to promote your music and doesn't clash with significant industry events or releases that could overshadow your launch.

5 Secure Your Rights

Before distributing your music, ensure you have the rights to all the elements in your tracks, including samples, beats, and any featured performances. Copyright infringement can lead to legal issues and potentially having your music removed from platforms. If you're using samples, obtain the necessary clearances or opt for royalty-free samples to avoid complications.

6 Create a Promotional Plan

Your distribution strategy should include a promotional plan to generate buzz around your release. This could involve social media teasers, music videos, singles released ahead of the album, or press releases to music blogs and magazines. Engaging your audience with compelling content leading up to and following your release can significantly boost your visibility and streams.

7 Utilize Pre-Save Campaigns

Many distribution platforms allow you to set up pre-save campaigns, enabling fans to save your upcoming release to their libraries ahead of its launch. This boosts your numbers right out of the gate and can help your music land on playlists. Pre-save campaigns also provide a way to engage with your fans and build anticipation for your release.

8 Monitor Your Analytics

Once your music is distributed, keep an eye on your analytics through your distributor's dashboard and streaming platforms. Understanding how and where your music is being listened to can inform your marketing strategies, tour planning, and future releases. Analytics can reveal valuable insights into your audience's demographics and listening habits.

9 Engage With Your Fans

Engagement doesn't end with distribution. Use social media, email newsletters, and live performances to keep the conversation going with your fans. Share stories behind your songs, host Q & A sessions, and offer exclusive content to keep your audience engaged and invested in your music.

10 Plan Your Next Steps

Finally, use the momentum from your current release to plan your next steps. Whether these involve recording new music, setting up a tour, or releasing merchandise, always be looking forward. The music industry moves fast, and staying proactive in your career will help you build on each success.

Navigating music distribution effectively involves much more than just getting your music on streaming platforms. It requires strategic planning, understanding the digital landscape, and engaging with your audience to maximize your reach and impact.

Podcast Distribution

Podcast distribution is a key element in reaching a wider audience and establishing a strong presence in the ever-growing world of podcasting. Here are 10 tips to effectively manage and optimize your podcast distribution:

1 Choose the Right Hosting Platform

Your choice of hosting platform can significantly affect your podcast's distribution and visibility. Platforms like Buzzsprout, Libsyn, and Anchor offer different features, including analytics, monetization options, and ease of distribution to major podcast directories. Evaluate each platform's offerings to find one that suits your needs, focusing on reliability, user interface, and integration capabilities.

2 Distribute to Multiple Directories

To maximize your reach, distribute your podcast to as many directories and platforms as possible. This includes popular choices like Apple Podcasts, Spotify, Google Podcasts, and Stitcher, among others. Each platform has its audience, and being present on multiple platforms ensures you don't miss potential listeners.

3 Optimize Your Podcast Metadata

Metadata, including your podcast title, description, and episode titles, plays a crucial role in discoverability. Use relevant keywords in your metadata to improve your podcast's searchability on platforms and search engines. Be descriptive and clear, and ensure your metadata accurately reflects the content of your podcast to attract the right audience.

4 Leverage SEO Strategies

Beyond metadata, employ SEO strategies to enhance your podcast's online visibility. This can involve creating a website or blog for your podcast, using keywords throughout your site content, and including transcripts of your episodes. These tactics can help your podcast show up in search results, drawing in listeners who are searching for topics you cover.

5 Engage in Social Media Promotion

Social media is a powerful tool for promoting your podcast and driving listeners to your episodes. Share updates, behind-the-scenes content, and snippets from your episodes on platforms where your target audience is active. Use relevant hashtags, engage with followers, and consider running targeted ads to increase your podcast's visibility.

6 Encourage Ratings and Reviews

Ratings and reviews can significantly impact your podcast's discoverability and credibility. Encourage your listeners to leave positive feedback on platforms like Apple Podcasts, which can help your podcast rank higher in search results and recommendations. Make it easy for listeners by providing direct links to review pages in your show notes or website.

7 Utilize Your Network

Leverage your personal and professional networks to promote your podcast. Guest appearances on other podcasts, collaborations, and mentions by influencers in your niche can introduce your podcast to a wider audience. Similarly, inviting guests with their own following can help you tap into new listener bases.

8 Consistent Publishing Schedule

Maintain a regular publishing schedule to keep your audience engaged and coming back for more. Consistency helps build a loyal listener base, as people appreciate knowing when to expect new content. Determine a realistic schedule you can maintain, whether it's weekly, bi-weekly, or monthly, and stick to it.

9 Monitor Your Analytics

Pay close attention to your podcast analytics to better understand your audience and what content resonates with them. Most hosting platforms provide data on listens, downloads, and listener demographics. Use this information to tailor your content, adjust your marketing strategies, and make informed decisions about the direction of your podcast.

10 Keep Your Content Engaging and High-Quality

Ultimately, the success of your podcast hinges on the quality and relevance of your content. Invest in good recording equipment to ensure clear audio quality, plan your episodes carefully to provide value and engage your audience, and be open to feedback for continuous improvement.

Effective podcast distribution requires a combination of strategic planning, marketing, and engagement with your audience. By following these tips, you can increase your podcast's reach, grow your listener base, and build a successful podcasting presence.

Posting Videos

Posting videos on social media can significantly enhance your engagement and reach, but it requires a strategic approach to stand out in the highly competitive landscape. Here are 10 tips to optimize your video posting strategy on social media platforms:

1 Understand Platform Specifications

Each social media platform has its specifications for videos, including aspect ratios, maximum lengths, and preferred formats. For instance, Instagram Stories and TikTok favor vertical videos, while YouTube is more flexible. Tailoring your videos to fit these specifications ensures they look their best and cater to the viewing habits of users on each platform.

2 Optimize for Silent Viewing

Many users scroll through their social media feeds in settings where audio isn't feasible, so your videos should convey their message clearly, even without sound. Use captions, engaging visuals, and on-screen text to make your videos accessible and understandable on mute.

3 Hook Viewers in the First Few Seconds

With the abundance of content vying for attention on social media, capturing your audience's interest in the first few seconds is crucial.

Start your videos with a compelling hook, question, or visual that draws viewers in and encourages them to watch the entire video.

4 Use Attention-Grabbing Thumbnails

Thumbnails act as the storefront for your videos; a compelling thumbnail can significantly increase your click-through rate. Use high-quality images, images of expressive faces, or intriguing visuals, and include minimal text to hint at what the video is about.

5 Leverage Trending Topics and Hashtags

Aligning your video content with trending topics, challenges, or hashtags can increase its visibility and engagement. Use social media tools to discover trends relevant to your niche and create content that contributes to these conversations in an authentic way.

6 Engage with Your Audience

Encourage and engage with comments on your videos to build a community around your content. Ask questions, solicit feedback, or prompt viewers to share their experiences related to the video topic. Interaction not only boosts your video's visibility through algorithms but also fosters a loyal audience.

7 Promote Your Videos Across Platforms

Don't limit your video's reach to a single platform. Cross-promote your videos on your other social media profiles, website, or email newsletters to maximize exposure. Tailor the messaging for each platform to fit the audience and context.

8 Monitor and Adapt to Performance Analytics

Use the analytics tools provided by social media platforms to track the performance of your videos. Look at metrics like view count, watch time, engagement rate, and audience demographics to understand what works and refine your strategy accordingly.

9 Schedule Posts for Optimal Times

Posting your videos when your audience is most active can significantly impact their initial engagement. Use insights from your social media platforms to identify peak times for your audience and schedule your posts accordingly to ensure maximum visibility.

10 Focus on Quality and Consistency

While frequent posting can help keep your audience engaged, sacrificing quality for quantity can dilute your brand's value. Invest in good production quality, and maintain a consistent posting schedule that aligns with your ability to produce high-quality content. Consistency in quality and posting frequency helps build trust and anticipation among your audience.

Implementing these strategies when posting videos on social media can help you capture attention, engage viewers, and grow your audience. Remember, successful video content is a blend of creativity, strategic planning, and audience understanding.

Nine

Thanks to Dr. Dan Hodges for written contributions to this chapter and overall counsel on music licensing.

In the modern digital age, social media offers unprecedented opportunities for musicians and content creators to monetize their talents and reach a global audience. This chapter explores the various strategies available for earning money through music placements. From leveraging copyright claims and memberships to engaging in direct sponsorships and selling merchandise, this chapter outlines practical steps for artists looking to maximize their online revenue streams.

The digital landscape provides a number of platforms (e.g. see Figure 9.1), each with unique mechanisms for content monetization. Whether it's through ad revenue, direct support from fans via amazing tools such as Patreon, or strategic partnerships and sponsorships, musicians have legitimate options to explore. The following contains a comprehensive overview of these methods, backed by platform-specific examples and insights into what to expect along the way.

COLLECTING ON USAGE OF YOUR MUSIC IN YOUR OWN CONTENT

In the digital realm, where content is constantly consumed and shared, musicians have a unique opportunity to monetize their creations directly on social media platforms. This section explores the mechanisms through which artists can ensure they are compensated for the use of their music when it is used in their own content.

Understanding Copyright

Musicians should understand their rights under copyright laws in order to effectively monetize their music. Registering music with copyright services is crucial as it ensures legal protection and facilitates the collection of royalties. Without this registration, artists may find it difficult

DOI: 10.4324/9781003416180-9

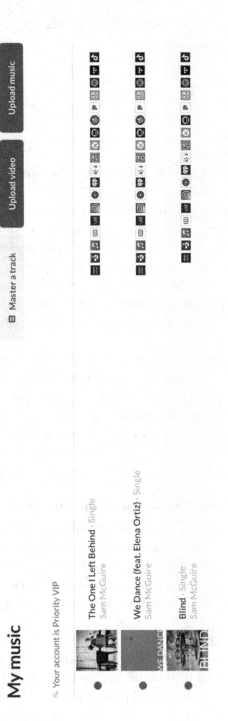

Figure 9.1 DistroKid Control Panel

to prove ownership and claim earnings. Knowledge of copyright law also helps in negotiating terms when partnering with labels or distributors. Ultimately, this understanding safeguards an artist's music from unauthorized use and ensures they are rightfully compensated.

Ownership needs to be secured by registering works with the appropriate copyright offices. This registration is crucial as it legally establishes their claim to the music and enables them to pursue royalties or other earnings. By holding the copyright, musicians can control how their music is used and negotiate terms for licensing and royalties effectively.

To collect royalties efficiently, artists should affiliate with PROs such as ASCAP, BMI, or SESAC, which track and collect performance royalties on behalf of their members. These organizations play a critical role in monitoring where and how music is used and ensure that artists receive compensation for broadcasts and public performances, including those on digital platforms.

Utilizing Content ID Systems

Platforms like YouTube have developed Content ID systems to help manage and automatically identify copyrighted material. When an artist registers their music with these systems, any instance where their music is used on the platform can be tracked, ensuring they receive established royalties. This system is beneficial for artists as it minimizes the manual effort required to chase down copyright infringement. It also streamlines the monetization process, allowing artists to earn passive income from their work. This technology helps maintain the integrity of copyrights on digital platforms.

Many social media platforms, including YouTube and Facebook, offer built-in monetization features, such as the Partner Program and Monetization Manager. These features enable artists to earn revenue directly from views and interactions with their music videos. By activating these options, artists can receive a share of the ad revenue generated from their videos. This method of monetization is particularly appealing as it provides a direct and quantifiable link between content popularity and revenue. It also encourages artists to create more engaging and high-quality content that attracts more viewers.

Affiliate Marketing and Direct Sales

Musicians can leverage their social media presence to include affiliate links in their video descriptions or direct links to purchase their music. This approach not only facilitates immediate sales but also allows artists to earn commissions on affiliated products or services. By strategically placing these links, artists can enhance their earnings beyond traditional content monetization. This method serves as an excellent supplement to other revenue streams, providing financial benefits from both music sales and related products. It also offers fans a direct way to support their favorite artists.

Artists can provide their music under a subscription model, where fans pay a recurring fee to access a curated library of tracks. This model can be facilitated through personal websites or platforms like Patreon, providing a steady income stream while also building a dedicated fan base.

Securing sponsorships for videos or live streams that feature an artist's music can be a lucrative way to monetize content. Sponsors pay to be associated with content that resonates with their target audience, which can be an effective way for musicians to monetize their music while enhancing their profile.

Platforms like Twitch and YouTube allow musicians to perform live, whereby they can earn money from ads, donations, or subscriptions. Live-streaming also provides an opportunity to promote merchandise or exclusive content available for purchase during or after the performance.

Using Analytics to Maximize Revenue

Understanding the analytics provided by social media platforms can help musicians identify what content performs best and strategize accordingly. By analyzing trends and viewer preferences, artists can create more content that engages their audience, increasing the likelihood of monetization.

By leveraging these strategies, musicians can effectively monetize the usage of their music in their own content across various social media platforms. This approach not only enhances their ability to generate income but also helps them maintain artistic control and build closer connections with their audience.

PROVIDING MUSICAL ACCESS TO OTHER CREATORS

Musicians can leverage their creations beyond personal uploads by granting other creators permission to use their music in various content across social media platforms. This strategy not only extends the reach of their music but also opens up additional revenue streams. In this section, we will discuss how musicians can provide access to their music to other creators, manage permissions, and ensure they are compensated appropriately.

Licensing Agreements

To provide their music to other creators, musicians must establish clear licensing agreements that define how their music can be used. These agreements should specify the scope of the license, including where the music can be used, for how long, and in what types of media. Licensing provides a controlled way for artists to monetize their work while protecting their copyrights. By setting terms that are mutually beneficial, musicians can ensure they receive appropriate compensation while allowing other creators to enhance their content with quality music.

Musicians can list their tracks in digital content libraries, which serve as marketplaces where other creators can find and license music. Platforms like Epidemic Sound, AudioJungle, and Artlist simplify the process for both musicians and content creators by managing the licensing, distribution, and royalty collection processes. By participating in these libraries, artists gain exposure to a broad audience of content creators looking for professional-grade music for their projects.

Some platforms offer revenue-sharing models, where musicians can earn a portion of the revenue generated from videos that use their music. For example, TikTok has initiated revenue-sharing programs where rights holders earn money based on the usage of their music in user-generated content. These models create passive income opportunities for musicians and encourage the use of licensed music over pirated copies.

For more exclusive agreements, musicians might consider offering custom licensing services directly from their websites or through contact points. This direct approach can be particularly lucrative when dealing with brands or larger content creators who seek unique music that aligns with their specific project visions. Custom licensing also allows for greater negotiation flexibility, potentially leading to better rates and more favorable terms.

As stated previously, registering with a PRO helps ensure that musicians are compensated for the public performance of their music, which includes digital streaming. When other creators use their music, whether in live broadcasts, videos, or other public performances, these organizations track usage and collect royalties on behalf of the musician. It is crucial for musicians to understand which PROs operate in their country and the specific terms of registration and royalty collection that apply.

Collaborations and Partnerships

Engaging directly with other creators for collaborations or partnerships can be an effective way to control the use of one's music while building relationships within the industry. These partnerships often lead to cross-promotion, which benefits all parties involved by amplifying reach and engagement across different audiences. Collaborative projects can also lead to new creative opportunities and innovations in how music is integrated into content.

To ensure compliance with licensing agreements, musicians should actively monitor how their music is being used across social media platforms. Tools and services that track music usage can help identify cases of unauthorized use, allowing musicians to take appropriate action to enforce their copyrights and secure their revenue.

Feedback and Adaptation

Musicians should regularly solicit feedback from other creators on their licensing processes and music offerings. This feedback can be invaluable in terms of improving the accessibility and attractiveness of their licensing options. Adapting to the needs and preferences of content creators ensures that musicians remain competitive and relevant in the rapidly evolving digital marketplace.

By understanding and implementing these strategies, musicians can effectively provide access to their music to other creators, benefiting from expanded reach and additional revenue streams while maintaining control over how their work is used. This approach not only enhances their financial gains but also contributes to a richer, more diverse media landscape.

PLATFORM-SPECIFIC EXAMPLES OF MEMBERSHIPS

Various platforms offer membership options that allow creators, including musicians, to monetize their content directly through subscriber fees. This section explores several platform-specific examples of how memberships can be utilized to generate a steady income, providing artists with the financial support needed to continue creating and sharing their work.

YouTube Memberships

YouTube offers a feature called Channel Memberships, where viewers pay a monthly fee to access exclusive perks such as custom badges, emojis, and members-only videos. Musicians can utilize this feature by offering exclusive performances, behind-the-scenes content, or first access to new music videos. This model not only fosters a deeper connection with fans but also provides a consistent revenue stream that is independent of ad revenue.

Twitch Subscriptions

Twitch, primarily known for live-streaming, allows creators to earn money through subscriptions. There are multiple tiers of subscriptions that viewers can choose from, each providing different levels of access to exclusive content, such as ad-free viewing or custom chat options. Musicians can leverage Twitch for live performances, music production tutorials, or casual interactions with fans, making it an effective platform for real-time engagement and monetization.

Patreon

Patreon (see Figure 9.2) stands out as a platform designed specifically for creators to receive financial support directly from their audience. Artists can set up different tiers of membership, each offering unique rewards such as early access to tracks, exclusive downloads, or personal interactions. Patreon is especially beneficial for musicians looking to fund ongoing projects or who want to focus on a niche audience willing to support their creative process.

Figure 9.2 Patreon

Facebook Fan Subscriptions

Facebook offers fan subscriptions which enable followers to pay a monthly fee in exchange for special perks like exclusive content, discounts on merchandise, or the ability to interact more closely with the creator. Musicians can use this feature to share exclusive video content, run live Q & A sessions, and to post special updates about upcoming projects, enhancing fan loyalty and providing a predictable income.

Bandcamp Subscriptions

Bandcamp provides an artist-friendly platform where musicians can sell their music and merchandise. Additionally, it offers a subscription service where fans can pay a set amount regularly to receive all of an artist's new music, often including back-catalog items and special releases. This model is particularly effective for independent musicians with a dedicated fan base and provides them with full control over their output and earnings.

OnlyFans

While widely known for other types of content, OnlyFans also serves as a platform where musicians can offer exclusive content to subscribers. This can range from exclusive performances, songwriting sessions, or even personalized content tailored to subscriber preferences. OnlyFans allows artists to set their subscription rates and offers a high degree of privacy and control over who sees their content.

Memberful

Memberful is a service that integrates with a creator's website to provide membership services without directing fans to a third-party site. This tool is ideal for musicians who prefer to keep their content on their own website but still want to offer subscription-based access. Memberful handles all the backend processes like payments and subscriber management, allowing artists to focus on creating content.

Substack

Originally known for newsletters, Substack now supports multimedia content and could be a unique avenue for musicians to combine written content with audio and video. This could include subscriber-only newsletters that offer insights into the music industry, combined with exclusive tracks or videos.

Ko-fi

Ko-fi is another platform that allows creators to receive money directly from their fans, either as one-time donations or ongoing subscriptions. For musicians, Ko-fi can be used to fund specific projects like an album or tour, with fans contributing directly to the cause they want to support.

Buy Me a Coffee

Similar to Ko-fi, Buy Me a Coffee offers a way for fans to support their favorite artists with one-time or recurring contributions. Musicians can use this platform to offer simple, straightforward ways for fans to contribute financial support, possibly in exchange for exclusive content or a mention in upcoming projects.

These platform-specific examples illustrate the diversity of options available for musicians to establish and grow a sustainable income through memberships. By choosing the right platforms that align with their content and audience, artists can effectively monetize their passion and ensure a stable financial foundation for their creative endeavors.

SUBSCRIPTION SUPPORT THROUGH PATREON

Patreon has emerged as a pivotal platform for artists, including musicians, seeking to harness the power of their community for sustained financial support. This section delves into how musicians can utilize

Patreon to engage with their fans and secure a reliable income stream through subscriptions.

A) Customizable Subscription Tiers

Patreon allows musicians to set up multiple subscription tiers, each offering different levels of rewards and content. This flexibility lets artists tailor their offerings to various fan commitment levels, ranging from basic support tiers offering exclusive updates to more premium tiers providing in-depth access to the music creation process or personalized experiences. Musicians can design their tiers to include anything from exclusive song releases, backstage passes, and signed merchandise to personal shout-outs and one-on-one video calls.

B) Direct Fan Engagement

Patreon is great at building a direct line of communication between artists and their fans. This platform uses a community-centric approach where people feel they are directly contributing to the success of their favorite artists. Musicians can use Patreon to share exclusive updates, behind-the-scenes content, and personal stories, creating a more intimate and engaging fan experience. This close interaction helps strengthen fan loyalty and increases the value of subscription content.

C) Consistent Revenue Stream

Unlike one-time sales or ad-based revenue models, Patreon provides artists with a predictable, recurring income based on monthly subscriptions. This model is particularly beneficial for musicians looking to fund ongoing projects or stabilize their income against the often sporadic earnings from gigs and album sales. The consistent financial support enables artists to focus more on creativity and less on financial instability.

D) Creative Freedom and Independence

By relying on fan subscriptions, musicians on Patreon often enjoy greater creative freedom than those who are under traditional music labels. This independence allows artists to experiment with their musical and artistic direction without being under pressure to conform to commercial expectations. Patreon's model supports a diverse range of musical projects, from experimental works to niche genres, giving artists the space to explore and innovate within their craft.

E) Multimedia Content Opportunities
Patreon supports various types of content, which means musicians can expand beyond audio tracks and offer video tutorials, live performance recordings, Q & A sessions, blogs, and more. This multimedia approach not only enhances the value of each subscription but also caters to different audience preferences, maximizing engagement across the board.

F) Workshops and Masterclasses
For educational artists, Patreon provides a platform to offer exclusive workshops or masterclasses. This can be particularly appealing for skilled musicians who wish to share their expertise on songwriting, instrument mastery, or music production. These educational offerings can serve as higher-tier rewards, adding substantial value to subscriptions and attracting serious students and fellow artists.

G) Collaborations with Other Artists
Musicians can collaborate with other artists on Patreon to create exclusive content, expanding their audience base. These collaborations can introduce musicians to new communities, potentially increasing their subscriber count and broadening their network.

H) Global Reach
Patreon's global platform allows musicians to reach an international audience, which is particularly valuable for niche genres or artists looking to expand their reach beyond local scenes. This worldwide accessibility helps artists develop a diverse and global fanbase, further securing their revenue.

I) Integration with Social Media
Patreon integrates well with other social media platforms, allowing musicians to promote their Patreon content across various channels. This integration ensures that their efforts to grow their Patreon community can benefit from their established social media presence, leveraging followers from platforms like Instagram, Twitter, and YouTube.

J) Analytics and Feedback

Patreon offers detailed analytics and feedback tools that help artists understand subscriber preferences and adjust their offerings accordingly. This data-driven approach enables musicians to refine their content strategy, optimize engagement, and ensure they meet the needs and expectations of their supporters.

K) Summary

By strategically utilizing Patreon, musicians can effectively monetize their passion and secure a sustainable, fan-supported career. This platform not only provides the financial backing needed to continue creating but also deepens the relationship between artists and their fans, fostering a supportive and engaged community.

VIEWS AND ADVERTISING THROUGH ADSENSE

AdSense represents a significant opportunity for musicians to earn revenue from their content on platforms like YouTube. This section explores how musicians can leverage AdSense to monetize their videos through views and advertising, providing a crucial income stream that complements direct music sales and performances.

A) Enabling Monetization on YouTube

To start earning through AdSense, musicians need to enable monetization on their YouTube channel. This process involves agreeing to YouTube's monetization policies, linking an AdSense account, and setting up monetization preferences. Musicians must ensure their content complies with copyright laws, as copyrighted music (unless it's their own or they have permission to use it) can lead to demonetization or account strikes. This initial setup is crucial for unlocking the potential to earn money directly from video views and ads.

B) Understanding Ad Revenue Share

YouTube pays out 55% of the advertising revenue to the content creator and retains 45% when it comes to long-form content. For musicians, this revenue is generated primarily through pre-roll, mid-roll, and display ads placed in or around their videos. Knowing how ad revenue is shared helps musicians to strategize their content production and release schedule to maximize their earnings potential, especially during peak viewer engagement periods.

C) Optimizing Videos for Higher Ad Revenue

To maximize earnings from AdSense, musicians should focus on creating high-quality videos that engage viewers for longer periods. Longer watch times can lead to more ad placements within a single video, especially with the mid-roll ads that appear in videos that are longer than 8 minutes. Additionally, using relevant keywords and engaging descriptions can improve video discoverability, increasing views and potential ad revenue.

D) Regular Content Release Schedule

Consistency is key in building and maintaining an audience on YouTube. Musicians should aim to release videos regularly to keep their audience engaged and attract new subscribers. A consistent posting schedule can also help improve the channel's ranking on YouTube, leading to more views and increased ad revenue over time. Seasonal content and participation in trending topics or challenges can also provide temporary boosts in viewership and ad impressions.

E) Leveraging Multiple Content Types

Besides traditional music videos, musicians can expand their content repertoire to include behind-the-scenes videos, vlogs, live performances, tutorials, and Q & A sessions. Diversifying content not only helps attract a broader audience but also increases the potential for monetization across different viewer interests and demographics. Each content type can appeal to different segments of an audience, thereby maximizing the overall engagement and ad revenue potential.

F) Engaging with the Audience

Interaction with viewers through comments, polls, and live streams can significantly enhance viewer loyalty and retention. Engaged viewers are more likely to watch videos for longer, increasing their ad exposure and click-through rates, which directly benefits ad revenue. Musicians can use these interactions to gain insights into what content works best, allowing them to tailor their offerings to audience preferences.

G) Cross-Promoting Content on Social Media

Promoting YouTube content on other social media platforms can drive additional traffic to videos, enhancing view counts and ad impressions. Musicians should integrate their social media strategies to include teasers, exclusive clips, or announcements on platforms like Instagram, Twitter, and Facebook, directing followers to their YouTube channels.

H) Analyzing Performance Metrics

Utilizing YouTube Analytics is essential to understanding which videos perform well and why. Metrics such as watch time, viewer demographics, and traffic sources provide valuable insights that can inform content strategy and optimization efforts. By analyzing trends and performance data, musicians can continuously improve their content to better cater to their audience, thus maximizing AdSense earnings.

I) Ad Placement Strategy

Musicians should consider the placement and type of ads in their videos. For example, skippable ads may provide a better user experience and potentially higher revenue than non-skippable ads, as viewers are less likely to abandon the video. Understanding the impact of different ad types and placements can help musicians make informed decisions that balance revenue generation with viewer satisfaction.

J) Summary

By strategically using AdSense, musicians can effectively monetize their presence on YouTube and potentially other platforms that support similar advertising models. This revenue stream, combined with direct fan support and other monetization methods, can help musicians build a financially sustainable career in the digital age.

SPONSORSHIPS: MONETARY SUPPORT

Sponsorships offer a valuable revenue stream for musicians on social media, providing them with financial backing that can significantly enhance both the quality and reach of their content. This section explores how musicians can attract and manage sponsorships that provide direct monetary support, allowing them to focus more on their artistic endeavors.

Understanding the Value of Sponsorships

Sponsorships involve financial support from brands that are interested in associating themselves with a musician's image and reach. For musicians, this means an opportunity to secure funding that can be used for various purposes, such as producing high-quality music videos, organizing tours, or enhancing overall production values. Recognizing the potential of sponsorships to elevate their career, musicians should approach these opportunities as both a financial arrangement and a partnership that can drive mutual growth.

The first step in securing sponsorships is identifying brands whose products or services align with the musician's audience and brand image. Musicians should look for companies that share similar values or whose target demographics overlap with their fan base. This alignment not only makes the sponsorship deal more organic and appealing to fans but also increases the likelihood of a successful and lasting partnership.

Musicians need to develop compelling pitch proposals that clearly communicate the benefits for potential sponsors. This includes providing detailed information about their audience demographics, engagement metrics, and examples of previous successful partnerships. The pitch should also highlight unique aspects of the musician's brand and creative projects that could enhance the sponsor's visibility and appeal.

Effective negotiation skills are crucial when finalizing sponsorship agreements. Musicians should strive for deals that offer fair compensation and that respect their artistic integrity. This might involve negotiating aspects like the duration of the sponsorship, the amount of control the sponsor has over content, and the specific obligations each party has. It's important for musicians to ensure that sponsorship terms do not compromise their creative freedom or alienate their audience.

Once a sponsorship deal is in place, musicians must integrate the sponsor's brand into their content in a way that feels natural and engaging (Figure 9.3). This could be through product placements in music videos, branded posts on social media, or mentions during live streams. The key is to incorporate the sponsor in a way that adds value to the content without overshadowing the musician's own brand.

Transparency about sponsorships helps maintain trust between musicians and their fans. Musicians should clearly disclose sponsored content to their audience, complying with legal requirements and

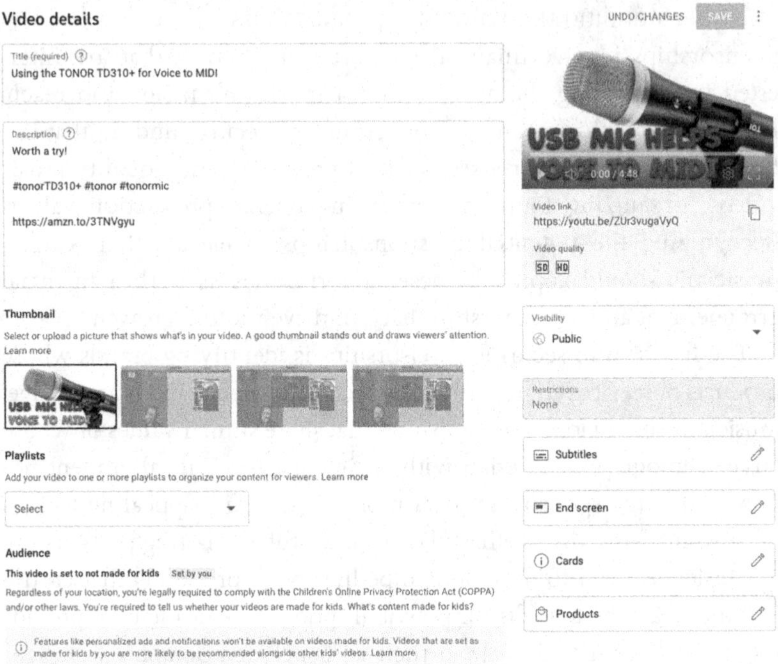

Figure 9.3 Sponsorship Example

maintaining ethical standards. Being upfront about sponsorships can prevent audience backlash and build a more loyal fanbase.

Beyond immediate financial support, sponsorships can be leveraged as part of larger strategic projects. For instance, a tour or a special album release might attract more substantial sponsorship deals that could cover more significant expenses. Musicians should think creatively about how to integrate sponsors into these larger projects in mutually beneficial ways.

To ensure continued success with sponsorships, musicians must monitor and report on the performance of sponsored content. Providing sponsors with detailed feedback on how their brand is being perceived and the impact of the sponsorship can help secure long-term commitments and possibly attract additional sponsors.

Strong, ongoing relationships with sponsors can lead to more opportunities and increased support over time. Musicians should regularly communicate with their sponsors, update them on project progress, and involve them in planning future activities. Good communication can turn initial sponsorships into long-term partnerships.

Finally, musicians should continuously seek new sponsorship opportunities to diversify their revenue streams. Keeping an eye on emerging brands or products that resonate with their audience, and attending industry events where they can network with potential sponsors, are good practices for expanding their sponsorship portfolio.

By effectively managing sponsorships for monetary support, musicians can secure the necessary funds to advance their careers while creating valuable marketing opportunities for their sponsors. This symbiotic relationship not only supports the financial aspects of a musician's career but also enhances their professional network and market visibility.

SPONSORSHIPS: PRODUCT SUPPORT

Product support through sponsorships is an opportunity for musicians to enhance their visibility and resources without direct financial transactions. This section explores how musicians can engage with brands for product sponsorships, which not only provide them with necessary equipment and services but also elevate their branding through association with established products.

Understanding Product Sponsorships

Product sponsorships involve receiving goods or services from brands in exchange for promotion or endorsement. For musicians, this can include musical instruments, recording equipment, fashion items, or other products relevant to their brand and audience. These sponsorships can significantly reduce the costs associated with music production and performance, allowing artists to maintain high-quality outputs without the associated costs.

Musicians must identify brands that align with their artistic identity and fan demographics. Compatibility enhances the authenticity of the sponsorship and increases audience acceptance. For instance, a musician known for a particular style or genre might partner with brands that align with that style, whether it's a specific type of instrument, apparel, or technology.

When approaching potential sponsors, musicians should prepare proposals that highlight the mutual benefits of the partnership. This includes detailing the musician's reach, audience engagement, and past successful collaborations. Proposals should clearly outline how the product will be featured in the musician's content and the expected exposure the brand will receive, making a strong case for why the partnership would be valuable for the sponsor.

Effective negotiation is crucial to securing product sponsorships. Musicians should discuss and agree on how often and in what context the products will be used or shown in their content. It's important to negotiate terms that do not overly restrict the musician's creative control or overwhelm their artistic content with promotional material, so as to preserve credibility and artistic integrity.

The integration of sponsored products into content should feel natural and relevant. Musicians can feature products in their music videos and social media posts, or during live performances, in a way that complements the content rather than detracts from it. Effective product placement can enhance the aesthetic of a piece while providing value to the sponsor.

Transparency about product sponsorships is essential so as to maintain trust with the audience. Musicians should disclose the presence of sponsored products in their content, ensuring that fans are aware of the promotional nature of the product placements. This transparency helps maintain the authenticity of the musician's brand and fosters a trusting relationship with the audience.

The products musicians choose to sponsor can significantly affect their brand image. By selecting products that enhance or are consistent with their public persona, musicians can strengthen their brand identity (see Figure 9.4). This strategic alignment helps solidify their niche in the market and can attract more dedicated fans.

Musicians should regularly monitor the effectiveness of their product sponsorships and the impact they have on their content and audience perception. Feedback from fans and changes in audience engagement metrics can provide insights into how well the sponsorship is received and whether it should be continued, adjusted, or terminated. Consistent reflection on each of these areas will help opportunities grow.

Cultivating long-term relationships with sponsors can lead to ongoing support and potentially more significant collaborations. Musicians should keep sponsors updated on the impact of their products and seek ways to deepen the partnership, such as through exclusive launches or co-branded initiatives.

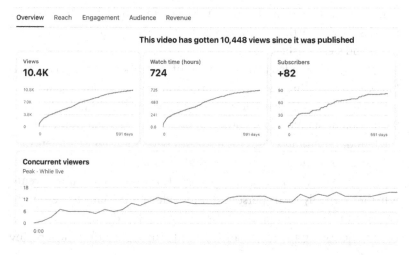

This video has gotten 10,448 views since it was published

Views	Watch time (hours)	Subscribers
10.4K	**724**	**+82**

Concurrent viewers
Peak · While live

Figure 9.4 Synthesizer V Association

As your career evolves, so too should your sponsorship strategies. Continuously seeking new and relevant product sponsorship opportunities can help you stay innovative and ensure you have the tools and support needed to grow and succeed. By strategically engaging with product sponsorships, you can effectively supplement your artistic endeavors, reduce production costs, and enhance your overall brand through carefully planned partnerships.

SPONSORSHIPS: EXPANDED EXPOSURE

Sponsorships can also significantly enhance a musician's exposure by connecting them with broader or even more targeted audiences, often beyond what they could achieve on their own. This section discusses how musicians can leverage sponsorships for expanded exposure, detailing strategies to maximize visibility and reach through collaborative efforts with brands.

Detailed Discussion on Leveraging Sponsorships for Expanded Exposure

Collaborating with well-aligned brands can extend a musician's reach to new audiences who might not have discovered their music otherwise. These partnerships should target brands with a customer base that overlaps with the musician's target audience or expands into new demographics. For instance, a musician known for their outdoor themes might partner with an outdoor apparel brand, tapping into the brand's established audience.

Creating co-branded content can significantly boost a musician's visibility. This might include special edition music videos, joint social media campaigns, or exclusive interviews featured on the brand's channels. Such content should highlight the synergy between the musician and the brand, providing value that resonates with both sets of audiences.

Brands often host events or live performances that can serve as platforms for musicians to gain exposure. Participating in these events, whether virtually or in-person, can introduce musicians to new audiences. Additionally, these events are often marketed extensively by the brand, increasing the musician's visibility through various advertising channels.

Musicians can engage in social media takeovers, where they manage a brand's social media account for a day or during a special event. This gives musicians direct access to the brand's followers, expanding their exposure and allowing them to showcase their personality and music in a new context.

Engaging in cross-promotional campaigns involves both the musician and the brand promoting each other's content. This reciprocal promotion can be particularly effective on social media, where content can quickly gain traction. Cross-promotion extends reach and visibility, potentially drawing in fans from the brand's customer base who have similar interests.

Many brands curate playlists on music streaming platforms, which can include tracks from sponsored artists. Being featured in such playlists can provide musicians with significant exposure, especially if the brand has a substantial following or a strong presence in the music industry.

Endorsement deals in which musicians use or mention specific products can lead to increased exposure through the brand's marketing efforts. These deals often include the brand featuring the musician in advertising campaigns, promotional materials, and even product packaging.

Brands typically have access to premium marketing resources and professional expertise that might be out of reach for individual musicians. Through sponsorships, musicians can benefit from access to high-quality promotional materials, professional photoshoots, and expertly crafted marketing campaigns. Musicians can achieve expanded exposure through integration into multimedia campaigns in which their music accompanies television ads, online ads, and public billboards. These campaigns often have extensive reach and can significantly boost a musician's profile.

Associating with reputable brands can lend credibility and prestige to your image, enhancing your profile in the industry. This association can attract attention from media outlets, industry leaders, and potential fans who trust the brand's judgment and endorsements. By effectively leveraging sponsorships for expanded exposure, you can both increase your visibility and enhance your reputation and marketability. These partnerships, when strategically chosen and managed, can open up numerous opportunities for career growth and audience development.

BRINGING AN AUDIENCE TO IN-PERSON EVENTS

Selling merchandise is not just about online transactions; it can also be a powerful tool to drive attendance to in-person events such as concerts, tours, and meet-and-greets. This section discusses strategies musicians can use to leverage their merchandise to enhance event attendance, creating a holistic approach to fan engagement and revenue generation.

Detailed Discussion on Using Merchandise to Boost In-Person Event Attendance

Offering exclusive merchandise that is only available at live events can be a significant draw for fans. These items could include limited edition apparel, signed memorabilia, or special merchandise bundles that include event tickets. The exclusivity adds value to the event attendance, encouraging fans to attend for the live experience and also to acquire unique merch.

Musicians can boost ticket sales by offering merchandise as part of the ticket purchase. For example, fans could receive a discount on merchandise when they buy a concert ticket, or vice versa. This strategy can increase early ticket sales and build excitement leading up to the event. Innovative ticketing options, such as wearable merchandise that serves as the event ticket, can enhance the fan experience and streamline event entry. As examples, wristbands, lanyards, or T-shirts could be designed with unique barcodes that act as entry tickets. This approach not only makes the ticketing process more exciting but also turns every attendee into a walking billboard for the event.

Encouraging attendees to share their merchandise purchases on social media can amplify event promotion. Musicians can create hashtags for event-specific merchandise or offer incentives for sharing, such as contests or giveaways at the event. This social media buzz helps draw larger crowds and increases merchandise visibility.

Offering early access to merchandise for ticket holders can enhance the value of buying tickets early. Fans might receive an opportunity to purchase merchandise before it becomes available to the public or get an opportunity to buy exclusive pre-event products. This tactic not only drives ticket sales but also boosts overall merchandise revenue.

Implementing loyalty programs that reward fans for attending multiple events or purchasing merchandise can create long-term engagement. Points could be earned with every ticket or merchandise purchase and redeemed for special rewards like backstage passes, VIP seating, or exclusive meet-and-greet opportunities. Exclusivity tends to play a large role in driving fan fever.

Combining merchandise with VIP experiences, such as soundcheck access or after-show parties, can provide added value for fans. These bundles can be priced higher, offering a comprehensive package that enhances the overall event experience.

Setting up pop-up stores at or near event venues can capture the excitement of the day and convert it into sales. These pop-up stores could offer a full range of merchandise, including items specifically branded for the event, which wouldn't be available elsewhere. Creating interactive displays where fans can see, touch, and try merchandise before purchasing can increase sales. These displays can be set up inside or near the venue, integrating seamlessly with the event atmosphere and providing an engaging shopping experience.

After the event, musicians can offer merchandise online as a reminder of the experience, possibly including items that commemorate specific moments of the event. This not only extends the lifecycle of the event's impact but also keeps the connection with the audience active, bringing fans back again and again to in-person events.

By leveraging merchandise effectively, you can significantly enhance both the appeal and profitability of in-person events. These strategies not only increase merchandise sales but also deepen fan engagement, turning each event into a multifaceted experience that extends beyond just the musical performance.

SPENDING MONEY TO PROMOTE CONTENT TO POTENTIAL AUDIENCES

Investing in content promotion (see Figure 9.5) is a strategic approach that musicians and other creators can use to enhance their visibility and reach potential audiences on social media platforms. This section explores the benefits of and strategies for effectively using paid promotions to maximize the impact and reach of influence.

Figure 9.5 Instagram Promotion Example

Detailed Discussion on Spending Money to Promote Content

Spending money to promote content involves taking advantage of paid advertising features offered on social media. These can include targeted ads, sponsored posts, or promoted content that appears in the feeds of users who are not yet followers but share characteristics with a musician's typical audience. This investment is crucial to breaking through the organic reach limitations often imposed by platform algorithms.

Selecting the right platforms for promotion depends on where a musician's target audience is most active. For instance, if a musician's audience skews younger, investing in promotions on platforms like TikTok or Snapchat might be more effective than on LinkedIn or Facebook. Understanding the demographics and behavior of the audience on each platform can help tailor the promotional efforts for maximum impact.

Effective targeting is essential to ensure that money isn't wasted. Social media platforms offer robust targeting tools that allow musicians to specify who sees their ads based on factors like age, location, interests, behaviors, and more. Precise targeting ensures that promotional efforts reach the most relevant audience, increasing the likelihood of engagement and conversion.

The success of paid promotions heavily relies on the quality and appeal of the content itself. Musicians should focus on creating visually appealing, engaging, and memorable content that resonates with their target audience. This might include music videos, behind-the-scenes clips, or interactive posts that encourage viewer participation.

Before launching a paid promotion, it is important to set clear objectives. Whether the goal is to increase followers, boost engagement, or drive traffic to a music streaming platform, having specific targets will help measure the effectiveness of the promotional campaign and adjust tactics as needed.

Determining how much to spend on promotions involves considering the overall marketing budget and expected return on investment. Musicians should start with a manageable budget to test different strategies and increase spending gradually based on what works best in terms of engagement and conversion rates.

Continuous monitoring of the performance of paid promotions is crucial. Platforms provide analytics tools that detail how well ads are performing in real time. Using this data, musicians can make informed decisions to tweak their campaigns, adjust targeting, or even pause and redirect funds to more successful strategies.

Paid promotions should be part of a broader marketing strategy that includes organic content creation and engagement. Integrating both paid and organic efforts can create a cohesive marketing push, as each can support and amplify the other.

Retargeting allows musicians to reach users who have interacted with their content but haven't taken a desired action, such as following their page or streaming their music. This is an effective way to maximize the impact of initial promotional efforts and improve conversion rates over time.

After running promotional campaigns, it's important to evaluate their success against the initial objectives and analyze the return on investment. This evaluation can help you understand how successful your investment was and inform future marketing decisions. By thoughtfully spending money to promote content, you can expand your reach and engagement, introducing your music to potential fans who might not have discovered it otherwise. With strategic planning, targeted advertising, and continuous optimization, paid promotions can be a powerful tool in your marketing arsenal.

DEMOGRAPHIC-BASED SPONSORSHIPS

Leveraging demographic-based sponsorships is a strategic way for musicians to align their marketing efforts with specific segments of their audience, ensuring that their promotional activities are as effective and targeted as possible. This section explores how musicians can harness the power of demographic insights to secure sponsorships that resonate with their core listeners and viewers, potentially increasing engagement and financial returns.

Detailed Exploration of Demographic-Based Sponsorships

The first step in leveraging demographic-based sponsorships is accurately identifying the key demographics of the musician's audience. This involves analyzing data on age, location (see Figure 9.6), gender,

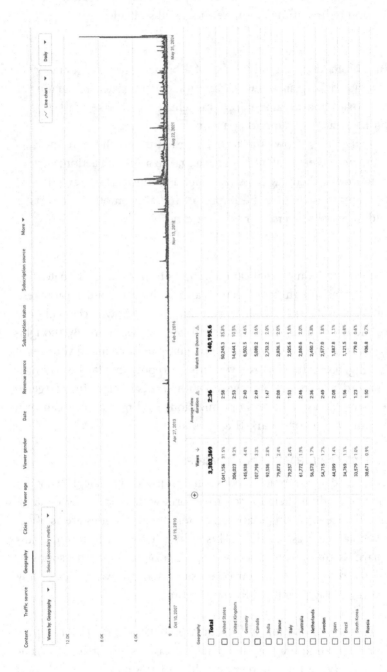

Figure 9.6 Looking at Demographics in YouTube Analytics

interests, and other relevant factors. Understanding these metrics allows musicians to tailor their content and sponsorship strategies to the specific needs and preferences of their audience.

Armed with detailed demographic insights, musicians can present a compelling case to potential sponsors who are looking to target similar demographics to theirs. A musician whose audience primarily consists of young adults in urban areas might attract lifestyle brands or tech companies interested in reaching the same group. Detailed data enhances a musician's pitch to potential sponsors by demonstrating a clear alignment between the musician's audience and the sponsor's target market.

With an understanding of their audience demographics, musicians can customize their content to better engage with specific groups. This might involve varying the content format, style, or the platforms on which it is shared, based on the preferences of different demographic segments. Tailored content increases engagement, making the sponsorship more valuable and effective.

When arranging sponsorship deals, musicians should highlight how their specific audience demographics align with the sponsor's targets. This can involve demonstrating past successful engagements and how these can be replicated or enhanced with the sponsor's support. Musicians can also propose specific, targeted campaigns that utilize demographic insights to maximize the impact of the sponsorship.

After securing sponsorships, it's crucial to measure the success of sponsored content through demographic engagement metrics. This includes tracking how different segments of the audience interact with the content, the conversion rates, and the overall reception. Keeping abreast of demographic trends within the audience allows musicians to anticipate changes and adapt their sponsorship strategies accordingly. This proactive approach can help secure sponsorships with brands looking to capitalize on emerging trends, providing an edge in competitive markets.

Musicians can create exclusive content or offers that cater to specific demographics within their audience. This could include special merchandise, exclusive digital content, or unique experiences that appeal to particular groups. Such exclusivity enhances the perceived value of the content and sponsorships.

Utilizing advanced analytics tools can help musicians gain deeper insights into their demographics. These tools can analyze audience behavior patterns, preferences, and engagement across different content types and platforms, further refining sponsorship strategies. By understanding their audience deeply, musicians can build more meaningful relationships with both their fans and sponsors. This deeper connection can lead to more authentic and effective sponsorship campaigns, which are beneficial for all parties involved.

Demonstrating flexibility in adapting sponsorship approaches based on dynamic demographic data can make a musician more attractive to potential sponsors. This shows that the musician is responsive and capable of evolving with their audience and the market, a valuable trait for long-term sponsorship relations. By strategically utilizing demographic-based sponsorships, musicians can enhance their appeal to potential sponsors, creating partnerships that are not only financially beneficial but also deeply resonant with their audience. This targeted approach ensures that sponsorships are effective, relevant, and successful in achieving their intended goals.

CASE STUDY SCENARIOS

The following examples are designed to demonstrate typical progressions and opportunities of earning money on social media in a variety of situations.

Traditional Band Live Streams on Facebook

In this case study, we examine how a traditional band utilized Facebook to host live streams, engaging their audience in real time and leveraging the platform's features to maximize their reach and revenue. This exploration provides insights into the strategies employed, the challenges faced, and the outcomes achieved, offering valuable lessons for other musicians considering similar endeavors.

A) Preparation and Promotion

Before the live streams, the band focused on extensive preparation and promotion to ensure a wide viewership. They created event pages on Facebook well in advance, shared teaser videos, and engaged with fans through posts and comments. They also utilized targeted Facebook ads to reach potential viewers who fit their audience profile but were not yet followers of the band.

B) Engagement During the Live streams
During the live streams, the band employed several strategies to keep the audience engaged. They interacted with viewers in real time by responding to comments, taking song requests, and sharing stories behind their music. This interactive approach helped maintain viewer interest and encouraged longer watch times, which were beneficial in enhancing Facebook's algorithmic promotion of the live stream.

C) Monetization Strategies
To monetize their live streams, the band used Facebook's built-in features such as Stars, which viewers can purchase during the live stream as a form of tipping. They also promoted their merchandise during the broadcasts, providing links to their online store and offering exclusive discounts to live-stream viewers. They also set up a virtual ticketing system for some special live-stream events, providing exclusive content to ticket holders.

D) Technical Setup and Quality
Recognizing the importance of production quality, the band invested in professional audio and video equipment to enhance the live-stream experience. They ensured that the sound quality was excellent and the video was clear and stable, which significantly improved viewer satisfaction and helped differentiate their live streams from less polished ones.

E) Post-Live-Stream Engagement
After each live stream, the band continued to engage with their audience by posting highlights, clips, and full replays. They encouraged viewers to share this content, extending the live stream's reach. The band also analyzed viewer data collected during the live stream to better understand audience preferences and adjust future content accordingly.

F) Building Community
The live streams served as a platform for building a stronger community among fans. The band fostered a sense of belonging and loyalty

by regularly acknowledging viewers, celebrating community milestones, and creating a welcoming environment for all attendees.

G) Collaborations and Guest Appearances

To keep the content fresh and exciting, the band occasionally invited guest musicians to join their live streams. These collaborations not only varied the musical content but also brought in fans of the guest artists, expanding the band's audience.

H) Future Streams

By maintaining a regular schedule for their livestreams, the band was able to cultivate a routine for their viewers, making it easier for fans to plan to attend. Consistency in streaming times helped stabilize viewership numbers and built anticipation for each event.

The band actively sought feedback from their audience regarding the live-stream experience and used this information to continually improve their performances and engagement strategies. This responsiveness to audience preferences contributed to an increase in viewership over time.

The band viewed their livestreams not as one-off events but as part of a long-term strategy to grow and maintain their fan base. Over time, they adapted their content and interaction based on technological advancements and changes in viewer behavior, ensuring they remained relevant and engaging.

I) Summary

This case study of traditional band live streams on Facebook illustrates the potential of live digital performances as a multifaceted tool for engagement, community building, and revenue generation. By effectively leveraging the platform's capabilities and maintaining a focus on quality and viewer interaction, musicians can significantly enhance their digital presence and fan base.

Composer Creates Composition Tutorials

This case study explores how a composer successfully used social media to create and monetize composition tutorials, providing insights into the strategies adopted to engage and educate an audience while generating income.

A) Choosing the Right Platform

The composer chose YouTube as the primary platform for posting composition tutorials, capitalizing on its audience reach and suitability for long-form educational content. YouTube's tools for creators, such as analytics and monetization options, make it an ideal choice for hosting detailed instructional videos.

The tutorials were designed to cover a range of topics from basic music theory to advanced composition techniques. Each video built upon previous tutorials, encouraging viewers to watch the series in order. This structured approach helps viewers progressively build their skills, increasing the learning value of the content.

B) Engagement and Interactivity

To maximize engagement, the composer included interactive elements in the videos, such as composing in real time, responding to viewer comments, and including suggestions from subscribers while composing. This interactivity not only made the learning process more engaging but also built a community of learners who felt directly involved in the creative process.

C) Monetization Strategies

The composer monetized the tutorials through YouTube's Partner Program, which primarily focuses on ad revenue. They also offered supplemental materials like sheet music and exclusive one-on-one coaching sessions through Patreon, providing multiple revenue streams. Sponsorships with music software companies and equipment manufacturers also supplemented income, aligning naturally with the content.

High-quality video and audio production ensured that the tutorials were clear and professionally presented, making them more effective as educational tools and more appealing to viewers. Investing in good quality production helped distinguish the tutorials from less polished content on similar topics, attracting a more stable set of income streams.

Maintaining a consistent release schedule facilitated building a regular viewership. The composer released new tutorials weekly, which kept subscribers engaged and helped maintain a steady flow of views and revenue. Regular releases might also have contributed to a better ranking in YouTube's algorithm, increasing visibility.

D) Community Building

The composer focused on building a community of musicians and composers through Q & A sessions, live streams, and community challenges. This fostered a sense of belonging among viewers, turning casual viewers into loyal followers. Viewer feedback was critical in the improvement of the tutorials. The composer adjusted the pacing, complexity, and content of the tutorials based on viewer comments and suggestions, making the tutorials more responsive to the needs of the audience.

The composer used other social media platforms like Twitter and Instagram to promote new tutorials and engage with the audience. Short clips from the tutorials were shared as teasers, and occasional behind-the-scenes content was posted to increase interest. These types of cross-platform engagement are very important to community building.

The tutorials were mostly designed to be evergreen-style reference content, providing value to new learners even years after the initial release. This long-term perspective on content creation ensured that the tutorials continued to attract new viewers, maximizing the lifetime value of each video.

E) Summary

This case study demonstrates the potential of using composition tutorials as a way to educate, engage, and earn. By effectively leveraging YouTube's platform capabilities and maintaining high standards of content quality and viewer interaction, the composer successfully built a sustainable revenue-generating educational series.

Singer-Songwriter Elicits Fan Participation Using Shorts Format

This case study examines how a singer-songwriter effectively utilized the Shorts format on platforms like TikTok and YouTube Shorts to engage fans and encourage participation, creating a vibrant community around their music and significantly boosting their profile.

A) Leveraging the Shorts Format

The singer-songwriter capitalized on the popularity of short-form video platforms by creating engaging, concise content that highlighted their musical talents and personality. The brief format was ideal for capturing the fleeting attention spans typical of social media users, making it perfect for showcasing catchy snippets of new songs, covers, or musical challenges.

To maximize fan engagement, the artist frequently posted interactive content such as call-and-response singing challenges, where fans were encouraged to duet with or respond to the artist's clips. This interactive approach not only increased viewer engagement but also fostered a sense of community among fans who viewed and participated in these challenges.

B) Using Hashtags to Boost Visibility

The singer-songwriter strategically used trending and relevant hashtags and topics to increase the visibility of their Shorts. This tactic helped their videos reach a broader audience, attracting new followers and increasing engagement rates. Hashtags were chosen based on the content of the video, trending topics, and the artist's unique musical style.

C) Encouraging User-Generated Content

By encouraging fans to create their own videos using the artist's music, the singer-songwriter effectively expanded their reach and influence. Fans would use segments of the artist's songs in their videos, which not only promoted their music but also had the wonderful side effect of creating a viral loop, as these fan videos attracted their own viewers. It's amazing when both side benefit.

D) Regular Posting and Engagement

The artist maintained a consistent posting schedule, which is crucial in platforms that favor frequent updates. Regular uploads kept the content fresh and maintained high levels of engagement. Additionally, the singer-songwriter made it a point to interact with fans by commenting on fan videos, sharing them, and occasionally featuring them on their own social media pages.

While engaging fans, the artist also utilized these platforms for monetization and promotion. They linked to their full songs and albums, driving traffic to music streaming services. Merchandise was occasionally promoted in the videos, and exclusive content was offered to viewers who followed the links provided in the video descriptions.

Active incorporation of fan feedback into content creation was a key strategy. The artist paid close attention to the types of videos that received the most engagement and adapted their content strategy accordingly, ensuring that the fans received more of what they enjoyed. They were careful not to rely on feedback for validation though, since comments both positive and negative are more a reflection on the viewer's state of mind and not always a commentary on the music itself.

E) Collaborations with Other Artists

Working with other musicians and influencers on these platforms helped reach different demographics and expanded the artist's fan base. These collaborations often took the form of joint Shorts, where both artists could showcase their talents and tap into each other's followers.

F) Building a Brand Beyond Music

The artist used the platform to build a brand that extended beyond just their awesome music. They shared personal stories, participated in popular nonmusical challenges, and engaged in trending conversations, which humanized them and built a stronger connection with their audience.

The singer-songwriter also used platform analytics tools to track the performance of their Shorts, analyzing metrics such as view count, likes, shares, and comments. This data was crucial for understanding what worked and what didn't, allowing the artist to fine-tune their strategy for future content.

G) Summary

This case study showcases the effectiveness of using the Shorts format to engage deeply with fans, encourage participation, and create a dynamic community that actively an artist's music career. Through strategic content creation, regular engagement, and clever use of platform features, the singer-songwriter was able to significantly enhance their profile and reach on social media.

Audio Engineer Builds an Audience of Student Producers Learning Work in Recording Studios

This case study focuses on an audio engineer who utilized social media to build an audience of aspiring student producers who were interested in learning about professional work in recording studios. It details the strategies employed to engage and educate this fairly niche audience, which turned the engineer's expertise into a valuable educational resource that also generated income. Extra income is always a good thing.

A) Content Strategy Development

The audio engineer developed a content strategy that focused on sharing detailed tutorials, behind-the-scenes videos of recording sessions, and tips and tricks related to audio engineering. This content was carefully tailored to be both informative and engaging, catering specifically to students and budding audio professionals interested in the technical aspects of music production.

Recognizing the visual and technical nature of audio engineering, the engineer primarily used YouTube to host their educational content. This platform allowed for the integration of detailed video explanations with demonstrations, which are crucial to teaching complex audio engineering concepts effectively.

To foster engagement, the engineer encouraged viewers to ask questions, request specific tutorial topics, and share their own production experiences. Regular live Q & A sessions and feedback reviews of viewer-submitted audio mixes were scheduled, enhancing the interactive learning experience and building a community around the content.

B) Monetization Through Educational Products

Beyond ad revenue from YouTube, the audio engineer monetized their expertise by creating and selling online courses, downloadable presets, and sound libraries specifically designed for novice producers. This not only provided additional value to their audience but also created diverse income streams. This is a crucial point; the monetization of expertise as a product that is the core element of a monetization strategy.

C) Collaborations and Guest Sessions

Collaborations with well-known producers and other professionals in the music industry were featured regularly. These guest sessions provided additional insights and perspectives, making the content more comprehensive and attracting a wider audience.

The engineer leveraged social media platforms like Instagram, Twitter, and Facebook to promote new content and interact with the community. Strategic use of hashtags, participation in relevant online groups/forums, and collaborations with music technology companies helped increase visibility and attract more subscribers.

The engineer actively sought feedback from their audience to continuously improve the content quality and relevance. Viewer comments and suggestions were regularly incorporated into new videos, ensuring the content remained responsive to the audience's evolving needs.

D) Building a Brand as an Educator

Establishing credibility was crucial, so the engineer consistently highlighted their professional experience and successes in the industry. This not only bolstered their reputation as an expert but also reinforced the educational value of their content.

The engineer fostered a sense of community among followers by creating spaces for discussion and collaboration, such as online forums and social media groups. This community became a valuable support network for student producers, facilitating peer-to-peer learning and networking opportunities.

Analytics tools provided by YouTube and other social media platforms were used to track viewer engagement, video performance, and audience growth. This data informed decisions about content direction, release schedules, and promotional strategies, optimizing overall channel performance.

E) Summary

This case study illustrates how an audio engineer successfully leveraged social media to create a niche educational platform, effectively engaging and monetizing their expertise. By combining high-quality, targeted content with strategic marketing and community building, the engineer not only enhanced their professional profile but also contributed significantly to the education of the next generation of audio professionals.

Harnessing Social Media for Musical Success

This chapter serves as a capstone to the exploration of modern musicians' paths to success, focusing on the pivotal role of social media in monetizing music. It's a narrative of transformation and opportunity, illustrating how artists navigate the digital realm to turn their creative output into sustainable income. The journey through various monetization strategies, such as leveraging copyright protections, engaging with fans through memberships, and forming strategic partnerships for sponsorships, reveals a landscape rich with potential.

A Symphony of Progress and Possibility

As we draw the curtains on this exploration, it becomes evident that the convergence of music and social media has orchestrated a new era for artists, a symphony of progress and possibility. From the "strings" of social media platforms to the "keys" of content monetization strategies, artists are equipped with more tools than ever to showcase their talent and sustain their artistry.

This journey has charted the evolution from traditional music distribution to the dynamic, interactive world of social media, where engagement directly translates into success. It has illustrated not just how artists can thrive in this new digital ecosystem but why mastering these tools is indispensable for anyone looking to make a mark in the music industry.

The path does not end here. The digital landscape is ever-evolving, and the strategies of those who wish to navigate it must be so too. As new platforms emerge and existing ones adapt, the potential for innovation in music monetization will only grow. Musicians and industry professionals must remain vigilant and adaptable, ready to tune into new opportunities and technologies as they arise.

In this symphony of the digital age, each musician has the potential to conduct their path to success, guided by the strategies and insights laid out in this book. Let the music play on, resonant and vibrant, in the vast concert hall of the digital world.

Printed in the United States
by Baker & Taylor Publisher Services